THE NEW DEMOCRACY
and
THE NEW DESPOTISM

THE NEW DEMOCRACY
AND
THE NEW DESPOTISM

by Charles E. Merriam
Professor of Political Science
University of Chicago

New York WHITTLESEY HOUSE *London*
McGRAW-HILL BOOK COMPANY, INC.

Copyright, 1939, *by the* McGraw-Hill Book Company, Inc.

All rights reserved. This book, or parts thereof, may not be reproduced in any form without permission of the publishers.

PUBLISHED BY WHITTLESEY HOUSE
A Division of the McGraw-Hill Book Company, Inc.

Printed in the United States of America by The Maple Press Co., York, Pa.

PREFACE

This is a statement of the assumptions of democracy and the validation of its program in general terms. I hope to follow this sometime with a more specific study of the American democracy.

The doctrines and the programs of the new despotism are less fully treated than those of democracy because they are not at this time fully and clearly formulated.

Portions of this volume have already appeared—"The Assumptions of Democracy" in the *Political Science Quarterly*, September, 1938; "The Assumptions of Aristocracy" in the *International Journal of Ethics*, May, 1938; and related material on planning in the *Role of Politics in Social Change* (New York University Press, 1936).

I am indebted to my assistants who have aided me from time to time in this inquiry, and particularly to my daughter Elizabeth, who made a very substantial and indispensable contribution to this study. I am also under obligation to my colleagues and others who have given me the benefit of their counsel, in particular to the sage Louis Brownlow of the Public Administration Clearing House in Chicago.

CHARLES E. MERRIAM.

UNIVERSITY OF CHICAGO,
  April, 1939.

CONTENTS

PREFACE... v

INTRODUCTION...................................... 3

PART I
THE ASSUMPTIONS AND PROGRAM OF DEMOCRACY

A. THE ASSUMPTIONS OF DEMOCRACY 11
   1. The Dignity of Man........................... 12
   2. The Perfectibility of Mankind................. 34
   3. Mass Gains and the Many 37
   4. The Consent of the Governed.................. 38
   5. Consciously Directed and Peaceful Social Change 42
   6. Summary..................................... 45
B. THE BACKGROUND OF RECENT DEMOCRATIC THEORY 50
   1. Ideology.................................... 51
   2. Science and Technology...................... 54
   3. Social Techniques........................... 57
   4. Democratic Experience....................... 60
C. VALIDATION OF DEMOCRATIC ASSUMPTIONS 71
   1. The Dignity of Man........................... 73
   2. The Perfectibility of Mankind................. 92
   3. Mass Gains and the Many 98
   4. The Consent of The Governed 104
      a. The Electoral Mechanism 105
      b. Common Counsel......................... 114
      c. Public Administration.................. 123
      d. Democracy and Decisionism.............. 132
      e. Plan Making............................ 145
      f. Criticisms of Planning................. 165
      g. Conclusions............................ 178
   5. Consciously Directed and Peaceful Social Change 180
      a. Change in Government................... 180
      b. Change in Industry..................... 182

CONTENTS

    c. Civic Education and Change. 182
    d. Force and Change. 183
D. Conclusions 187

Part II
THE NEW DESPOTISM

A. Beginnings of the Anti-democratic Movement. 191
    1. The Superman and Caesarism. 198
    2. The Noble Few. 202
    3. Economic Inequality. 205
B. Postwar Defences of the Few 208
C. The Theory of the New Despotism 217
D. Analysis of the Doctrines of the New Despotism 231

Part III
CONCLUSIONS

A. General Considerations 243
B. The New Despotism. 250
C. The New Democracy 252

Index. 263

THE NEW DEMOCRACY
and
THE NEW DESPOTISM

INTRODUCTION

Political associations, commonly called states, commonwealths, or nations in our day, have many continuing tasks in common. They must provide a system of cohesion that will hold together the personalities and groups within their segment of human population; they must provide for an organization of force, an organization of consent or morale, an organization of intelligence in the special tasks of policy and management; they must provide for a balance between order and justice; they must provide for a balance between stability and change; they must provide a balance between equality and inequality; they must provide for a method of the zoning of power and for the centralization of authority; they must provide a balance between liberty and authority; they must provide for conferential and consultative functions, for adjudicative functions, for administrative functions and their working interrelation; they must develop a system of common defence and of interrelations with the other members of the family of nations; they must minimize the maladjustment between the political values and needs of men and other values and needs of mankind at particular times. In short, they must promote the general welfare—the common weal—through positive or negative measures as from time to time may seem appropriate.[1] The maintenance of what I have called a "moving equilibrium" of complex social forces at all times challenges the capacity of states for adjustment, for statics and dynamics as well.

[1] See my *Political Power* (1934), Chap. VII on "The Survival of the Fittest," Chap. IX on "The Morbidity and Mortality of Power," and Chap. X on "The Emerging Trends of Power."

THE NEW DEMOCRACY

Whether these complex problems of adjustment are to be solved in a system based on the consent of the Many or of the Few, has been a central point in political thought for many centuries—from the days of Plato and Aristotle down to the times of the modern theorists and proponents of despotism and democracy. One position defends the irresponsible determination of the policies of commonwealths by the Few or the One; the other the responsible determination of the policies of commonwealths by the bulk of society. Needless to say, there are many intermediate stages and forms between these competing systems.

I intend to analyze these ideas in their modern forms, to examine their assumptions and their implications, to appraise them in the light of modern political theory and in the presence of emerging trends and problems.

I have not considered in full detail the specific doctrines of noted defenders of democracy, such as Dewey, Lindsay, Kelsen, Bouglé, Bryce, and others, not to speak of the earlier defenders of democracy from Aristotle down. To all of these thinkers I am greatly indebted for their contribution to the discussion of the present problem. If I have appropriated their arguments at any point without giving them due credit, I hereby make my apology and venture to hope that I may have bettered their instruction here and there.

Can democracy survive in the present world, or must it go down before other types of political association?

From the broadest point of view there can be little doubt that forms of democracy will emerge in the world from time to time. Whether democracy rides the present storm depends upon whether it is able to develop a program and an organization adapted to the needs of our day.

I have indicated the methods of validating the democratic assumptions in our time. It is plain to any clear-eyed observer that our problem is deeper than the reorganization

INTRODUCTION

of the machinery of political association. It reaches into economic structure, into human ideals and goals, into reconciliations between tradition and modern science. If democratic association can adapt itself to modern conditions, making use of modern productive forces and interpreting modern ideals, it will survive; otherwise it must yield to auspices under which the ideals and practices of fellowship are supplanted by rougher methods with the domination of the Many by the Few.

The problem of our time is not merely, as many assume, one of democracies or despotisms, but a question of the relative roles of the Many or of the Few in our whole society, economic as well as political.

Our underlying problem is a deeper one than the personality of powerful men, who are common symbols of wide and deep social movements. It involves the role of the Few and the Many in outlining and directing the conditions that modern technology has developed.

Who shall decide, and in what manner, how the gains and values of civilization shall be allocated in the commonwealths that produce them and what shall be the principle of distribution? This is a paramount question of our day, cutting below the glamorous imperialism of nations or the shrill ambition of adventurous individuals.

Obviously the form of political association is not one to which a universal answer, applying to all conditions, can be given. There are situations that make popular rule impossible; there are also situations in which the Few are less adapted to the guidance of the commonwealth than the One. The level of political civilization, the trend of historic events in a given time and place, the sharpness of the crisis are always significant factors in considering the type of political association. There are also many transition stages characterized by the retreat of the Few and the advance of the Many, or

THE NEW DEMOCRACY

by the abdication of the Many and the rise of the One or the Few.

Theoretically and practically the ideal situation is one in which mastery and slavery alike disappear and the consent of the governed is the key to action. Whenever the optimum social conditions are found, education, political maturity, prosperity, the common good is the cooperative concern of the commonwealth.

The following statement of guiding considerations may prove useful in appraising the subsequent discussion:

1. I affirm the possibility of vast gains in social production, in the light of modern science, and of speedy advance in standards of human living, within the forms of free society.

2. I affirm the relative advantages of rational discussion and of general consent and cooperation as against force and violence as a means of social reorganization and human progress. Both Marx and Mussolini overemphasize the role of violence as a contributory factor in modern advancement.

If, however, force and war are the arguments, my position is that they can be and will be effectively answered in their own terms.

3. I repudiate the doctrine of the Few as the irresponsible lords of human destiny and emphasize the value of the fraternal, equalitarian, and libertarian way of life, and the permanent values of common judgment in common affairs.

4. I affirm the values of conscious control over the development of our social life in contradistinction to the brute struggle for survival. The American Constitution put an end to the age-old argument that political institutions could not be constructed by men. *Laissez faire* applied to nineteenth-century conditions has now been generally repudiated, but in diluted form still survives as a nucleus of opposition to forms of social control, and especially to any movement labeled as a "plan."

INTRODUCTION

I affirm that democratic social planning wisely conceived may be directed toward the release of human capacities and the opening of opportunities for human liberty and personality through agencies of common consent and cooperation.

5. I repudiate the doctrine of those who invoke democracy and liberty as defences of special privilege in our industrial society, and are willing to surrender both democracy and liberty to any political system that will protect their vested advantages.

I affirm the possibility of organizing liberty and equality within the framework of democratic society and institutions.

6. I repudiate the doctrine of despotism in government, either (1) in the form of the totalitarian state, right or left wing, or (2) of the centralization of irresponsible authority in the hands of One or of the Few.

These new systems labeled dictatorial are actually despotic in form and principle. These despots are wholly irresponsible to the community, except as they themselves interpret the community interest. Their doctrine is not merely (1) that of the concentration of national as against local authority, or (2) the concentration of all national governmental powers in one or few, but (3) of the irresponsibility of the government to the community.

7. I repudiate the point of view that places "economics" alone as the lord of our social life. The doctrines of Mill and Marx alike have overemphasized the role of ill-defined "economic" factors in our civilization—the one as the basis for "collectivism" and the other as a basis for "individualism." The basic troubles of our time are not fundamentally "economic" only, but are scientific and technological, territorial-racial, sociopolitical, philosophical, psychological, as well. Our problems involve forms of behavior, value systems, ideas, and institutions beyond the bounds of "economics" in any ordinary use of that term. The organization of the complexity

of old-value systems and the new science in workable forms and practices is the root problem of the present time.[1] Our age is an industrial age, but our problems transcend industry.

8. I affirm the validation of democratic assumptions by a comprehensive program vigorously directed toward the attainment of democratic principles.

[1] See my *Role of Politics in Social Change* (1936), Chap. II.

Part I

THE ASSUMPTIONS AND PROGRAM
OF DEMOCRACY

A. ASSUMPTIONS OF DEMOCRACY

Democracy is a form of political association in which the general control and direction of the political policy of the commonwealth is habitually determined by the bulk of the community in accordance with appropriate understandings and procedures providing for popular participation and consent.

Democracy is contrasted with other forms of political association in which the control and direction of the political policy of the commonwealth are habitually determined by a relatively small group in accordance with appropriate understandings and procedures providing for autocratic, aristocratic, oligarchic, or other forms of minority control and direction.

The principal assumptions of democracy are as follows:

1. The essential dignity of man, the importance of protecting and cultivating his personality on a fraternal rather than a differential principle, and the elimination of special privileges based upon unwarranted or exaggerated emphasis on the human differentials.

2. Confidence in a constant drive toward the perfectibility of mankind.

3. The assumption that the gains of commonwealths are essentially mass gains and should be diffused as promptly as possible throughout the community without too great delay or too wide a spread in differentials.

4. The desirability of popular decision in the last analysis on basic questions of social direction and policy, and of recognized procedures for the expression of such decisions and their validation in policy.

5. Confidence in the possibility of conscious social change accomplished through the process of consent rather than by the methods of violence.[1]

I. *The Dignity of Man*

1. *An assumption of the doctrine of democracy is that of the essential dignity of all men and the importance of protecting and cultivating personality primarily on a fraternal rather than on a differential basis.*[2]

It is, of course, quite possible that under various systems of social or political order the dignity and worth of all men should be fully recognized and amply protected; or per contra that mass rule might give merely lip service to the doctrine. But in general the practice has been otherwise. In a caste system such as that of India the lower castes may be respected but in a very lordly manner; and when we reach the pariahs the dignity remaining is very minute. The untouchables must not even cast a shadow upon the higher types of mankind—their betters. Slaveowners may also manifest deep interest in their slaves and respect the dignity of their slave personality, but in other instances sell them like chattels or beat them like dogs. Patrimonial rulers may also exhibit fine types of patronage to their serfs and tenants, but again there are many pictures of sad neglect and haughty treatment unworthy of the dignity of the race.

---

[1] For some general discussions on the assumptions of democracy see James Bryce, *The American Commonwealth* (1888), *Modern Democracies* (1921); Hans Kelsen, *Vom Wesen und Wert der Demokratie* (1929); Alexander D. Lindsay, *The Essentials of Democracy* (1929); Harold J. Laski, *Democracy in Crisis* (1933); John Dewey, *The Ethics of Democracy* (1888), *Democracy and Education* (1916), *Individualism Old and New* (1930), *Liberalism and Social Action* (1935), *The Public and Its Problems* (1927); Richard Henry Tawney, *Equality* (1931); Celestin Bouglé, *Les Idées égalitaires* (1899), *La Democratie devant la science* (1923). Max Lerner, *It Is Later Than You Think* (1938); Thomas Mann, *The Coming Victory of Democracy* (1938); Eduard Benes, *Lectures on Democracy* (1939, forthcoming).

[2] Emile Durkheim, *De la Division du travail social* (1902), Book I.

ASSUMPTIONS AND PROGRAM

Even the nineteenth century attitude toward the majority of the people—the poor—in England seems almost incredible today, so callous was it in nature. Preachers, economists, lords, and ladies thought of the "lower classes" only to scoff at their ill manners, and to assail them for daring to protest at their God-given lot. Lord Shaftesbury, in a speech before Parliament in 1864, quoted "a lady who complained that she could not have her chimneys swept in the afternoon, because the boys were at school: 'A chimney sweep indeed, wanting education! What next?'"[1] And there are many other instances of the same type of reaction.

Even the clergymen became infected with the spirit of the times. On the poor laws the Rev. Townsend commented

> It seems to be a law of nature that the poor should be to a certain degree improvident, that there may always be some to fulfill the most servile, the most sordid, and the most ignoble offices in the community. The stock of human happiness is thereby much increased, whilst the more delicate are not only relieved from drudgery, and freed from those occasional employments which would make them miserable, but are left at liberty, without interruption, to pursue those callings which are suited to their various dispositions, and most useful to the State. As for the lowest of the poor, by custom they are reconciled to the meanest occupations, to the most laborious works, to the most hazardous pursuits; whilst the hope of their reward makes them cheerful in the midst of all their dangers and toils. . . . When hunger is either felt or feared, the desire of obtaining bread will quietly dispose the mind to undergo the greatest hardships, and will sweeten the severest labours. The peasant with a sickle in his hand is happier than the prince upon his throne.[2]

It is quite evident that all such rulers felt relatively little or no responsibility for the condition of the majority of the human beings under their governance. Nor were they far removed in spirit from those individuals who showed their idea of the nature of poverty by enacting in 1697 a law to

---

[1] J. L. Hammond and B. Hammond, *Lord Shaftesbury* (1925), p. 232, speech on Climbing Boys' Bill, June 3, 1864.

[2] Joseph Townsend, *A Dissertation on the Poor Laws* (1785), quoted in Sidney Webb and Beatrice Webb, *English Poor Law History* (1927), Part II, Vol. I, pp. 8, 9.

deter "idle, sturdy, and disorderly beggars" from seeking public aid, an act by which every pauper—man, woman, and child—was made an object of public notice and scorn. For on the shoulder of the right sleeve of the outermost garment each was obliged to wear, in red or blue cloth, a Roman P, as well as the initial of the parish of which he was a resident—a veritable badge of poverty and shame.[1]

Later on, when the question of a ten-hour day for adults was raised, Bright, a prominent employer, objected.

> Why are we mill-owners . . . to be selected as subjects of interference? Why is a Scotchman to be sent to see how I work my people, while the farmer, and the carpenter, and the builder, and the tailor is left to the ordinary responsibilities of law and public opinion? . . . I have advised my partners, if this machinery Bill passes, to set the example of turning the key on the doors of our mills, and to throw on the legislators the responsibility of feeding the millions whom they will not allow us to employ with a profit.[2]

The nineteenth century is rich in examples of upper- and middle-class indifference to the welfare of the masses. Brute force was the favorite remedy for popular misery: intelligent understanding was rare.

> Typical of the ideas of the monarchs of the time is the following statement of Charles Felix of Savoy, "At the beginning of my reign (1820) everything was a mystery to me. I did not know what to write or what to answer. Then I made the sign of the cross, recommended myself to the adorable Trinity, and God willed that my decisions should be worthy of a Christian prince."[3]

To believe in the concepts underlying democratic government was a criminal offense.

> The words liberty, justice, happiness of the greatest number are infamous and criminal: they give to the mind the habit of discussion and of

---

[1] 8 and 9 W III, c. 30, s. 2 (1697).

[2] Quoted in A. V. Dicey, *Lectures on the Relation between Law and Public Opinion in England* (1905), p. 235.

[3] F. B. Artz, *Reaction and Revolution* (1924), p. 2, note 1.

ASSUMPTIONS AND PROGRAM

distrust. This fatal habit of distrust once contracted, human weakness applies it to everything, man comes to distrust the Bible, the orders of the Church, tradition, etc., etc.; from then on he is lost.[1]

In France the upper classes felt that "action is more persuasive than words ... to discuss the laws in public is to rob them of that respect which is the secret of their power."[2]

In Austria the same view prevailed. Robert Owen, for example, relates his conversation with M. Gentz, secretary of the Congress of Sovereigns, in 1817.

> I stated that now, through the progress of science, the means amply existed in all countries, or might easily be made to exist on the principle of union for the foundation of society, instead of its present foundation of disunion, to saturate society at all times with wealth, sufficient to amply supply the wants of all through life. What was my surprise to hear the reply of the learned secretary! "Yes," he said, and apparently speaking for the governments, "we know that very well; but we do not want the mass to become wealthy and independent of us. How could we govern them if they were?"[3]

In Russia conditions were even worse. "'Why in the world should you be interested in our mujik?' a French traveller was asked by a lady on the Lower Volga. 'He is a brute of whom you will never make a man.'"[4]

"'Very good,' the Grand Duke Mikhael said once of a regiment, after having kept it motionless for one hour presenting arms, 'only, *they breathe!*'"[5]

It must also be readily conceded that under nominally mass-rule systems, attention to the lot of great groups of population may leave much to be desired in factory, mine, and farm. Indeed in the earlier forms of popular rule the bulk of the population was excluded from the voting circle and

---

[1] H. Beyle (Stendhal), *La Chartreuse de Parme* (ed. 1853), pp. 121–22.
[2] A. L., marquis de Custine, *Russia* (trans. 1854), p. 16.
[3] R. Owen, *The Life of Robert Owen* (1857), p. 183.
[4] A. Leroy-Beaulieu, *The Empire of the Tsars and the Russians* (1893), p. 408.
[5] P. Kropotkin, *Memoirs of a Revolutionist* (1899), p. 9.

slavery remained for many. This was done, it might be maintained, not because the mass was in power but because they were not in fact effectively in authority; a relatively few interpreted their own private interest in terms of the relatively many. Nevertheless the system of democracy points steadily in the direction of this goal, even if it is not reached thus far. Lincoln said of the Declaration of Independence, it is an ideal "constantly looked to, constantly labored for, and even though never perfectly attained, constantly approximated, and thereby constantly spreading and deepening its influence, and augmenting the happiness and value of life to all colors everywhere."[1]

The fraternal basis of life has been weakened in recent years by such influences as race hatred and the doctrines of the racial differentials, notably in Germany, and further by the tendency toward private regimentation and exploitation in great concentrations of economic power reaching over into the political field. In many areas sad ravages have been made on the doctrine of human comradeship. But on the other hand, sweeping progress has been made through the emancipation, in part, of womankind, through mass industries, through the organization of labor, through the democratizing of many spheres of life formerly held as the preserve of few. In the field of transportation, of dress, of art, of education, of recreation, of health, the status of the individual has been elevated materially and in many ways so gradually that the advance of social democratic mores has not been perceived.

The French Revolutionary adoption of *citoyen* was a symbol of the larger mass movement toward the recognition of the essential dignity of mankind, and the meaning of human personality in our modern world. Of this larger movement the egalitarian and the libertarian ideas are

[1] Abraham Lincoln, *Complete Works*, ed. Nicolay and Hay (1915), Vol. I, p. 232.

ASSUMPTIONS AND PROGRAM

parts, important parts, but not the whole unless they are broadly interpreted.[1]

Equalitarians and libertarians are essentially concerned with the free development of the human personality in its richest and most creative possibilities. The political equalitarians and the economic libertarians alike have before them the unfettering of human abilities and their full and free expression in social relations. Their external scheme of instruments is designed to bring about this emancipation, to create a world realizing the innate possibility.

The doctrine of liberty underneath its procedural trapping is essentially that of opportunity for free development of personal desires for expression. Who says liberty says life—richer and more abundant life. Liberty, Bryce has said, is an end in itself, but it is more than that. It is also a means of arriving at other ends, a method of expression of personality, a mode of obtaining recognition and possibly rising in the hierarchy of values in the society.

When the alleged procedures of liberty stand in the way of the throbbing interests of life, it is time to reconsider their form and application, to see whether what was intended as a release has become a restriction, whether Shylock is demanding his pound of flesh according to the law, but contrary to the basic purposes of the law. When the rich and the powerful publicly invoke liberty as a means of private exploitation of the poor and weak, it is time to examine the nature of the forms and procedures and the spirit in which they are applied before we accept these invocations at their full value. The variation of social forces must be accompanied by a covariation of the libertarian forms that express them; otherwise liberty becomes only a convenient word twisted to the purposes of tyranny.

[1] *Cf.* Bouglé, *Les Idées égalitaires;* Dewey, *Individualism Old and New,* and Tawney, *op. cit.*

THE NEW DEMOCRACY

It is not necessary to the doctrine of the dignity of mankind that every man should be equal to every other man in everything, or that every man should be able to do everything he may desire at any time. These are no part of the assumptions of democracy, and only stand in the way of the achievement of the larger program.

It is the larger and ampler regard for the position of the human personality in the general scheme of values that lies at the root of the assumptions of democracy. This persistent factor in all of its program includes insistence upon placing the substance of human personality above the forms of its protection—often a puzzling phenomenon to those who see the personality, apparently protected by the letter of the law, cruelly exposed in practice.

Again the democratic movement is directed against the unwarranted or exaggerated emphasis on the human differentials in various forms. The conclusion from the fact of human inequality that there should be set up a caste system or a slave system, or serfdom, or special legal privilege, or private exploitation in some other form, even in the name of economic liberty—this is contrary to the general doctrine here set forth.

That there may be an inequality in the distribution of values does not mean that this must be unlimited in its spread. Nor does it contemplate that the beneficiaries shall be the unrestrained judges of their own importance in the value system of the community. That personalities will develop only when and as they are allowed unlimited and completely self-determined rewards is not a realistic explanation of the incentives to human activity.

The doctrine of democracy is not one of leveling down primarily, but of building up to a minimum level, and of cultivating the possibilities in all ways of life. It discards traditional status and emphasizes creative capacity or

ASSUMPTIONS AND PROGRAM

dynamic ability. Far from crushing out talent, democracy may place the highest premium upon it and strike at all artificial limitations.

Most differentials are not inherited, but must be established and earned pragmatically in the given society in a given cycle of its development and in the given direction of its social objectives. In the democratic political world, selection should not be determined merely by the fact of inheritance, but by the test of demonstrated capacity. In general the dead hand is not presumed to control the living present.

It is always possible, as critics have repeatedly pointed out, that the human differentials may be too jealously or suspiciously regarded in a democracy and that their inappropriate recognition may be the result, with consequences unfortunate for the functioning of the society. This must be set up against the possibility of favoritism on the part of those who administer the doctrine of aristocracy and failure in the impartiality of the distributors.

It is an essential in any mass program that differentials in ability be recognized and that they be given an appropriate place in the grand intervaluation of human services. The emphasis of democracy is not on the flat egalitarianism of all men, but on the equality within certain fields, such as equality before the law, equality in suffrage, equality in opportunity, in dignity, in basic minimum ways of life. It has further been asserted that many types of inequality are not the inexorable outcome of human nature, but of brutal conditions under which human nature has been trained and developed. It was Rousseau who said, "If then there are slaves by nature, it is because there have been slaves contrary to nature."[1]

Said Markham in the *Man with the Hoe:*

[1] Jean Jacques Rousseau, *Social Contract*, trans. Rose Harrington (1898), p. 6.

THE NEW DEMOCRACY

> How will it be with kingdoms and with kings,
> With those who shaped him to the thing he is,
> When this dumb Terror shall reply to God,
> After the silence of centuries?

If the possibilities of modern science and modern organization were utilized in practice, there would be an end of "masses" in the sense in which that term is sometimes employed, namely, of a great mass of population unformed or malformed in body and mind and soul. There is no excuse for the existence of a "Lumpenproletariat" in our day, except that of our inattention or greed—or of cynical acceptance of a condition now outgrown. This might well be blazed in letters of fire wherever modern civilization holds sway, and made the first step in the formulation of any modern social policy.[1]

When this objective is once realized, there will still remain differentials in human capacity in many ranges of activity. Some of these differences will be found in the field of political competence, some in science and invention, some in art, some in the field of production and organization of commodities and services. These differences in ability will be differently rewarded in accordance with special needs in differing phases of development. The effort of the mass movement has been in the direction of seeing that the differentials were in fact the outcome of genuine variations and not of a privilege-creating environment,[2] producing and recognizing artificial inequality.

It is easy to say that all men are not created equal. It is easy to find widely disparate I.Q.'s, and far-ranging differences in skill and capacity or taste in almost every walk of life. But on the other hand, it is easy to see that many bruised and broken lives might have been saved if society had taken

---

[1] Edwin Grant Conklin, *The Direction of Human Evolution* (1921); Winterton C. Curtis, *Science and Human Affairs* (1922).

[2] C. Bouglé, *La Démocratie devant la science*.

ASSUMPTIONS AND PROGRAM

its obligation to mankind more seriously. Any physician is furnished with proof of this, and, indeed, he need not be a physician or a psychiatrist to observe that man's inhumanity to man has blunted many lives.[1] Indeed, this sensitiveness to the lot of others has been one of the distinctive characteristics of the modern democratic movement as contrasted with the underlying philosophy of the founders and exponents of the caste system, which has held sway over so many millions for so long a time; and as contrasted with the philosophy of slavery, which likewise condemned men to permanent subjection on the ground that they were incapable of improvement and must be held as wards of the more competent. There are many worlds in which many types of prestige may be developed so that the leader in one world is a follower in another. There may be and indeed are many true types of preeminence in the many ways of life in which differentials are found. These differentials do not or need not stand in the way of a system of democracy except as men acquire positions of undue privilege and begin to obstruct the opportunity of others.

No dead-level system has ever been seriously advocated by any responsible person, since the range and variety of human attainments are such as to make this psychologically impossible even if desired. Even the most successful system of conservation of the old could not prevent mutations in the direction of the new of infinite variety. Even the most despotic and determined power could not reverse the trend toward variation in all phases of human life, under any system of conditioning yet devised.

It is not the purpose of a system of democracy to iron out all human differentials, but on the contrary it is a part of the program to cultivate and enrich human capacities and variations at many points where they are kept back by

[1] *Cf.* Paul de Kruif, *Why Keep Them Alive?* (1936).

neglect. It may be found necessary from time to time to review and revise those differentials that bear directly on the general purpose of the system, as is seen in minimum-wage legislation or progressive income taxes, price or profit regulation, or other adjustments touching closely the inner workings of the commonwealth.

Although the fluid forms of prestige such as that represented by money income may be more easily regulated by the state, the special types are far less readily reached. The governor cannot well regulate the prestige of the musician, the poet, or the artist or fix the range of esteem for the scientist and the inventor. He may say what salary the great general may have, but cannot much depress the esteem in which he stands in the community. The limits here are soon reached, and prestige may retreat into inner domains into which the most penetrating authority cannot find its way.

The charge that popular rule involves the wholesale crushing out of human differentials, or indifference to variations in ability, is not sustained by observation of what has happened in such systems, and will be found in general to be the accusation of some special-privilege group which fears the attention of the public to its large rewards. It is of course true that the mass in power may be indifferent to or oppressive of special forms of talent, but this has also been true of all competing types of rule, aristocratic and autocratic. The persecutions of the Jews with their enormous treasures of intelligence have been the work of the aristocratic systems of Spain in its tragic era of persecution and of the Nazis in their glorification of race superiority and individual differences. The encouragement of education, science, and invention has never been more conspicuous than in the modern democratic states. The basis of popular rule is indeed a high level of education, which of itself inevitably emphasizes variations and differentials in those who pass through its channels.

ASSUMPTIONS AND PROGRAM

We may inquire, what are the premises upon which an aristocratic system is constructed and operated? What are the underlying considerations in the ideology of anti-democracy.

The first premise of aristocracy as a type of political association is that there are well-defined differences in the political capacity of individuals, and that these differences may be identified and validated. What are these political differentials?

The differentials in human ability—and especially in political ability—must be well defined and commonly understood; and they must be validated by general understanding of their soundness and by general acceptance as a basis of authority. What shall be, then, the special qualities of the few by which we shall identify them and, having identified, worship them or accept them without worshiping? Birth, seniority, wealth, arms, special skills, personality, attitudes, habits may alone or in combination supply such a basis of widespread acknowledgment. Heredity is by this time discredited and abandoned by some of the apostles of elitism themselves. Wealth is a fluid claim to service—if honored by those to whom addressed—but more uncertain in modern times than in earlier years. Arms are an element of strength. But the fact that rulers have arms is not enough. Long ago Rousseau said: "The strongest is never strong enough to be always master, unless he transforms his might into right, and obedience to duty."[1] We yield to the force of the robber, but at the first opportunity turn to entrap him and disarm him. If a few Great Ones had title to every last penny in the world, would they feel secure? Or if a few Great Ones commanded an army containing every able-bodied man and woman in a given state, would they be or feel secure—or shiver a little as they reviewed their own? A great commander

[1] Rousseau, *op. cit.*, p. 8.

might feel secure—a Caesar, an Alexander, a Napoleon—but not one who merely dreamed the dreams of these men. A great producer of human wealth might feel some confidence in his security, but not a fortune hunter such as Insull or Kreuger—a dreamer of Croesus dreams in a world of speculation, running close to the borders of fraud and gambling.

The credentials of the aristoi are not easily read thus far, whatever later theorists may develop in the form of indices of difference. The heir apparent in China was told that a special mark on the palm of his hand indicated that he was predestined to rule. In India there was the story that, if a child was seen protected by the hood of the cobra against the sun, he was destined to become a great ruler; and it is said that rulers have been so discovered.

Aristotle lamented that there was no sure distinguishing mark to serve as the infallible index of the slave nature, although he thought that in general this might be observed in the cringing manner of the inferior. Slaveholders of the South found the missing link, they said, in the color of the Negro. In more modern times the Germans have found the mark of superiority in the alleged characteristics of the Aryan.[1]

Plato faced this difficult situation squarely and set up his indicia of superiority, further indicating the ways and means by which selection of the adequate might be made. But in this he has had few successors who have been willing to face the tests he set up.

Much study has been given recently to the nature and causes of human differentiation. The problem has been attacked from a scientific experimental point of view by the

[1] H. S. Chamberlain, *Grundlagen des 19. Jahrhundert* (1899); Count A. J. de Gobineau, *Essai dur l'inégalité des races humaines* (1853-1855); Madison Grant, *The Passing of a Great Race* (1916); H. F. K. Gunther, *The Racial Elements of European History* (1927), *Adel und Rasse* (1927); Adolf Hitler, *Mein Kampf* (1932); Alfred Rosenberg, *Der Mythos der 19. Jahrhundert* (1933).

ASSUMPTIONS AND PROGRAM

geneticists, endocrinologists, psychologists, psychiatrists, and social scientists. The geneticists have been concerned with the role played by heredity in human differentiation; the endocrinologists with the influence of the ductless glands, and the problem of medical treatment of glandular functioning; the educational psychologists have attacked the problem from the point of view of the measurement of nervous and mental traits. The psychiatrists have been specially concerned with the causes and treatment of mental abnormalities, but have also developed a theory of personality development which is of the highest importance for the understanding of psychic differences and their causation.

Anthropologists, sociologists, and geographers have been deeply concerned with the influences of culture and class and surroundings, physical and social, upon the development of human personality. The relative roles of heredity and environment have been much contested in the course of this discussion,[1] with strenuous advocacy of the priority of one or the other of these factors in shaping man.

The consensus of judgment on the question of the relative roles of biological and environmental determinants takes this question out of the naive "either or" context. Every human characteristic, it is held, depends for its development upon hereditary material in a conditioning environment. It is impossible to give exact "weights" to these two factors. There is no hard and fast distinction between qualities and characteristics that are biologically and environmentally conditioned.

The case of the extreme environmentalist cannot be supported by genetic findings. All human characteristics, physical, physiological, and psychological, have some biological basis. Jennings, in drawing the political conclusions from

---

[1] See my *New Aspects of Politics* (1931), Chap. V, "Politics in Relation to Inheritance and Environment," also Preface.

his investigations, maintains that generally the superior elements of the population will produce a greater number of superior offspring than the same number of inferior parents. But in terms of absolute number the mediocre elements of the population are more productive of mentally superior offspring, since they constitute a far greater proportion of the population. Biology does not support a theory of absolute equality, nor does it support the theory of aristocracy.

The fallacy of those who would support a theory of aristocracy on a biological basis is that "like produces like; that intellectuals produce intellectuals; genius produces genius; morons produce morons; good people produce good people; criminals produce criminals; that each grade of ability, of superiority, or inferiority reproduces itself."[1] Any group of human beings, however equal they might be in external conditions, will produce descendants differing in mental and physical characteristics. Some will be superior, some mediocre, some inferior. These biological findings are far from supporting a theory of traditional aristocracy, just as they are far from justifying a theory of absolute equality. "But," states Jennings, "if one means by a democracy, such a constitution of society that any part of the mass can in time supply individuals fitted for all its functions—in that sense the biological situation is that of democracy."[2]

In the last decades psychologists have begun to develop tests of intelligence that have pointed to great differences in native "intelligence" between different occupational, race, and cultural groups, and between individuals. The more sanguine of the psychologists have maintained that these tests isolate native "intelligence," and therefore show great and permanent differences in intelligence between these social groupings. The more sober conclusion seems to be

---

[1] H. S. Jennings, *The Biological Basis of Human Nature* (1930), pp. 220–221.
[2] *Ibid.*, p. 221.

ASSUMPTIONS AND PROGRAM

that these tests do not adequately isolate the inherited factor. Thus a student of the problem of environment and heredity after covering all of the literature in this field concludes: "It is now recognized that all tests are highly charged with environmental content and that they offer a fair measure of individual differences only when used *within* groups having a similar environmental background."[1]

In other words, although it is clear that heredity influences intelligence, the differences in the intelligence of different occupational, cultural, and racial groups do not reflect only differences in heredity. The role of family life, cultural level and values, and formal education have seriously influenced these results.

Furthermore, the possession of high "general intelligence" does not guarantee its effective political use. Many individuals never realize their potentialities because of personality difficulties. These factors have not yet been subjected to measurement. Conclusions as to the role of heredity and environment in producing differences in character and personality must be based upon the psychological and psychiatric theories of personality development. Setting aside differences in theories of personality formation, psychiatrists generally agree on the importance of various types of environmental influence on the formation of character and personality. Schwesinger describes the various schools of personality theory as agreeing on the role played by biological equipment, but also on

> ... the necessity of social interaction for development; differentiation with experience; the importance of the earliest years of life in the formation of habits, attitudes, ideas, overt reactions, many of which are set even before speech is established; the consolidation of "original," "acquired" and modified responses to a point of complete metamorphosis. ... [2]

[1] Gertrude C. Schwesinger, *Heredity and Environment* (1933), p. 70.
[2] *Ibid.*, p. 443.

THE NEW DEMOCRACY

The geneticists, the psychologists, and the theorists dealing with personality agree to the importance of environmental factors in producing differences in physique, intelligence, and personality. They oppose any point of view that considers the potentialities of individuals as fixed by birth. Although they recognize the importance of heredity as setting certain limits upon individual development, scientists generally do not contend that they have developed any methods or techniques whereby the biologically superior may be distinguished from the inferior.

A precise study of the human differentials is said to be on its way, but is still far from the goal of adequacy. The psychologists, the biologists, the psychiatrists, and psychoanalysts have developed tests and "batteries" of tests of many types. But the battle still rages even on the relatively simple ground of the I.Q., although little advance has been made in dealing with complex social characteristics and aptitudes, and still more scanty is the material dealing with the narrower range of political capacities. And in the political field, though progress has been made with personnel studies revealing individual differences and skills in public administration, the determination of the traits and abilities of governors in the larger sense of the term is not yet developed to the point of exact or approximate identification. If the making of the administrator is understood or by way of being understood, there still remains a long road to the identification and training of the leader.[2]

---

[1] For studies in heredity and environment see H. S. Jennings, *Prometheus* (1925); *The Biological Basis of Human Nature* (1930); J. B. S. Haldane, *Heredity and Politics* (1938); Lancelot Hogben, *Genetic Principles in Medicine and Social Science* (1931). See also bibliographies in Francis W. Coker, *Recent Political Thought* (1934), pp. 333–335 and 376–378. The literature in the field of the measurement of intelligence is listed in Schwesinger, *op. cit.*, pp. 72–85; on personality measurement and theory, *ibid.*, pp. 140–155, 445–454. See also *Psychiatry: Journal of the Biology and the Pathology of Interpersonal Relations, passim.*

[2] Analysis of leadership qualities is presented in my *Political Power*, pp. 31*ff.*, and

ASSUMPTIONS AND PROGRAM

The analyses of writers commonly associated with the idea of aristocracy are meager in the range and precision of their descriptions of the aristoi whose rule they advocate. Close inspection of their interpretations of the chosen few are indeed so disappointing as to make it well-nigh incredible that these doctrines should ever have been accorded any serious consideration. This is notably true of Pareto, foe of democracy, whose analysis of the characteristics and skills of the elite can scarcely be considered as more than elementary, if not indeed trivial.[1] It would not be far from the truth to say that in Pareto's theory the elite are the elite. Those are competent to rule who do rule, and the test of their capacity is the fact of their governance. But, obviously, the fact that the rulers rule gives no answer to the question as to how we should proceed technically to learn who are our leaders. It is interesting to note that the two founders of elitism differed widely on whether the Fascists were really the elite or not. Mosca said no, and Pareto said yes. The doctrine of *Führerschaft* is not subjected to acute analysis. If we ask how these leaders are to be known, the theoretical answer is not clear.

Since it may be assumed that some of the superior will always be found on the outside of the governing circle, may it not be possible to define the governing class in group rather than in individual terms?

The readiest answers from this point of view are found in birth, property, occupation, some common cultural mark. Seniority and intelligence might perhaps be included in this list but are not seriously considered in the modern presentation of the claims of aristocracy, at least not as distinctive marks. The bonds of birth and blood are emphasized

---

reference is there made to other studies in this field. General theories of political leadership are treated in a forthcoming study I have under way.

[1] Vilfredo Pareto, *Les Systèmes socialistes* (1902), Vol. I, Chap. I; *Mind and Society* (1935), Vol. III, pp. 1421*ff*.

in the German Nazi theory, but until recently were rejected in the Italian version as irrelevant. Hitler finds a special criterion of aristocracy in a "pure race," Aryan in its German setting, whereas Mussolini discovers no such mark. "Race," said Mussolini, "is a feeling, not a reality; ninety-five per cent at least is a feeling. Nothing will ever make me believe that biologically pure races can be shown to exist today."[1]

However, on July 14, 1938, the Ministry for Popular Culture issued a manifesto declaring that races are a reality and that Italians belong to the Aryan race. Commenting upon Mussolini's declaration on the racial problem, the *Difesa della Razza* (Aug. 5, 1938) stated that "Mussolini says 'Race . . . this is a feeling, not a reality. Ninety-five per cent is feeling.' But the fact remains that race exists biologically and sentimentally, that is spiritually; feeling also is a reality."

The theory of racial or national superiority does not solve, however, the problem of individual position within the nation, or help to draw the sacred circle around the naturally endowed rulers. The question still remains, even in Germany, Who are the *Führer* intended by nature for leadership, and how shall we find a classifying principle? What is it that marks out Hitler, Goering, Goebbels, as over against Bruening, Braun, Severing, making one set the leaders and the other not?

The doctrine of "personal" biological descent is repudiated in the modern systems. If hereditary differentials were firmly established on a scientific basis, and if it were shown that political qualities were transmissible, the geneticists might be called upon to trace the biological transmission of such predispositions, if any. But none of these steps has thus far been taken, and there are no data upon which a system of

[1] Herman Finer, *Mussolini's Italy* (1935), p. 221.

ASSUMPTIONS AND PROGRAM

aristocracy may now be constructed. Nor is there yet any assurance or reasonable expectation that such discoveries will ever be made in the domain of biology.[1]

The same thing may be said of the psychoanalysts' development of master-slave natures or inferiority-superiority complexes as distinctive marks of capacity and incapacity for rulership.[2] These attitudes or dispositions are set in the framework of a many-sided system of personal and social values, and are not specifically political in their significance. Recognition and satisfaction may prove adequate to the needs of the individual in any one of a long series of prestige systems, and the political may not be of prime significance in a particular individual's scale of values. He may prefer to lead an orchestra or a bowling team, be well paid in the applause of his fellow men for any one of a thousand skills found in the wide range of work, of play, of art, of relationships innumerable. But thus far none of these developments plays any role whatever in the emerging theories of aristocracy as they are actually developed. However important ultimately, they may be dismissed from the field of present consideration.

Property as a distinguishing characteristic of the ruling group is rejected by the modern aristoi along with biological descent. When the land and the title to rule went together, the description of the "lord" was relatively easy, but in the present system of aristocracy neither of these factors is admitted as decisive. No system sets up the possession of wealth, measured in our pecuniary order, as a title to political recognition in the official sense. Hitler has indeed announced that he has not even a bank account. Nor do the traits and

[1] See Aldous Huxley's ingenious outline for organization in the event that such discoveries are made, as described in his *This Brave New World* (1932). See also Jennings, *opera cit.*
[2] See notable studies of Harold D. Lasswell, *Psychopathology and Politics* (1930); *World Politics and Personal Insecurity* (1935); *Politics* (1936).

skills by means of which wealth is obtained play a large part in the description of the natural elitist. It may be borne in mind that the large holders of property and industrial power often regard these possessions and position as evidence of their right to influence and even to control the ordinary government, but this rarely enters into the modern theory of aristocracy. In many instances, further, the special qualities and skills exhibited by the *de jure* rulers would not be highly valued by the industrialists, who may give a low social rating to political capacity in general.

It may be noted that the Soviet system attaches a negative significance to property, in that the possession of property used for the purpose of enabling the owner to live on the earnings of others is set up as a disqualification for political activity of every type, including even suffrage. From this point of view high rank in the pecuniary wealth scale is set up as a characterizing mark of the nonelite, whereas "nonproperty" is made a mark of the politically responsible.

Nor has any occupational basis been accepted as a means of entrance into the charmed circle of the aristocracy. Plato proposed the creation of a special class of guardians and specifically set up their characteristics, but this early advice has not been followed by the modern apostles of aristocracy. The use of technical experts in the direction of administration is important but does not reach the problem of political leadership. The nearest approach is that of the technocrats.

In a situation where the direct appeal to force enters largely into the argument, it might be presumed that the military profession would automatically be counted in as a part of the governing elite. But there has been no disposition thus far to accord theoretical recognition to the occupation of arms or any natural right to political leadership, although many instances might be cited as evidence of the meaning

ASSUMPTIONS AND PROGRAM

of the military in the establishment of the superior. Democratic states also have given military figures recognition. In none of these cases, however, was there any development of the underlying philosophical assumptions of the Fascists or the Nazis. Mussolini and Hitler reached the rank of corporal. In the philosophy of neither of these men is there any effort to incorporate the military class into the inner circles of the upper superiors. In their tactics is clearly seen an effort to utilize the armed forces while keeping them away from the center of actual political authority—a balancing feat of supreme difficulty, especially where there is the enormous prestige of the army in the background.

The development of technocracy as a proposed system of industrio-political government gave an opportunity for the elaboration of a theory of the superior, but little progress was made in this direction by the proponents of the new system.

It may be concluded that the identification of the aristoi is far from satisfactorily developed thus far. The Platonic analysis, by far the most complete yet presented in defense of the rule of the few, is disregarded almost as if it did not exist. It is a far cry from Plato's guardians to Hitler's assertion that the basis of authority must be popularity and force, or to Mussolini's fierce scowl, outthrust jaw, pouting lips, and heavy tragedian manner. One might almost conclude that the chief skill of the elite was histrionic, and hence the ablest actor the most desirable leader.

The most conspicuous of the modern elites have been somewhat embarrassed by the fact that their leaders were set forth as *sui generis*, genii of an exceptional type. In such instances the leader cannot be replaced, and even to suggest this is to question the superhuman basis of the whole plan of political salvation. There can be no other Mussolini, or other Hitler, it is argued.

Indeed, aristoi do not need dictators, who are more likely to betray and devour them than to nourish them.

2. *The Perfectibility of Mankind*

It is assumed that there is a constant trend in human affairs toward the perfectibility of mankind. This was plainly stated at the time of the French Revolution and has been reasserted ever since that time, and with increasing plausibility. Inventions and discoveries which Condorcet could not have foreseen or even imagined have created a new world of abundance, alike in the fertility of soil, in the productivity of machines, in facility of organization and management.[1] The era of plenty has taken the place of the era of scarcity in many parts of the world, although not in all; but human thinking lingers in the earlier phase of our tragic experience stretching over the centuries of want.

The early philosophies of democracy must either have ignored the condition of great masses of humans or have looked forward, idealistically, to the progressive improvement of the human type. One hundred years ago there might have been room for argument upon this question, and critics of democracy might in the light of experience have challenged the competence of the mass of the people to understand enough of government or public policy to undertake the responsibility for any kind of important decision. There are indeed many such comments vividly expressed.[2]

But the unparalleled advance of technology in our time has revolutionized the conditions of production and made these older contentions more difficult to sustain. Not only

---

[1] *Technological Trends and National Policy*, Secs. III and V, Report of the National Resources Committee, 1937.

[2] See Henry J. S. Maine, *Popular Government* (1886); Émile Faguet, *The Cult of Incompetence* (trans. 1914); Ortega y Gasset, *The Revolt of the Masses* (trans. 1932); and many others.

ASSUMPTIONS AND PROGRAM

have enormous advances been made, but the soberest view of the future indicates a continuance of the stream of invention and discovery—of a continually broadening range of human controls over the forces of physical nature and over man himself.[1]

When the forces of nature are still more thoroughly mastered, when the possibilities of eugenics and education are better understood, when social invention shall have done more perfect work, then the full possibilities of human perfectibility will be more nearly seen and better understood. In the light of such a progressive unfolding of human possibilities democracy was developed, and still continues to set as one of its cardinal principles the assumption of the indefinite extension of this development.

What is the ultimate goal? The goal is the leveling up of the standards of human living to a point far beyond any thus far attained even by the aristocrats themselves. Dr. Mayo says the outcome is not the triumph of the proletariat, but its extinction, using proletariat to mean a mass of ignorant and incompetent persons, incapable of assuming serious responsibilities. Since the days of the French Revolution the doctrine of the continuing perfectibility of mankind has glimmered in the minds of the leaders of the mass movement, and has animated them to continue the struggle in this direction. Thus far the human lag has been very great.

In one sense poverty may be considered a relative term on any scale of income, but there are sordid desolations of humanity that may be eliminated forever from the experience of mankind. That there will always be differentials in capacity is not a valid pretext for the most obvious handicaps to the unfolding of human personality and for low-level

[1] *Recent Social Trends in the United States*, Report of the President's Research Committee on Social Trends (1933), Vol. I, Committee's Findings, and Chaps. II and III.

forms of education, housing, diet, medical care, surroundings that are a disgrace to the human race in our day.

In the broadest sense, liberalism and prosperity should be happy companions. Democracy is committed to their union. One of the goals of democracy is the ideal of prosperity. But what is prosperity? Prosperity is achieved in a community when men realize in large and increasing measure the values they cherish, material or otherwise—commodities, services, or satisfactions. Prosperity looks to the highest possible levels of economic and social productivity and the widest possible distribution of the resulting gains, awarded in accordance with the nearest possible approximation to the principles of social justice and the realization of the common good.

Prosperity includes, on its positive side, an era of plenty, abundance of physical goods and comforts, rich intellectual achievement and expression, assurance of economic and political security, fullness of artistic and spiritual life, ample recognition of the unique and exquisite place of creative instincts and talents.

And, negatively, prosperity tends to exclude war, famine, disease, poverty, scarcity of goods and meagerness of services, social and economic unbalance, individual and social frustration and distress.

Prosperity denotes an era of abundance, but with emphasis on the quality as well as the quantity of goods and values, on harmonious and desirable interrelations as well as growth in the scale of magnitude. Prosperity in the democratic system of values means not merely sheer power of intelligence, science, organization over nature, but also the application of such controls for the central purpose of social life—fulfillment on the widest possible scale of human aspirations and potentialities.

ASSUMPTIONS AND PROGRAM

3. *Mass Gains and the Many*

Democracy assumes that the gains of commonwealths are essentially mass gains and should be diffused through the mass by whom they were created as rapidly as possible. In a political unit such as a modern nation this becomes clear in time of great national stress, as in war. Men are called upon to give up their ordinary occupations, to risk their lives, in defense of what is clearly recognized as a common cause. In these moments the meaning of the commonwealth stands out clearly, without any successful rival. Likewise in other moments of tension such as famine, plague, flood, depression, this is clear.

Individuals and groups are not presumed to assert the priority of selfish claims over the community as a whole in case of conflict, just as no individual in time of war may demand exemption of his special interest. The nation has not only the right of eminent domain over land, but also the right to draft persons for war, and the right to make rules for what it conceives to be the common good.

There are those who demand the public protection, heritage, and advantages of the nation and are not willing to subordinate their private claims to it. There are those who seek all the profits and none of the losses in a common enterprise. There are those who insist that the gains of civilization are essentially the creation of a few men who are the real foundations of the nation or society in which they live, and that others contribute only in a minor and subordinate way. But from the mass point of view the land, minerals, energy resources, human resources of the nation are of and for the people as a whole.

The assumption of democracy is, then, that the total gains of commonwealths are mass gains produced by the common effort and that these gains are to be enjoyed by the mass that made them possible. This is not to deny that either contributions or rewards may be unequal, but to assert that broadly speaking national gains are nationally produced, the outcome of a joint effort in war and peace, pointed toward the common good.

4. *The Consent of the Governed*

The next assumption is the desirability of popular control in the last analysis over basic questions of policy and direction, with recognized procedures for the formulation of such controls and their execution.

Under all systems there is some attention given to popular feeling, popular morale, popular protest. This may be roughly measured by the applause for the king or his aides, or by the breadth and strength of popular discontent and murmurs, or by other evidence known to the skilled observer of the "temper" of the mass. The king himself may even visit his people incognito to find out what they are saying or how they are feeling. The assumption of democracy goes far beyond this rough sampling, however, to the conclusion that basic questions should be determined by the mass; or as many questions as the people care to consider, and in such form of consultation and assent as the nation may decide upon.

The special forms, times, and modes of consultation are of subordinate importance in the face of the major problem of consent in the large. These forms and modes are not unimportant either in the field of fact or in the field of symbolism, but they yield in significance to the broader principle involved, namely, the assertion of popular decision in ultimate analysis. As to the type forms in which assent is obtained there may be wide difference of opinion and practice, but here again the mass decision is final and controlling.

ASSUMPTIONS AND PROGRAM

In passing over a detailed discussion of the numerous and competing forms of organization of popular government I do not intend to minimize their importance, but only to lay the greater emphasis on the larger principle involved and its contrast with the assumption of aristocracy.

It is also true that the detail may become extremely important if it involves the actual distortion of the general principle. The special mechanism may indeed be little more than a cunning method of defeating the very principle involved, as in the case of a controlled plebiscite or a deceptive form of representation, in which twisted appearance takes the place of reality.

It may be asked, Who shall decide what are "basic questions," and who shall determine whether the ways and means of expressing the mass will are appropriate and effective? We cannot go farther back than the "general understandings" of the community, always the judge of the form and functioning of the legal order in which the system is set. Locke's doctrine that the people are always sovereign although "not under any form of government" has puzzled many political mechanics, but it contains an element of truth which cannot be disregarded. Participation in the making of decisions upon basic questions is one of the protections of the amateur against the professional, of the mass against the specialized class who take on the function of administration for them, and sometimes forget who is master. The responsibility of the ruler to the ruled has been one of the historic battlegrounds of popular government, and its instrumentation appears in many forms in many lands and times. Mass judgment as a means of determining community policy is vigorously resisted both in theory and in practice by the apostles of aristocracy.

Evidently no political association would be concerned with the fixation of all human value systems, for many of these are so intimate in their nature as to be inaccessible except in times of extraordinary tension, and others are so numerous and varied as to be incapable of successful administration by any one kind of grouping.[1] Some human values will be sharply fixed by the government; others more remotely regulated or affected; others will be supervised in a general way; others regarded only as they seem to interfere with the course of the nation, threatening it in some important particular.[2]

If a given system seems to imperil the community by overweight in the economic field, or in the ecclesiastical field, or becomes defiant of the association's basic principle in any field, the group may care to take appropriate action to restore the balance of social values.[3]

The wisdom of the government will under such circumstances be measured by the balance kept between its actual needs and the degree and type of regulation exercised. Every overregulation will bring its own antidote in the form of resistance, sabotage, low morale, and possibly overthrow of the powers that be, whereas failure to act will jeopardize the position of the state and destroy its unity of purpose and vigor.

In times of stress and storm this function of the state is readily recognized, as in war and disaster, but it is equally important in other periods of the group's development, when the implications of such differentials are not as apparent.

In an absolutistic state such powers may be exercised ruthlessly, without general consultation and without any real participation of the community in the program. "Autoc-

---

[1] See Huxley, *op. cit.*, for a satirical treatment of the complete regulation of human life.
[2] Dewey, *The Public and Its Problems*, Chap. I.
[3] See my *Role of Politics in Social Change*, Chap. V.

ASSUMPTIONS AND PROGRAM

racy tempered by assassination" was the old phrase applied to such rule. In a system of democracy broad powers may likewise be used ruthlessly, but not without opportunity for general counsel and participation, or ultimate review. Consent will be necessary and consent freely given under fair conditions.

In an autocratic state the same principle will be followed, but with this difference, that the policy of intervaluation will be determined by the few frankly rather than by the many. The few will be the judges of whether their value system is advantageous to the whole community and to themselves. If it is difficult for the mass to deal fairly with the few, it must also be admitted that it is even more difficult for the few to deal fairly with the many.

This assumption of popular control necessarily involves confidence in the value of mass judgment on basic community problems. The usefulness of any such judgments has been denied for centuries in varying terms and forms, down to the present day when the folly and futility of the mass is widely and loudly proclaimed. From the days of Aristotle, however, the social value of mass judgments has been asserted and defended. A man may not be able to make a poem, said the Greek, but he can tell when a poem pleases him. He may not be able to build a house, but he can tell when the roof leaks. He may not be able to cook, but he can tell whether he likes what is prepared for him.[1]

This is what Lincoln called "government of the people, by the people and for the people." In its more modern form this assumption rests upon the values involved in cooperative

---

[1] Rousseau has reformulated this doctrine in his *Social Contract*, stating: " . . . the general will is always right, and always tends toward public utility; but it does not follow that the deliberations of the people always have the same rectitude. The people wishes its own good always, but it does not always see it; the people is never corrupted, but it is often deceived, and it is then only that it seems to desire what is evil." *Op. cit.*, p. 40.

effort and concomitant morale—upon the significance of good will in participatory enterprises—and negatively on the fear that aristocratic decisions may be unduly weighted by the interests of those who are judging.[1]

5. *Consciously Directed and Peaceful Social Change*

The next assumption is that of confidence in the possibility of conscious social change, accomplished normally by consent rather than violence.[2]

Down to the nineteenth century, it was denied in high quarters that society could consciously and deliberately alter the form of its political institutions, or that this could be done wisely; and certainly not by the mass of the community. Count de Maistre, forgetting Philadelphia, declared that the constitutional convention was the modern Tower of Babel—attempting the impossible and the divinely forbidden. Constitutions, it was said, are not made, but grow—the work of history or of divine decree. A modern formulation of this same reactionary point of view, challenging the possibility of the conscious and deliberate shaping of political institutions, is to be found in the writings of contemporary German constitutional theorists, especially Ernst Rudolf Huber.[3]

---

[1] Dewey says: "A more serious objection is that expertness is most readily attained in specialized technical matters, matters of administration and execution which postulate that general policies are already satisfactorily framed. It is assumed that the policies of the experts are in the main both wise and benevolent, that is, framed to conserve the genuine interests of society. The final obstacle in the way of any aristocratic rule is that in the absence of an articulate voice on the part of the masses, the best do not and cannot remain the best, the wise cease to be wise. It is impossible for highbrows to secure a monopoly of such knowledge as must be used for the regulation of common affairs. In the degree in which they became a specialized class, they are shut off from knowledge of the needs which they are supposed to serve." *The Public and Its Problems*, p. 206.

[2] See my *Role of Politics in Social Change*, Chap. III.

[3] Ernst Rudolf Huber, *Verfassung* (1937); *Wesen und Inhalt der Politischen Verfassung* (1935).

ASSUMPTIONS AND PROGRAM

Democracy assumed on the contrary that governments could be made and remade by the will of the community. The American Constitution was a symbol of this belief in the possibility of conscious political change directed by the community as a whole.

An aspect of democracy is confidence in the utility of government as a social organizer. At one time, in the nineteenth century, the anarchistic doctrine tended to prevail, and it was widely believed that the ideal condition would be that in which there would be no organized political order whatever. This still remains the anarchism of Proudhon and of Tolstoi, and a conspicuous point in the creed of the Soviets, who foresee the end of all governmental organization, remote as it may appear at the moment. In various periods also government was identified with tyranny, and efforts were made to provide restrictions against government on the theory that whatever it did would be bad, and that the less done the better.

In more recent times, however, it has been realized that government may be the friend of the community as well as its foe; that popular government is not to be confused with arbitrary or personal or aristocratic government; that a weak government face to face with social situations in which action is urgent may be a danger to the stability and progress of the nation. When governments have not acted vigorously and progressively in moments of distress, they have exposed themselves to danger of overthrow, as in Italy and Germany, where more vigorous political action might have averted revolution. The unpardonable sin of government is inaction in emergencies. To do nothing is to abdicate. The distrust of government as an alien force, which a century or so ago was characteristic of the Many who feared the encroachments of the Few, is now more characteristic of the Few who fear the encroachments of the Many upon their special set of values.

Furthermore, it is assumed that conscious social change is to be brought about in the main by the process of peaceful consent rather than by the methods of violence. Freedom of discussion, freedom of association, in a relatively peaceful atmosphere, are the conditions making popular decisions possible. Obviously it is impossible to obtain a mass decision if those who decide are intimidated, if they are not in a position to consider the questions of policy or personnel at stake, if violence and duress and the distortion of facts through the agencies of communication take the place of deliberation and free choice. It was Bentham who once said that the liberty of a people is measured in the ultimate analysis by the facility with which acts of government may be criticized, discussed, and reversed.[1] A plebiscite following a period in which freedom of association and of discussion are repressed is no plebiscite at all, but a cynical imposition of authority. The assertion that the people have voted and approved a policy or a person under such circumstances is of no significance except that those who have used force have mislabeled it consent. No intelligent person need be deceived by consent obtained in "robbery with a gun."

This does not involve abdication of the use of organized force in democratic communities, but the predominance of emphasis on peaceful and persuasive methods of political action. This in turn implies the general willingness to accept the mode of consent, rather than the method of imposition, and to abide by the decisions rendered by mass verdict.

Democracy is not a set of formulas, or a blueprint of organization, but a cast of thought and a mode of action directed toward the commonweal as interpreted and directed by the common will.

[1] Jeremy Bentham, *A Fragment on Government* (1891), pp. 216–217.

ASSUMPTIONS AND PROGRAM

Democrats differ from time to time as to local and special aims, particular platforms, and specific operating plans, but have in common a general attitude and method in arriving at social decisions, a general spirit in which social policies are administered, a devotion to a general framework within which order and justice serve the common good and follow the common will.

The formula of democracy for dealing with social tensions is that of resolution by the orderly processes of reason and discussion rather than by arbitrary decision; by adjustment, compromise, and good will rather than by inflexible intolerance and brutal repression of opposition; by hopefulness and persuasion rather than by pessimism and violence.

The use of force by democracy in moments of irreconcilable stress is not directed at the repression of opposition, but at the preservation of the liberal attitude itself, at reasonable approach toward social conflicts, at patience in the modes of their adjustment.

Unwillingness to inquire into the underlying elements of conflict, impatience in interpretation and conclusion, flat arbitrariness in decision, cruelty in repression of minorities, violence as a usual mode of conversion—these are contrary to the liberal spirit.

In general the tools of democratic liberalism include intelligence, education, persuasion, adjustment, administration, adjudication, directed hopefully and patiently by the community toward the common good, through accepted forms of community action and control.

6. *Summary*

These assumptions constitute the theoretical basis of democracy. The program of democracy is directed toward their validation through specific mechanisms, and in particular programs. But the underlying principles are standards by which special procedures and the policies of the moment are to be evaluated. These assumptions taken together make up the working philosophy of democracy, as it is evolving historically.

We may raise the question, How shall these assumptions be tested in the light of our present knowledge, and how do they differentiate democracy from other alternative types of political association? The validity of these assumptions is, of course, subject to examination by any of the means we utilize in the testing of knowledge. For the proof of some of them we should look primarily to rational and perhaps to ethical analysis and for others to the body of observations, analyses, and conclusions accumulated by modern social science; or both methods may be applied.

Thus, the dignity of the human personality may be regarded either from the ethical-rational point of view, or from the point of view of the student of groups in their relation to their members, or of a student of morale such as Dr. Mayo or Major Urwick who considers the meaning of the satisfied personality in the organization of association. The "continuing perfectibility" of mankind may be explored from the point of view of data developed by science, technology, personality studies and seen in the ranges of social science. Likewise the generalization of mass gains may be approached from the point of view of studies of the nature of associations, as seen in the students of groupism, or from the point of view of a rational analysis of the nature of a community and the commonweal. The same process is applicable to the assumptions regarding the possibility of conscious control of social affairs and to the role of violence in this field. The assumptions regarding the value of mass judgment and the meaning of the consensual arrangements designed for that purpose may be scrutinized by a variety of

ASSUMPTIONS AND PROGRAM

approaches, including rational analysis, observation, experiment. All of these types of treatment have been applied from the days of Aristotle down to modern times.

Or we may take the whole body of assumptions together and consider them in their cumulative aspect, as a joint characterization of the general premises of democracy. We should then find that not all defenders of democracy agree with this statement of democratic theory. We should find on the other hand that defenders of alternative systems of association will declare their acceptance of some of the assumptions set up as democratic.

Thus we find that there are democrats who intimate that democracy can exist only within a capitalistic society, as in the case of Rappard, and those who, quite to the contrary, intimate that democracy cannot exist in capitalistic society, as in the case of Laski.[1] There are, of course, those who contend that democracy can exist neither in a capitalistic nor in any form of industrial or other society, as in the case of the Fascists.

We must, of course, allow for the historical fact that many regimes, absolutistic, aristocratic, and other, have proclaimed from time to time their adherence to one or more of these democratic assumptions, but in practice have paid little heed to them. Benevolent despots have arisen who took seriously the task of protecting their subjects and nourishing them as they would their flocks and lands—and perhaps with right good will. But they wished to remain irresponsible to their people—and ordinarily their regime at best was neither fraternal nor peaceful.

---

[1] See William E. Rappard, *The Crisis of Democracy* (1938), Chap. VI; Harold J. Laski, *The Rise of European Liberalism* (1936), concluding chapter; *The State in Theory and Practice* (1935), Chap. IV. See also the position of Hans Kelsen interpreting democracy in terms of a special form of liberty in *Vom Wesen und Wert der Demokratie* (1929), Chap. I; and Bryce on democracy as a type of governmental mechanism, *Modern Democracies* (1921), Vol. I, Chap. III.

THE NEW DEMOCRACY

The governments of the Few or the One have often assumed a general paternal attitude whether from the patrimonial point of view or the military, the industrial, or the religious, or the more modern view of nationalistic proprietorship. But commonly they were unconcerned with liberty, or equality, or the protection of human personality; or with normally peaceful change; or with ways and means of responsibility of the ruler to the ruled. Sometimes indeed they were practically unconscious of these ideas, or were indifferent or cynical; or again were positively antagonistic to them; or in a more cheerful mood looked upon them as ideals impossible of attainment in any practical span of time. All of this attitude was set of course in a framework of vested interest which made the rejection of democratic ideas not only logically inevitable, but also profitable and pleasant in the immediate present.

It is also true that so-called "democracies" at various times have fallen far short in practice of the goals indicated in the assumptions of their basic form of political association. Even in our own day there are nominal democrats who do not intend to allow their democracy to interfere with their preferred position in society, and the protection of the special values they cherish whether in the form of property or prestige.

The democrat will maintain that on the basis of his analysis and observation the general assumptions indicated may be most readily and surely achieved through the democratic form of association and the democratic way of life. He will not deny that some of his assumptions may be developed from time to time in partial fashion in some alternative system, but he will note that the whole body of democratic aims is not even avowed in other systems, and further the assurance that they will be carried out is lacking where the means for consulting the community are missing. Rulers who are

ASSUMPTIONS AND PROGRAM

judges in their own cause tend to twisted interpretations of human dignity, of human shares in social values. They tend to see through colored glasses the fundamentals of order, justice, and liberty.

On the whole the democratic theory affirms that the democratic group of assumptions, both as to ends and means, constitutes a unified program which may be taken as a way of life, within the range of values that may be classed as political. Other systems are differentiated from it either by the specification of different ends or means, or both. The disunity of ends and means constitutes one of the most serious obstacles to the development of democratic institutions.

The prime factor in the maintenance of democracy is the unification of the assumptions of democracy in a working program—in the general recognition of the meaning of these assumptions and of the importance of realizing them in practical affairs, internal and international as well.

Democracy will be at its weakest when these assumptions are imperfectly or weakly carried through, and strongest when they are energetically advanced in comprehensive, systematic, and persistent fashion.

B. THE BACKGROUND OF RECENT DEMOCRATIC THEORY

There is little difficulty in piling up mountains of evidence to indict mass governments for incompetence and corruption upon many counts.[1] And yet the democratic tide sweeps forward in recent centuries with increasing breadth and momentum, reaching through the ways of life.

We may ask the question, What are the chief contributory causes to the spread of the democratic idea? What caused the decline of the caste system? What are the basic situations that ended slavery and serfdom as well? What has developed the new regard for great masses of persons who for centuries were passed by as scarcely human?

What is there in the nineteenth and twentieth centuries that effected this fundamental change in human attitudes and social relations? The main influences and forces may be classified as follows:

1. Ideology
   Ethical
   Political
2. Science and technology
   Discovery
   Production
3. Social technique
   Education
   Social participation
4. Democratic experience

---

[1] For the best literary pictures see William E. H. Lecky, *Democracy and Liberty* (1896); Emile Faguet, *The Cult of Incompetence* (trans. 1914); Vilfredo Pareto, *Mind and Society*, ed. Arthur Livingston (1935).

ASSUMPTIONS AND PROGRAM

At the basis of the system of democracy there lie an ideology, a system of technology, and a set of social techniques in the field of social relationships—inventions in social behavior corresponding to inventions on the material side.

1. *Ideology*

The political ideology of the democratic movement was stated early in the doctrines of Aristotle. Lost for hundreds of years, his *Politics* was rediscovered in the eleventh century and became the subject of liveliest discussion. The Roman law doctrine that the ruler has power since the people had transferred it to him likewise obtained wide vogue with the revival of interest in the study of the Roman law in the thirteenth century. Later, the Old Testament version of the popular establishment of the kingdom of Israel aided in directing attention to the democratic principle in setting up government. The feudal relationship itself made contract an important element in authority and compelled interest in the nature of such agreements.[1] By the end of the fourteenth century the doctrine was universally accepted that the consent of the governed is the theoretical basis of all authority, and although not carried out in practice this idea became firmly fixed in the minds of the theorists of the day.

The ideology of democracy on its ethical side is as old as the doctrines of Stoicism and Christianity.[2] The early struggle of these humane doctrines is now easily forgotten, but they once competed with the caste idea accepted by a great portion of the world, as in India. Historically, democracy met systems resting upon human slavery and systems of racial superiority. Stoicism, proclaiming the brotherhood

---

[1] On the relation between form of church government and civil government in New England see my *American Political Theories* (1920), pp. 32*ff.*, and Alexander D. Lindsay, *The Essentials of Democracy* (1929), p. 13.

[2] On Confucian theory see E. D. Thomas, *Chinese Political Thought* (1938), and Pao Chao Hsieh, *The Government of China*, 1644–1911 (1923), Chap. I.

of man, arose as the philosophy of the Greek "Bastards" who "did not belong." Christianity proclaimed the equality of all men in the sight of God.

Religion might and did at times turn the idea of the dignity and fellowship of man into toleration of slavery in actual life, and build up defences for arbitrary and oppressive authority as in the union of the altar and the throne. But the basic meaning of human spiritual equality swept on slowly through Western civilization, developing most rapidly in the theories of the social contract and of the moral basis of the right to revolution against an unjust or tyrannical government—a doctrine in which both Catholic and Protestant controversialists joined heartily.

The apostles of religion constantly reiterated the doctrine that on moral levels of human behavior each human being must be considered as possessing a soul and a destiny of vast importance—possessing the moral right to judge of the conduct of his governors, upon points involving ethical problems at any rate.

Church government was not based upon hereditary transmission of ecclesiastical power. The new officials were recruited at large, and continuity of government in the church was brought about without regard to inheritance.

The ecclesiasts were thus aiding in the spread of a basic ideology of human interrelationships which was not on the whole either a philosophy of submission or a philosophy of inequality, whatever the actual practices might have been, and however subservient the church might become at times. That these ideas were twisted by designing persons into convenient defences of their special plans does not alter the basic fact with which we are dealing; we are concerned with the long-time march of the idea.

The next stage was the application of this idea to the theory that government originates in some formal govern-

ASSUMPTIONS AND PROGRAM

mental or social contract by which the fundamentals of authority and popular control are set up. After a bitter struggle with the opposing theories, the divine right of kings and the historical customary basis of power, the contractual theory obtained a sweeping victory and was almost universally accepted in Western Europe as basic in political reasoning.[1] There followed the question of the delineation of the constitutional limitations upon autocratic governments, and the construction of types of popular organization or representation most appropriate under special conditions. But the foundation theory was almost universally accepted.

The transition from the private proprietary state to the public state shifted the basis of public affairs from private law to public law—from the doctrine that one individual owned the land and the people on the land, with the private right to govern them and regulate their affairs, to the doctrine that the ruler became the first servant of the state rather than its master.[2]

There followed the transition from the *Machtstaat* to the *Rechtstaat*, from the power state to the legal state, from the doctrine of legal irresponsibility to the doctrine of limited powers and special procedures for the definition and protection of civil rights of individuals, from the arbitrary rule of those who might call themselves the servants of the state and act quite otherwise, to a system in which legal responsibility applied even to the conduct of the persons in power.

The development of the doctrine of democracy was aided on the ideological side by the concurrence of theories that were not primarily concerned with democracy, but that when brought together contributed to the strengthening of

---

[1] See William A. Dunning, *A History of Political Theories: From Luther to Montesquieu* (1905), Chap. II, on the Monarchomachs.

[2] See Friedrich Meinecke, *Die Idee der Staatsräson in der neueren Geschichte* (1924), for an analysis of the transition from the doctrine of the private proprietary state to the theory that the ruler is the trustee of the community.

the mass position. Among these were the philosophies of Hegel, who lifted the state out of artificiality by declaring it to be the highest form of human association;[1] of Austin, who developed the idea of the juristic omnipotence of the state;[2] of the group who found the state to be organic in nature, or at least a real, as distinguished from an artificial, person;[3] of another group of "societarian" theorists who emphasized the meaning of the society in its relation to the individual member of the association.[4]

Along with these ideas came the emerging theories of liberal nationalism and of economic collectivism, both of which inevitably emphasized the role of the mass in political theory and practice, although neither was necessarily directed toward the advocacy of democracy. Nationalism might become anti-democratic, indeed, as in Germany in the latter part of the nineteenth century. Collectivism might be anarchistic or welcome the dictatorship of the proletariat. Both these ideologies tended to bring into the foreground the importance and meaning of the mass movement of the time. The nation was not a class but the mass, and the economic collectivity, although calling itself a class (the proletariat), was essentially the mass.

2. *Science and Technology*[5]

One of the consequences of the development of science and technique was the discovery of new worlds and their settlement. In many colonial developments this process was carried on with little or no contribution to any program of Democracy; on the contrary, brutality and exploitation were the chief characteristics of the movement.

[1] Georg W. F. Hegel, *Naturrecht und Staatswissenschaft im Grundrisse* (1822).
[2] John Austin, *The Province of Jurisprudence Determined* (1832).
[3] Francis W. Coker, *Organismic Theories of the State* (1910).
[4] See William A. Dunning, *A History of Political Theories: From Rousseau to Spencer* (1920), Chap. IX and bibliography at conclusion of chapter.
[5] See Celestin Bouglé, *La Démocratie devant la science* (1923).

ASSUMPTIONS AND PROGRAM

In the case of the English colonies, however, opportunity was given for the rise of a new group of immigrants whose organization and procedure turned in the democratic direction, all the more easily because of the preoccupation of the home government with the revolutions and readjustments of the seventeenth century. The institution of nobility weakened, the hereditary transmission of political power ended, and primogeniture and entail on which that system rested was likewise eliminated in the course of a few generations. The reaction of these American developments was first marked in the French Revolution and later worked powerfully in the other peoples of Western Europe.

These new discoveries shattered the closed world of that day, wrecking the traditional view of human geography, the influence of which it is now difficult to reconstruct, so accustomed are we to another view. But the new world also facilitated the growth of a vast democratic base of development in America, Canada, and Australia, apart from the social background and traditions of the Old World. At the same time, the South American development was made democratic in form if not always in substance, at any rate distinctly not made a part of the traditional line of European aristocratic, autocratic organization.

An equally striking triumph of human intelligence was the amazing discoveries of science and their equally amazing applications in the form of technology which incredibly increased the control of man over the forces of nature. The productivity of the soil and the productivity of the machine were alike increased beyond the wildest dreams of the human imagination. The output of the soil was increased manifold, and the output of the machine increased the power of the hand manifold.[1]

---

[1] See National Resources Committee, *Technological Trends and National Policy* (1937).

THE NEW DEMOCRACY

This spectacular triumph was in large measure the work of the scientists and the inventors who carried through the most revolutionary conquest in human history within a century—a revolution so basic in its effects and implications as to leave the world still unable to interpret or organize it. Scientists, inventors, engineers played the grand roles in this fairyland of accomplishment, in many cases remaining relatively obscure men, in a few instances recognized and rewarded by their contemporaries. These chief actors were in the main not an acknowledged part of the economic or political order of their day, but stood apart from it, absorbed in the immense task of advancing the frontiers of human intelligence over hitherto untamed forces of nature. They were not primarily concerned with questions either of power, profit, or prestige, leaving these to the exploitation of others. Their efforts made possible the greatest of historical revolutions, that which overthrew the regime of scarcity and enthroned in its place a regime of plenty—a plenty in the domain of food products and plenty in the realm of machine production of commodities and services.

The new era was based on science and technology and the new technique of mass production. The triumph that produced so fruitful a world as to embarrass sections of it by a superabundance of goods was a triumph of technology and social organization. The new economic and social system to which these developments gave rise brought with it its own injustices and inequalities. The owners of capital became the new aristoi, enjoying a disproportionate share of political and economic power, either in their own right or in collaboration with the older landholding aristocracies.

Prior to this development it might be said, and was said, that there was not enough to go around, not enough land or production from the land, not enough commodities produced or producible; and therefore some must be hungry and

ASSUMPTIONS AND PROGRAM

probably some would starve. The poor were given by God, it was said, in order to stimulate and exercise the philanthropic impulses of others, which else would shrivel and die away.

That the masses of the people immediately obtained all of these possible new advantages is not true. On the contrary, they were sometimes worse off than before, as in mines and factories, where new forms of "white slavery" were found. But the way was made possible for a program of democracy based upon a new type of abundance. And by and large the consumption per capita of units of commodities and services was increased substantially.

3. *Social Techniques*

Significant advances were also made in the invention and organization of social techniques. Among many a few may be indicated.

The invention of printing opened new worlds to the masses and tended to make difficult an unquestioned regime of caste or slavery. The way of emancipation from ignorance was opened out to many. And what challenges sprang up in their minds as they looked upon the hitherto closed world around them, a world revealed only by the authentic interpreters of tradition and proprietors of power.

The next step was the universalization of education throughout the Western world, over a constantly widening range of years, approaching universal obligatory education. Education ceased to be a privilege of the few and became not merely the right but the duty of everyone, and that for an increasingly higher age group.[1] In the United States the "high school" level was generally adopted as the minimum of education. It is true that a literate people may not be

---

[1] On the development in the United States see Charles H. Judd, *Problems of Education in the United States* (1933).

democratic, but even more true that a democracy rests upon a basis of popular intelligence and education.

A part of this new trend was attributable not alone to the desire for more education but to the increasing amount of leisure time available in an era of abundance; but this does not affect the meaning of the process of education in examining the background of the recent democratic development. Caste or class education inevitably tends to hold the mass of people helpless where they are—as in the long-standing caste system of modern India, where generation after generation follows the same dark course.[1]

Under all systems, to be sure, or most of them, the youth of very superior intelligence may perhaps break his bonds. But this leaves many forgotten talents never recognized or utilized in the society.[2] Under a universal system of education the range of recruitment is wider and the circle of critical judgment is also widened—an equally important consideration in any democratic society.

Modern education leaves much to be desired, but when compared with an era in which only a few were given the opportunity of training, the gap between the old and the new is seen to be enormous. Of particular importance is the broad basis of education in its relations to the continuing flow of natural and social invention, increasing the range and effectiveness of our knowledge of natural forces and human behavior alike.

Out of the field of science and education emerged the body of inquiry, experiment, and reflection known as "social sciences." The developing range of knowledge regarding the principles and techniques of social behavior tended to increase human confidence in conscious social control. The tendency was not merely to accept the environment as

[1] Celestin Bouglé, *Essais sur les régimes des castes* (1908).
[2] *Cf.* H. S. Jennings, *Biological Basis of Human Nature* (1930), p. 220.

ASSUMPTIONS AND PROGRAM

given, but to understand it, then to devise appropriate methods and techniques for the guidance of social forces.[1] It cannot, of course, be said that social science has achieved more than an imperfect understanding of social forces, but in various fields, notably in those of health, welfare, education, and administration, great forward strides were taken. In other directions significant progress was made toward a more adequate working knowledge of social relationships and an approach to various forms of social technology.

The democratic movement was further advanced by the development of techniques of participation in political affairs. One of these took the form of equality before the law, another of universal suffrage, another of responsible representative government and the accompanying growth of the party system. Another was the recruitment of administrators from the mass. These mechanisms turned the average man and later woman first into a "person" and then into a potential critic and creator in the domain of government, however crude and inexpert he might appear or actually be.

Even in the Middle Ages it had been generally agreed that government rests theoretically upon the consent of the governed, but practically the implications of this brave theory were very slight. The person might actually be a serf or a slave, or be entirely ignored in political decisions, or confined to a very narrow range of them.

The earlier democracies themselves strictly limited the number of eligibles, without serious challenge in many cases. The area of general participation came later and slowly. By the twentieth century, however, this zone of participation had been extended to include practically all of the adult population and usually women as well as men.

[1] See my *New Aspects of Politics* (1931), especially Chaps. I, VI, and VIII; and Reports of the Social Science Research Council, *passim*.

Significant steps were also taken in the direction of the organization of a jural order of the world in which the importance of decisions by violence would be diminished. It cannot be said that these efforts were crowned with success; but on the other hand it cannot be denied that the growth of international law, the establishment of the Hague Tribunal, the organization of the League of Nations, the setting up of the International Labor Office and of a series of international organizations were the most significant attempts at formulating a world order in the history of mankind. They had a distinct relationship to the development of the background of a democratic system in which persuasion rather than violence was emphasized as a normal mode of arriving at political decisions.

4. *Democratic Experience*

In the course of practical experience of recent generations there has been a notable shift in the type of anti-democratic argumentation. Among the older hobgoblins were the oft repeated assertions by eminent authorities:

a. That democracy cannot exist except on a small area with a small population.

b. That democracy cannot maintain itself in time of military emergency because of its inherent incapacity to act promptly and effectively.

c. That democracy is essentially the rule of the ignorant mob, unable to set up any competent organization of administration.

But before looking at these theories, it is important to take a broad view of the labors and the obligations arising from recent experience on the part of democratic states.

The tasks of the newly developing democracy were such as might try the temper of any political order since history

ASSUMPTIONS AND PROGRAM

began. These obligations of the nineteenth and twentieth centuries involved such weighty tasks as the following:

a. The extension of democracy over many new lands, and the democratization of democracy itself in many states.

b. The transition from rural agrarian economy to an urban industrial economy for millions of population, and the adjustment of new urban and old rural ways of life.

c. The development and application of science and technology on the vast scale commensurate with their depth of meaning for modern life.

d. The equitable diffusion of the gains of civilization through the masses of the community without too great delay or confusion.

e. Adjustment of the educational personnel and equipment to the new order of things.

f. Adaptation of governmental and social instruments to the shifting economic and social structure and changing human values.

g. The construction of a jural system of world order in which nations and industry might function without interference from international violence.

These were the burdens imposed upon an imperfectly developed system of mass rule hardly prepared for the sudden accession to power and responsibility under swiftly changing conditions,[1] and including in its peoples only a small percentage of the world's population.

On the other hand, no group seemed better prepared to take over the responsibility of the possession of political power in most jurisdictions. The burden of these adjust-

---

[1] See James Bryce, *Modern Democracies* (1921), Chap. LXXVIII; Francis W. Coker, *Recent Political Thought* (1934); Chap. X; Edwin L. Godkin, *Unforeseen Tendencies of Democracy* (1898); C. E. Merriam, *American Political Ideas* (1920), Chap. I; C. E. Merriam and H. E. Barnes, editors, *Political Theories: Recent Times* (1924).

ments fell heavily upon the democratic or semi-democratic political societies of Western Europe, who were obliged to find some line of unified political leadership in a world of divergent beliefs and of clashing mechanisms alike in the field of science and of social organization. Class conflict, national rivalries, struggles between skills and value systems presented almost insuperable difficulties in the way of prompt, equitable, and acceptable solution.[1]

It is, of course, the recurring task of every political society to administer not merely the normal problems of the period in which it exists, but also the abnormal, unusual, and difficult ones. But the complexity of the case must also be taken into consideration; unless this is done, what is attributed to a special form of control may be overemphasized, and what is due to special circumstances underestimated. The conjunction of problems in the nineteenth and twentieth centuries would have tried the temper of any government, and many of the failures of the day, politically speaking, are the outcome of the conflict of ideas and technologies in a phase of social evolution rather than the product of any particular form of association.

In the light of all this experience, it is important to observe that many of the older criticisms of democracy are no longer seriously considered.

a. In view of the far-flung territory and population of the United States and of Great Britain, it is absurd to maintain the older thesis of the incompatibility of democracy and the large-scale state. Yet as late as the end of the eighteenth century and even in the United States at that time, doubts were expressed as to the possibility of any other than a small-sized democracy.

There is democracy in relatively small areas such as Switzerland and Sweden, but there is also democracy in

---

[1] See discussion of emerging trends of authority in my *Political Power*, Chap. X.

ASSUMPTIONS AND PROGRAM

Australia and Canada. In neither instance does the area or the numbers seem to be the conclusive consideration.

b. It is no longer confidently asserted that a democracy cannot survive in military struggle against monarchic or aristocratic contenders. In modern times the life span of mass rule seems as good a risk as that of any competing form of government, and better than some. In the recent World War it was Russia, Germany, Austria who collapsed under the strain of the long-drawn-out struggle. France and England were able to weather the storm, to organize and utilize vast military and naval forces, to maintain their morale under very difficult circumstances. Whether or not the essential differential was the form of government or not, it cannot be denied that the democracies were not shown incapable of maintaining themselves over a long period of intense military activity.

c. It is no longer confidently asserted that democracy can produce nothing beyond the rule of incompetence and ignorance, as was positively declared in earlier times by the advocates of the Few. In the face of competent governments such as those of Sweden, Holland, England, France, and the United States such a position is no longer tenable, and indeed is no longer advanced seriously. There are clouds of criticism of the weaknesses of democracies in special cases— most effectively developed within democracies themselves— but the old-time generalized assertion that no democracy can ever produce types of competence under any circumstances is now difficult to sustain.[1]

In short the classical arguments against democracy based upon necessary limitation to small size, based upon inability to survive military struggle, based upon general ignorance

[1] A prewar wholesale indictment of this type is found in Wilhelm Hasbach, *Die moderne Demokratie* (1912), an unfortunate date of publication. Compare Bryce's comparison of the strength and weaknesses of democracies in *Modern Democracies*, Vol. II, Part III, as judged by the "canons" he set up and applied to them.

and incompetence have been abandoned as a result of the experience of recent generations with democratic types of association, even when not fully democratic in horizon of participation. Democracy has been acquitted of these charges and a new indictment framed.[1]

Much confusion has been caused by failure to distinguish between the essential elements of democracy and special features of democratic organization, program, or social background. The general principle of community control over essential community problems is in this way lost in the controversy over special and temporary features of a general system.

In general political theory, democracy is not identifiable with:

a. Any special size or area such as a city, state, nation state, world state.

b. Any special form of economic organization, agrarian, industrial, capitalistic, socialistic, state capitalistic, or otherwise.

c. Any special form of centralization or decentralization of powers or functions, as federal or centralistic, or any special form of the separation or balance of power among agents of authority.

d. Any particular form of representative or executive organization, such as unicameral, bicameral, multicameral, regional or occupational representation, or special type of administrative or managerial arrangements.

Of course, in different historical situations—American, Swiss, English, Swedish—democracy is associated with special types of machinery, program, cultural background. But the general principle of democratic association and purpose lies deeper down than these special forms and problems, however important they may be in a given phase of social

[1] For discussion of "Postwar Defences of the Few" see below, p. 208.

ASSUMPTIONS AND PROGRAM

development in a particular territory or people. The principle and the practice of democracy may be found in any kind of social, economic, religious, racial, cultural situation; or it may be found in many varying types of governmental organization; or it may be found with many widely ranging programs designed to carry out the principle of democracy under very different circumstances.

But these different social settings, varying mechanisms, and diverse programs are not to be confused with the underlying system of common determination of the commonwealth organization and action.

Further confusion arises from the wider or narrower range of democratic participation in various times and places. From time to time the horizon of democracy varies. A small section or a very large section of the community may be excluded from political participation in community affairs, and the remaining section may constitute the area of democratic effectiveness. The inclusion of the adult population is a relatively recent phenomenon, for most historic democracies so-called did not include more than a minority, sometimes a very small minority of the political community.[1]

The fact that within these narrower ranges of population with imperfect democracy much of the practice of popular government has developed often tends to confuse the general principle of democracy with special times, places, and programs. What we often observe historically is the development of democratic principles and forms within aristocratic society, which affirms the theory of democracy while retaining the aristocratic form of association and tradition.

The modern problem arises from

a. The establishment of genuinely democratic participation in community affairs.

---

[1] Bryce declares that the eligibility of three-fourths of the adult community is necessary to establish the democratic character of the society, *op. cit.*, Vol. I, p. 22.

b. The development of a democratic program corresponding to this wider range of interest and activity.

What for centuries was the theory of democracy—in practice its dream—now tends to become its everyday program. Under these conditions aristocracies or oligarchies which entertained the doctrine of democracy in the abstract, with the understanding that the idea would not seriously be carried out, now face new realities. A transition from the implications of democracy to the applications of democracy is the problem of our time.

In more recent years it has been the habit of economic determinists and others to relate the democratic system of government to a special form of industrial organization, and in particular to capitalism. It has been held that there is a close analogy between the free competition of the economic world and the electoral process of the political, and the conclusion has been drawn that one rises or falls with the other.

A view of the historical development of democratic ideology and institutional forms shows that they have sprung up under a variety of conditions, sometimes rural and agrarian and at other times urban and industrial. Aristotle enumerates different varieties of democratic rule in his politics; a democracy of husbandmen; of shepherds and herdsmen; of mechanics, exchange men, and hired servants.[1]

The history of the world since the great Greek illustrates still more fully the possibilities of varied types of democratic states, as in Switzerland, in Australia, in Canada, in America, rural and urban industrial—under a wide variety of economic backgrounds so numerous as to make it perfectly clear that essentially democracy is not dependent upon any particular form of industrial or economic organization. Jefferson indeed declared that only a rural democracy was

---

[1] *Politics* (trans. Jowett, 1905), Book VI, Chap. IV. See also classification according to modes of choosing officials, Book VI, Chap. IV. Book IV, Chap. VI.

ASSUMPTIONS AND PROGRAM

capable of surviving,[1] whereas others have maintained to the contrary that the urban community is the best ground for the development of a democratic system. Others have asserted, more recently, that true democracy is possible only under a society not capitalistic in nature.

During the nineteenth century the development of democracy was carried on in many places in which industry was operated upon a laissez-faire basis, and later on a modified basis in which monopoly and regulation had materially changed the character of the original system.

All of the burdens of unorganized urbanism and of unorganized laissez-faire economics were imposed on the development of mass rule, and the inevitably ensuing problems were charged wholly to these democratic institutions without regard to the special circumstances under which one form of democracy grew up. Additional basis for this position was given by the fact that the natural-law theory of government bore some resemblance to the natural laws of economics, as they were called. There was an effort to identify liberty in the political sense with economic liberty. It soon became evident, however, that the "natural-law" system in politics led straight to the establishment of government, whereas that of economics led to the boycott of government; and further that the "natural liberty" of politics soon resolved itself into a system of political order and justice, whereas the "natural liberty" of the economic world resisted governmental and social regulation at almost every point.[2]

Within modern economic society there developed concentrations of wealth which began to menace at many points the workings of a political system which had not presupposed such powerful elements of opposition. These new industrial

---
[1] See my *American Political Theories*, p. 166.
[2] See Frank H. Knight on the similarities between democracy and the prevailing economic order in *The Ethics of Competition* (1935), pp. 293*ff*.

units in a sense took the place of the old landed group—the landlords—who in the preceding period had dominated the economic and the political life of the community. Mobilizing quickly and often acting with great ruthlessness, these new forces were able in many instances to dictate terms to government and to obtain either special privilege or immunity from regulation by the state. Their powers over trade and commerce enabled them to fix wages and salaries, to determine prices, and to control the amount and type of output over wide ranges of industrial activity. Under the protecting shelter of *laissez faire*,[1] they often made politics in a sense a branch of economics. What emerged in various situations was in effect a plutocratic aristocracy.

This situation led many to the conclusion that democracy was only another name for oligarchy—or, in the later terminology, plutocracy—using the forms of democracy while enjoying the substance of aristocracy. Marxians indeed were so confused that they identified the entire state with a mechanism for the use of violence in support of the bourgeoisie. They therefore demanded its destruction. The neo-elitists attributed to democracy all of the ills of the recent postwar period, both economic and governmental as well. These problems were presented primarily, not by any form of economic or governmental organization, but by the emergence of human science and by the development of new and dazzling forms of technology.[2]

Others drew the conclusion that formal mass rule could signify nothing but plutocracy, more or less thinly disguised, and that not as a passing phase but as a permanent relationship. That America, the amplest home of democracy, was also the home of industrial concentration in its amplest form was cited as an additional proof of the intimate and

---

[1] See my *Role of Politics in Social Change* (1936), Chaps. I and II.
[2] *Ibid.*, Chap. I.

ASSUMPTIONS AND PROGRAM

necessary interrelationship between the form of government and the form of concentration of capital. That capitalism had developed in like form in Germany under another system and in Japan under still another was blandly ignored in these hasty calculations. This type of reasoning often made it possible for opposites to unite in attack upon popular rule, one side denouncing democracy on the ground that it was not democratic enough and the other because it was or threatened to become too democratic. Thus the Communist and the Nazi might combine against the democratic government, as they did in Germany in the period just before the advent of Hitler.

In general political theory, however, there is no necessary relationship between democracy as a form of political association and any special form of economic association or organization. Whatever the form of government, it is obliged to bear the burden of adjusting the balance between modern technology, industry, and government.

Equally naive are those who assert that democracy cannot survive in an industrial society in which large-scale production is found or widely found. It is somehow discovered that only on small farms and with small-scale industry can popular rule be maintained successfully. This is not unlike the earlier doctrine that democracy cannot work on a widespread territory, but must be confined to tiny lots of land.

The size and complexity of industrial production do not condition the operations of the consent of the governed. The broad decision as to the function of the democracy may be made equally well whether the industrial organization or territorial area is small, middle-sized, or large. The task of the people consists in outlining the broad policies to be followed and in exercising general and not detailed supervision over the personnel and the policies they have set up. It is no more difficult to accomplish this result in a large territory than in a smaller one, or in a large-scale industrial organization than in a smaller sized one.

An underlying problem in respect to industrial units is the optimum size of operating units from the point of view of the commonwealth, and this may vary widely in different ranges of industrial production.

The real difficulty arises in the minds of those who are so bewildered by size, or confused by complexity, or overwhelmed by nostalgia for the primitive that they are unable to apply organizational principles to the essential problem—which is the organization of policy-determining bodies for the statement of general laws and principles, and the organization of administration for the purpose of management, and the counterrole of the policy-determining agency in general supervision of the administrative agencies.

C. VALIDATION OF DEMOCRATIC ASSUMPTIONS

The program of democracy follows from its principles. Popular government must adapt itself to widely differing conditions in various stages of cultural development, in various periods of tension, and in various phases of the dynamics of development. In an agrarian era, the program would develop its details in one form and in an industrial era in another fashion; in emergencies, pestilence, war, famine, depression, one pattern may appear, and in times of peace, prosperity, and content, when the tension is easier, quite another type of policy might be shaped.

This is true of the mechanics of democracy as well as of its policies and program. The organization of the selection and continuity of officialdom may vary from time to time; the organization and methods of representative bodies will inevitably shift with changing social factors and needs; and if we were to run through the various power "patterns" we should find wide room for democratic variation in practically all of these power relations.

Mass rule is primarily a principle and secondarily a special form of organization; it is an idea or an attitude rather than a mechanical institution. A structure is also a function in process of action, and a democratic "institution" has no validity except as it serves a democratic purpose—as a means, not an end. At all times both assumptions and institutions are open to challenge, but the institution cannot well be defended against the basic assumption on which it rests. When the forms of mass rule are habitually used to defeat its fundamental purposes, there is need for reexamination of these mechanical arrangements, of their workings in a given social situation, and there is need of revision to ensure adaptation of form to function. Here as elsewhere it may be said that the letter killeth, but the spirit giveth life. If the forms of legal liberty stand in the way of substantial liberty, if nominal justice covers substantial injustice, if "rights" become the continuing defences of vested wrong, then the validity of the system is *pro tanto* subject to challenge and review. If then it is found that such abuses are typical and characteristic, that they tend to recur on a wide scale, then the institutional arrangements become a subject of readjustment.

I have dealt with the basic assumptions of mass rule. I now address myself to the task of considering the positive program of mass-governed political society.

This program is considered in the light of the assumed objectives of democracy and is directed primarily at these objectives rather than at the special machinery through which the mass acts, although this is no mean part of the plan of democratic society. In the light of such considerations the program of democracy may be shaped.

This program, in order to have any general validity, must be couched in very broad terms and subject to many local modifications and adjustments to meet changes in time, place, and tempo of growth. It includes an examination of the following:

1. Validation of the assumption of the essential dignity of man and the importance of treating the human differentials on a fraternal basis.

2. Validation of the assumption of the continuing perfectibility of mankind.

3. Validation of the assumption that the gains of civilization are essentially mass gains and should be distributed throughout the community as rapidly as possible.

ASSUMPTIONS AND PROGRAM

4. Validation of the assumption of the desirability of mass decision on basic policies by establishment of procedures, forms, and understandings adapted to this purpose.

5. Validation of the assumption of the desirability of deliberate social change, typically non-violent in method.

1. *The Dignity of Man*

The essential dignity of man and the importance of protecting and cultivating his worth upon a fraternal rather than a differential principle may be validated partly through a wide range of attitudes.

It is easy to lose this way at the very beginning. Starting with actual inequalities among men, it is a short step to the fixed establishment of permanent status, and then to the hereditary transmission of status. The actual differentials become formal differentials not necessarily corresponding to the actualities any longer. The son of the military hero, or the son of the man of economic genius, or the son of the savant takes over the advantage of the superiority of a past generation. He may take for granted a status once based upon genuine capacity for a status not at all related to capacity. Groups of such individuals may be formed and may forget the foundation upon which their standing rests. In a fluid money economy this is especially easy, as broad claims to power are concealed under the protective coloration of gold or its equivalent in credit. In such instances the dignity of all mankind may be forgotten—on both sides indeed—in the deference owed to the nominally distinguished. Manners, accent, garb, the phenomena of "conspicuous waste" may all add to the false position of the favored status. Political power and military position may in large measure be determined by the same type of consideration.

"Sharp contrasts of opportunity and circumstance," says Tawney, "which deprive some classes of the means of development deemed essential for others, are sometimes defended on the ground that the result of abolishing them must be to produce, in the conventional phrase, a dead-level of mediocrity."[1]

Once developed in a social system, the inequality of the equal becomes difficult to modify. Indeed the more the nominally superior are uncertain of their actual superiority, the more arrogantly they may emphasize the external evidences of their nominal superiority.[2]

The aristocratic spirit tends in general to

a. Overemphasize the significance of differentials in the pattern of social organization.

b. Regard the differentials once established as permanent in nature—transmissible, hereditary, or even purchasable.

c. Resist changes in the social and political rules that alter the meaning of types of differentials—as in the case of wealth, birth, social standing, education, or other indices.

The guaranty of respect for the dignity of the person and for the fraternal treatment of human differentials will be validated partly by guaranties of civil rights, partly by suffrage, partly by free participation in the shaping of public policy, partly by education, partly by basic standards of human existence, partly by a democratic way of life, partly by an opportunity to participate in the common gains of our civilization, partly by rules and regulations designed to prevent the rise of privilege or undue concentration of prestige, particularly in permanent form.

We cannot measure accurately the differences between men as a basis for rewards until we have determined to what extent society is responsible for the differentials. But we need not be so influenced by the assertion that men are

---

[1] See R. H. Tawney, *Equality* (1931), p. 97.
[2] T. V. Smith, *Democratic Way of Life* (1926); *The Promise of American Politics* (1936).

ASSUMPTIONS AND PROGRAM

variously unequal as to forget policies that will tend to equalize opportunity.

Laws forbidding primogeniture and entail, prohibiting perpetuities, providing for progressive inheritance taxes have been directed against undue concentrations of prestige, as a means of preserving the position of the average man. From time to time it has been found necessary to reexamine the laws of inheritance and to study more thoroughly the conditions under which the holding of properties with their possibilities for good or evil may be justified.[1] Property is a bundle of rights, it has often been said judicially, and there is no absolute right to utilize ownership against the interest of the community.

The enduring protection of the dignity of mankind is not, however, primarily a question of laws and orders. It is a problem of avowed and energized attitudes and objectives in the given society. If the aim is democratic and the attitude is democratic, prevailingly, the outcome will be democratic. In the doctrine of Nietzsche this theory of human recognition is the gospel of weakness, but in the doctrine of Lincoln it is the counsel of strength. The doctrine of fellowship pervaded the Stoic and the Christian philosophy, expressing itself, however, primarily in the inner refuges of the soul, rather than in external relations.

The wide-ranging area of liberty in democracy has been attacked

a. Because it placed too great emphasis on liberty, as asserted by the Nazis and Fascists.

b. Because of its alleged hostility to liberty, as declared by Lecky and others.[2]

---

[1] Laws provide for judicial examination of the capacity of an individual to act as the custodian of property, even his own, and the appointment of a guardian if he is found incompetent.

[2] Thomas B. Macaulay, letters to Henry S. Randall, Jan. 18, 1857, reprinted in *What Did Macaulay Say about America?* (edited by Henry M. Lydenburg, 1925);

THE NEW DEMOCRACY

c. Because of the denial of liberty in democratic association operating in a free industrial association, as charged by the Soviets.

How can it be possible, we may inquire, that democracy at one and the same time gives too much liberty, gives too little liberty, gives no liberty at all? Perhaps the answer may be found in the differing uses and meaning of "liberty," or in the exclusive consideration of one or more limited aspects of what is called "liberty," or in the general system of doctrine held by various commentators upon liberty, or in the nature of the national tension in which different states are caught for the moment.

The world's literature is rich with erudite discussions of the nature and implications of liberty. The philosophers have emphasized unendingly the struggle between determinism and voluntarism, the theologians the status of liberty in the relation between the personality and God; the social psychologists have dwelt upon the relation between personality and the surrounding culture; others the relationship between inheritance and environment, or between total environment and man; and the students of government have dwelt upon the conflict between the citizen and the state.

In the political world at this moment, interest centers around the forms and the understandings favorable to the fullest development of liberty.[1]

W. E. H. Lecky, *Democracy and Liberty* (1896); Ortega y Gasset, *The Revolt of the Masses*, Chap. VII; Ralph Adams Cram, *The End of Democracy* (1937), pp. 38*ff.*; William E. Rappard, *The Crisis of Democracy* (1938), Chap. VI.

[1] Among the outstanding studies in the field of the relation of the state to the freedom of the individual are John Stuart Mill, *On Liberty* (1859); de Tocqueville, *op. cit.;* T. H. Green, *Lectures on the Principles of Political Obligation* (1895); Stephen, *op. cit.;* J. E. Acton, *The History of Freedom and Other Essays* (1907); F. C. Montague, *The Limits of Individual Liberty* (1885); J. W. Burgess, *The Reconciliation of Government with Liberty* (1915); Harold J. Laski, *Liberty in the Modern State* (1930); Leon Duguit, *Souveraineté et liberté* (1922); H. M. Kallen, editor, *Freedom in the Modern World* (1928); G. B. Logan, *Liberty in the Modern World* (1928); T. V.

ASSUMPTIONS AND PROGRAM

In democratic theory and practice, liberty has had a negative and a positive side. On the negative side, mechanisms have been set up with the design of protecting the citizen against arbitrary and oppressive conduct. The apparatus of civil rights was devised for this purpose. In earlier days emphasis was laid upon small-size states, upon decentralization, and upon the separation and balance of powers, following Montesquieu, as guaranties of the liberty of citizens. Positive mechanisms were also set up, providing for participation in the affairs of the state, as in suffrage and in representation, giving to the electors control over the general direction of the policy of the state.

But the terms "liberty" and "individualism" were taken captive by the economic world at times, even under democratic or semi-democratic forms of association. The techniques of government were turned to the fostering of a special type of "economic" freedom—one among many—even at the expense of the civil or political liberties of the citizen, who might be and was oppressed by the very machinery he set up to emancipate himself.[1] It was Anatole France who referred to "the majestic equality of the laws, which forbid rich and poor alike to sleep under the bridges, to beg in the streets, and to steal their bread."

In democratic theory, however, liberty is not merely negative, but also positive in its nature. Liberty connotes the fullest and richest possible development of the possibilities of the personality of the citizens. In a sense liberty is life, the "good life" of the Greeks, the "spiritual" life, the "more abundant life" of our time. But the personality is set in a framework of social and spiritual interests and values. Even anarchism in its later phases as developed by

---

Smith, *The Democratic Way of Life* (1925); Jacques Maritain, *Freedom in the Modern World* (1936); Dorothy Fosdick, *What is Liberty?* (1939).

[1] Reginald Heber Smith, *Justice and the Poor* (1919).

THE NEW DEMOCRACY

Kropotkin recognized the values of association and cooperation.[1]

Liberty involves a wide range of alternative choices in which autonomy is possible—choices that are not confined to industry, but reach far beyond. "Individualism" and "enterprise" are not limited to an economic area, but run through the whole gamut of human living. "Individualism," "individuality," "personality," have many facets, including the economic, but not ending there. It is the function of a democratic association to give the widest possible play to the widest possible range of choices by its citizens—to encourage intellectual and creative enterprise. There are producers' choices, there are also consumers' choices, and workers' choices, and leisure-time choices, and cultural choices of a wide variety.

Much confusion has been caused by the struggle for priorities in liberty—or perhaps more accurately by the failure to recognize the many competing human-value systems in each of which there is an area of alternative libertarian choices. This area is expanding and contracting with the time and the tension of the social situation—external and internal.

Political liberty, economic liberty, religious liberty, social liberty, artistic liberty, liberties of many modes and tenses are all involved in the whirling social equilibrium. And we must reckon further, not only with personal liberties, but also with corporate liberties of endless types in the given society. Racial, regional, occupational, cultural associations of widely varying forms and purposes are intertwined in the complex movement of the period, whatever it may be.

These liberties are not necessarily exclusive, one of the other. The state provides the setting for all of them, bal-

[1] *Mutual Aid a Factor in Evolution* (1902).

ASSUMPTIONS AND PROGRAM

ancing their impact upon each other, and adjusting and adapting otherwise more severe collisions and conflicts.

If all of these competing types of life could agree upon the field and priorities of their "liberty" or "liberties," there would be no need for the political association. They might pursue their peaceful ways, revolving in their own orbits without clash or conflict. But it is precisely one of the functions of the state to balance these ways of life and to prevent an anarchy of liberties, rudely crashing against each other, and leading to an intolerable form of life.

Any of these systems of liberty may assert itself against the others, drawing in as it were all liberty to itself, as in religion, economics, art, science, culture. And each, of course, tends to give itself at least a high rank in the scale.

From time to time one or another attains such a position of trust or preponderance that it may in effect direct the action of the state and, without assuming technical responsibility, determine the lines of governmental function.

In most discussions the problem of liberty is oversimplified. In reality there are many liberties balanced against each other, or revolving around each other in plural fashion. The personality lives in a complicated, whirling system of choices, not always related to each other in the realm of conscious personality. Furthermore there are many other factors in the social equilibrium and movement. Liberty must be balanced against order; against justice; against equality; against the rate, type, and direction of social change or social tension; against internal, international, racial, religious, regional interests and demands.

Even in the citizen's own personality he must himself balance his own liberty against his own sense of justice, his own sense of order, his own sense of social interrelations, and his own responsibility to them. If "my mind to me a kingdom is," it presents all the problems of a kingdom, from which the personality cannot escape even by abdication. He cannot flee himself, his own inner constituency and constitution. The personality itself contains a cross section of anarchism, another of despotism, one of tolerance, another of intolerance. Hence, the statesmanship of personality is also a perennial problem of life. In the larger society the problem is much the same on a vaster scale, but with much the same elements struggling for position.

In a sense, liberty is life. In the political sense this liberty is attained in the framework of mechanisms, procedures, understandings we call "government." It is not primarily negative, although there is an element of negativism in it, but primarily positive. It is not no, but yes, in the main—not prohibition, but release.

Free choices may be blocked not merely by law but by custom. Not only do the power holders themselves unduly magnify the importance of their office, or seek to prolong their brief authority, but the bulk of the community bears down heavily upon variations from established habits and customs.[1] An invention of intelligence such as the school may itself be used to repress the spontaneous development of other ideas from other intelligences. Tendencies toward stability and conformity, which possess important elements of value in the functioning of a community, may operate against the life and vitality of the nation by becoming an obstacle to adaptation to new conditions. The graves of ancestors may not only block the building of railways in China but the reorganization of international relations in the

---

[1] See Mill's admirable analysis of this tendency toward mass oppression, not governmental in nature, but social in its characteristics, *On Liberty* (1859), Chap. III. See also J. C. Merriam, "Conservation and Evolution in a Changing Social Program," *Proceedings, American Philosophical Society*, 73: 351; *The Inquiring Mind in a Changing World*, Rice Institute 121, No. 3; Adolph Löwe, *The Price of Liberty*, Day to Day Pamphlets, No. 36, 1937.

ASSUMPTIONS AND PROGRAM

interest of human happiness. Education itself may be used to stifle free thought.

It is probable that in the future larger use will be made of quantity production in many commodities and services; and this itself may tend to operate against human variation and spontaneity.[1] To guard against the fatal inroads of a deadening spirit, it is imperative that the community deliberately devise ways and means to protect the attitudes and activities of those who might otherwise be crushed down or frightened out by the mere weight of the mass. Otherwise the creative spirit, which lies at the base of modern technical progress and which must also underlie the growth of social invention, will not flourish. It is easier to order silence than to order imagination and invention.

One of the greatest causes of confusion in our own time is the identification by some persons of democracy with a special form of liberty, notably with economic liberty. In some instances the demand for economic liberty takes priority over political liberty. There are those who are not in reality interested in democracy except as it provides a shield for a particular form of industrial organization in which what is called "economic liberty" is provided, and what is more important a special economic status is preserved.

From this not uncommon point of view, an aristocratic or absolutistic system of political organization which preserved special industrial privilege might be taken in preference to a genuinely democratic system which placed the general welfare of the community ahead of a special industrial system; and if democracy is not the protector of plutocracy (designated by the term economic liberty), it will be given up for

[1] At the English Special Schools Conference of 1937, it was stated that "there were firms in London . . . who made a point of employing mentally defective girls" because they "make steady employees in a monotonous job," *Planning:* A broadsheet issued by PEP (Political and Economic Planning), No. 131, p. 14.

whatever form of government will provide the necessary protection.

There are some elements in modern industrialism that prefer Fascism or its equivalent to the Labor party, or the Popular Front, or the New Deal for this reason. They see in so-called "economic liberty" the *summum bonum* and are willing to defend and support democracy only to a line within which their economic advantages are given priority in the given scheme of things.

What is to happen when we must choose between liberty and equality, it may be asked. The possible rivalry between the ideas of equality and the idea of liberty is based upon the assumption of an absolutely flat or quantitative form of equality in a democratic association.

But this, as has been shown, is neither possible in fact nor necessary for the purposes of democratic association. In all societies there are widely ranging types of equality and inequality and there are widely ranging forms of liberty. The systems of liberty and the systems of equality are not necessarily exclusive, but may be complementary. Formal and proportional liberty as well as formal and real liberty may be and are compounded in varying proportions in human societies, but the essential problem is no more difficult in a democratic association than in any form of human political grouping and government.

Equality involves a recognition of a certain status, and capacity to act—to choose—within the framework of that recognized status. Equality is not identity so much as it is similarity. Liberty does not carry with it the right to interfere with the choices of others within the general assumptions of democracy. My unlimited freedom of choice—liberty—may, to be sure, interfere with the free choices of others, with their liberty, or with social justice, or with public order and the commonweal itself, or with their equality. If my

ASSUMPTIONS AND PROGRAM

system of free choices interferes with the dignity of man, with the possibility of his development, with his fair share in the gains of civilization, my system must be revised in accordance with the systems of others in a democratic society at any given stage of its development.

Democracy, and indeed any other type of association, may interfere from time to time with one form or another of a person's liberty as expressed in a person's unlimited will to act as he wishes. This may indeed be a condition of the survival of the commonwealth, but such restriction is not peculiar to democracy. It is, on the contrary, common to all forms of human political association, in which the interest of the part must yield to the interest of the whole. For this is the condition of political association and not merely a special problem of one form—in this case the democratic.

Many of the regulations attributed by Lecky and others to democracy are the result of modern technology and the problems precipitated by the changing situation of mankind. Building codes are not peculiar to democracy—or sanitary regulations, or housing and recreation and education, or provisions for social security and economic stabilization.

Here again much of the criticism of democracy is not really based upon a love of political liberty as such, but on a fear that liberty and governmental regulation may affect special forms of industrial organization deemed desirable in general or personally.[1]

Government is not in reality wholly negative. Power as repression speaks in force and expresses itself in commands, rules, laws; but power as creation speaks in terms of invention, of spontaneity, of creative faculties; and in this role power may plant and water, cultivate and encourage the

---

[1] See the edition of Herbert Spencer's *Man versus the State* with special introductions to each chapter by well-known and competent defenders of modern large-scale industrialism (1916).

precious seeds of variation, with their incalculable values for the growth of the productive power of the nation.

It is important accordingly that there be formal recognition of this fact and an appropriate policy of the commonwealth, and that the declaration of policy be followed by proper instrumentation in terms of institutions, attitudes, and material support.

This, it may be said, and truly, is a hard task for any government, and it may be further said especially for a democracy, with the consciousness of power in its huge masses. It is really easier, however, for the Mass than for the Few to recognize spontaneous and creative ability. The Few are constantly concerned about the continuity of their line, fearing that the thread will weaken or break. The Mass, on the other hand, need have no fear that their power will end because of any shift in special talents within their numbers.[1] They will go on, whatever the variation in the immediate holders of power. They may look with toleration on the activities of those whom they have encouraged to study variations. In this sense the Many can better afford to be tolerant than the Few.

Thus democratic association may make possible free choices in the light of

a. The essential dignity and worth of all mankind.

b. The consent of the bulk of the community to the conduct of the commonwealth, freely expressed.

In democratic society, regard for the dignity of man stands behind the throne of public order, a constant reminder of the need for liberty and justice as well as order, a constant plea that the human personality shall not be forgotten in the multiplications of law, in the ramifications of administration, or in the antiquarianism of formal justice. Other systems

---

[1] See H. S. Jennings, *The Biology of Human Nature*, 1930, p. 221, on the recruitment of new talent from the mass.

ASSUMPTIONS AND PROGRAM

may, as lords, leaders, masters, teach respect for their serfs, their slaves, their subjects, or their inferiors. Democracy breathes respect for all men and for their choice of a way of human life.

The democratic doctrine of consent comes in just at this point to aid in the process of balance and adjustment—as a lubricant for the reconciliation of group and personal interests with each other. The real conflict of personalities is not with the state and with authority as such. On the contrary, this authority is only a symbol, or a formula for the reconciliation of their own interests in the easiest manner.

That the state may use force is important, but not the most important factor in the situation. The vital and prime point is the meaning of interest and choice, conciliation and equilibration. It is important for the state to have other bases than violence—to have wisdom, insight, diplomacy, managerial facility. The insignia of technical sovereignty, which it may constantly brandish and proclaim, are not enough. For at this point the poverty of power may lead to the shame of power, and to the weakening of the whole state fabric.

The chief difficulties, then, centering around the discussion of liberty arise from the failure to realize the pluralistic nature of liberties and the widely varying types of situations under which they are operating. Competing forms of liberty must be brought together and reconciled not only in the general framework of the state—always a difficult problem—but also under widely varying kinds of crises in the life of the state itself and in the life of the various constituent citizens and groupings operating within the state, or partly within the state. How to reconcile competing interests and their value systems, how to reconcile order, justice, liberty, stability, variation—these are continuing tasks of the state; and the allocation or recognition of wide-ranging areas of free choice is a perennial problem of democratic statesmen from which they cannot escape.

The problem of democracy is not merely absolute, but also relative; not merely negative, but also positive in character. It is not merely political, or merely economic, or merely ethical, religious, or merely racial, regional, occupational; not merely artistic, scientific. It is a general task which calls for the general view of the total situation, requiring insight, judgment, sense of balance and proportion in a dynamic, moving situation.

On one hand democracy protects its citizen against arbitrary governmental intervention, and on another against encroachments upon his personality. It strives to foster the optimum conditions for the unfolding of all human personalities positively and aggressively.

The mechanisms of democracy are designed to be constant reminders of the nature of human association and the importance of an expanding range of free life. Its popular forms and procedures refer to the understandings and objectives of fraternal association and cooperation as a way of life.

Frames and forms of government are essentially psychological in nature. They rest upon and induce understandings, reactions, conditionings, operating with enough regularity to make possible forecasting of behavior and counterbehavior. The symbols of democracy are the symbols of liberty, of free life, of wide choice, of the expansion and expression of the personality of its citizens.

In a non-democratic system the Superiors—one or few—assume the trusteeship of the community, with a general undertaking for the well-being of the nation or other political unit in which they function. They must determine their own position in the general scheme of things political, and they must observe the relative position of all others in a broad scheme of values over which they stand in general charge.

ASSUMPTIONS AND PROGRAM

What is the bearing of this system, we may ask, on the preservation of the dignity of men?

It is not clear in the first place what responsibility the overlords will assume.

Shall the supermen assume that the welfare of mankind is best served by their own superdevelopment, with the benefits trickling down to others as time goes on? Or shall they undertake some more immediate and direct diffusion of the gains of greatness for the weak? Or shall they perhaps assume that their own glorious development is itself a flower that may well satisfy the imagination and the desires of all the others? Perhaps others do not matter at all, but merely serve as the clay from which the figures of the truly superior are shaped, they may say.

What theoretical account of themselves shall the politically unaccountable give in their philosophical moments? And what shall be their program?

Shall they decide to educate the masses of the people in such a way as to fit them ultimately for the aristoi, or in such a manner as to render them ineligible and content with a humbler lot? Shall they educate for class status on the whole or for mass status? At this point they may predetermine the destiny of the oncoming generation in great measure.

What type of race will they choose to breed, if they better understand the art of eugenics? Will they give preference to breeding of superior types, or might they conclude to grow morons as once suggested by a psychologist—morons to do the hard work of the world, while others live upon the fruit of their labors? Shall they breed a class or a special race, or breed for mass development upward toward final universal eliteness?[1]

---

[1] See Huxley, *op. cit.*, for ingenious suggestions as to possible policy; H. G. Wells, *The Shape of Things to Come* (1933), has described the "Air Dictatorship" and the "Modern State Fellowship."

Shall they begin early to train men for special occupations, adapting them to some standard of status; or shall they leave the door of hope open to all? Shall they approximate something of a caste system, or assume that modern society requires more opportunity for adaptation and advancement on the part of the Many?

Shall they regard the economic field as essentially a free struggle for survival of the fittest, or supervise it to the extent at least of making sure that it does not undermine the prestige or position of the aristoi, political and otherwise?

How far will they go in the assumption of responsibility for direction of control over the instruments of production, the processes of distribution and consumption, and of standards of living?

What shall they say to capitalism and to communism in developing national policies appropriate to the domination of the Few? Theoretically they might go either way—a long way—or they might go another way which was neither one nor the other in form or process.

Practically, recent Italy and Germany have balanced capitalism against socialism, although favored and supported by the former, but in so doing it must be observed that they have made an appeal to another form of loyalty in the shape of modern nationalism. The nation itself is, however, a mass phenomenon; and continuing appeal to the mass is full of peril for an association based upon the principle of the few, even if repudiating any specific responsibility to the masses. This accounts undoubtedly for the retention of the forms of plebiscite and pseudo-voting in these cases.

There can be no question that the anti-democrats of our day have been utilized for the purpose of crushing out mass movements in the form of socialism, trade-unions, and democracy; but the ultimate outcome is still in the future, and the trends of nationalism are not so easily or securely

ASSUMPTIONS AND PROGRAM

forecast as some have thought. In its time nationalism captured Christianity or phases of it. Later democracy, at first cosmopolitan, became nationalistic. Nationalism might take over conceivably any form of economic or social organization, such as communism or socialism, if deemed important for the national interest by those with whom the decision lay.

Nor is there anything to prevent a small group of lords from taking on a religious color and affiliation, improbable as this might seem in view of the warfare with the church in Italy and in Germany. It might indeed be maintained that the only sure basis for an elite lay in the cultivation of religious values and interests as a continuing bond of allegiance. The caste system, which held sway over the world for a long period of human history and still dominates the daily lives of millions of our fellow men, was given the aura of religion and found this the strongest support in its most difficult hours. It is entirely possible that a state church may emerge, to bless the new leaders, as in earlier days the Anglican and Gallican churches emerged.

The foes of democracy must make a series of fundamental decisions in the establishment of their authority. Their relations to religion, to science, to industry are involved; still more difficult their relations to the mass movement are involved in nationalism, with its heavy trend back to massism and democracy. What is their program? What safeguards shall they build against the shock of military defeat, against the cycles of economic depression, against the outbursts of suppressed freedom of speech and thought, against the silent persistence of religious values? If autocracy is merely another name for personal adventure, if its methods are chiefly violence and propaganda, if it reflects largely national impatience in a moment of despair, then it may be judged from this point of view. But if the government of the best fitted to govern is really the generalized goal, then the criteria of excellence must be identified, ways and means of selection and continuity must be developed, the relation of the Few to the Many must be defined and interpreted, and types of programs must be developed.

Thus far indeed in modern times the advocates of autocracy have been more conspicuous for the use of violence than for reason, for bombastic appeal to the very masses they affect to despise, for pseudo voting rather than genuine electoral processes, for attacks upon rational political choices rather than for their recognition and incorporation in a system preeminently requiring these traits and skills.[1]

If the superior are really superior in the light of modern intelligence and science, why do they employ so extensively the weapons of force and ballyhoo? Why have they so little confidence in their own inherent qualities? If it is qualities of will and of activism they seek to emphasize, then the question may be asked: Has it been found impossible to unite intelligence and will in a formula of personality or a pattern of behavior? If the loudest shouting and the bloodiest shedding of blood give the title to the new leadership, will not the trend be in the direction of still louder shouting and still more savage policies?

The historic categories of true aristocracy point either in the direction of intelligence and personality demonstrated by long training, as indicated by Plato, or in the direction of a group inspired by religious ideals, as seen in various forms of religious organization; but neither the philosopher-king of the classical period nor the prophet-priest type is seen

---

[1] "If you want to get men to act reasonably," says Huxley, "you must set about persuading them in a maniacal manner. What we want is a sane and reasonable exploitation of the forces of insanity." [*Crome Yellow* (1922), p. 229.] For this purpose he suggests three main species of men: the directing intelligences, the men of faith, and the herd. *Cf.* H. G. Wells's prescription for recruiting the new elite, *What Are We to Do with Our Lives* (1931) and *The Shape of Things to Come.*

ASSUMPTIONS AND PROGRAM

in the oligarchies of the modern day. Neither military force nor economic wealth offers a solid and enduring basis of groups that profess to rest upon any rational view of life.

It may be said that nationalism or proletarianism affords support for a group of leaders, but the underlying trends of modern nationalism and of modern proletarianism are at bottom mass driven, and over a long period of time are untrustworthy for those who affect the cult of aristocracy. Dictatorships of the few, resting upon mass movements, are built upon foundations of sand, for ultimately the nation or the class may decide to take charge of its own estate. If the test of the validity of authority is force, then the mass may ultimately have the superior argument; and if it is ballyhoo, how long and how effectively may it be maintained?

We conclude that we are a long way from knowing the differentials in human capacity and in political capacity, from knowing adequate methods of selection and continuity of such persons in political leadership, from being in a position to outline the scope and method of their "irresponsible responsibility" to the commonweal.

The curse of aristocracy is not that great men fill great places, but that small men fill great places and piece out their inferiority with arrogance. Truly great natures are likely to find a response in the mass of mankind. They need not fear the Many as much as the jealous Few. In the very nature of aristocracy it is difficult, if not impossible, to appraise the position of the aristoi properly, to be as expert and responsive to the problems of equitable distribution as of production. Aristocracy tends to identify the public good with its own material and spiritual values. Can aristocrats know what justice is when they are judges in their own cause?

Of course, those who are in power may always say, "We are in power"; and if they are, then indeed this is the case.

But this of itself is no proof of their competence. Political realism is never wholly realistic if it disregards the foundations upon which continuing authority must rest.

We may sum up this discussion by concluding that the chief defect of anti-democracy as it actually develops is that of choosing the Few, but not the best. The institutions or machinery set up to choose the Few tend to emphasize status rather than ability. A group made up in formal manner on the basis of land, or of birth, or of property, or of force does not tend toward the choice of the most competent, but tends to draw in one generation of competence and many generations of incompetence or even of impotence. Autocracy may choose the great and the good at times, but it tends to substitute standing for reality, form for substance.

2. *The Perfectibility of Mankind*

During long periods of time the advocates of democracy relied upon their faith that human conditions would continually improve, until the political consciousness, interests, capacity of man made it possible to assume the responsibilities of self-government. Under Stoicism the externals of a democratic or fraternal life were unrealized, but equality was attained in Stoic rationality, in philosophical reflection, in physical renunciation. In Christianity all men were held to be equal in the sight of God, but the full enjoyment of this reality was postponed until the other world. In the period of Rousseau the environment was blamed for inequality, and men were to be treated *as if* they were equal; they were accorded the accolade of humanity in theory even if not in fact. For centuries this hope must have seemed a desperate one, remote in the possibilities of its realization.

But in recent times a livelier faith animates mankind, as they come nearer to a long distant goal. For this purpose

ASSUMPTIONS AND PROGRAM

it is important that careful attention be given to such areas as

a. The development of science and the practical application of its results to human affairs.

b. The fullest possible development of educational and guidance facilities, both for the young and for the adult, and the completest utilization of these facilities.

c. Insistence upon the highest standards of human living possible in a given stage of development.[1]

Every effort may be made toward the encouragement of science and technology and of social invention as well; for these are the continuing bases of progress. Science in all of its phases may be regarded as one of the nation's very greatest resources, and stimulated in every possible way, directly or indirectly, to the end that the very highest level of achievement may be obtained.[2] There is no prospect that science will take a holiday, but on the contrary, every reason to anticipate its increasing development.

The transmitted and developed skills and insights are in fact the very greatest of our national resources. They are indeed the basis of modern civilization and the bulwark of any democracy. Research itself is a national asset of priceless value in the national economy. Without our modern intelligence and apparatus the whole vast structure of our civilization would fall of its own weight.

It will be found essential to lay yet greater emphasis on the scientific attitude in the great process of education. The trend of modern times is in the direction of democracy and of science—of mass rule and of high intelligence on a scale hitherto never approached. Science itself will have

[1] See following paragraphs on mass gains, p. 98.

[2] J. C. Merriam, "Some Responsibilities of Science with Relation to Government," *Science*, 80: 597; Karl T. Compton, "The Social Implications of Scientific Discovery," *American Philosophical Society*, March, 1938.

THE NEW DEMOCRACY

neither meaning nor security unless it is reflected not only in higher standards of living, but in richer values of human life and in bettered attitudes toward life.

It is the responsibility of those in command of the necessary facts to present the reasonable possibilities of the future in the language of technology and of social organization. Men wish to know whether there is a way out, and where that road leads. It is not impossible to make estimates of this type from time to time, subject to revision with the progress of intelligence and of organization.

This has sometimes been resisted or ridiculed either from lack of faith in the future, or from fear that such estimates might become the basis of discontent among the less fortunately situated.

One of the weaknesses of many recent systems of politics and economics has been the failure to present a picture of what might reasonably be attained within a not too distant future. In modern times no system can rest upon its past alone. It must develop a future or suffer the consequences. And it must be a future in terms of the social-scientific possibilities indicated by the present and increasing knowledge of our social world, and the possibilities of social engineering within that world. There are value systems and emotional drives that grow out of the past, but there are others that beckon out of the future. They come out of hope and expectation of another and a better day.

It is important accordingly that the scientific developments of the present situation be fully and vividly portrayed, in order that mankind may be made aware of what lies ahead. It must be assumed that adequate social engineering can be found and can be supported by the masses with whom the ultimate power of disposition lies.

A new world is well within our reach if we can organize and act to obtain it. Men do not believe this; they do not see it;

ASSUMPTIONS AND PROGRAM

they do not heed, perhaps, even the words in which such a scene is developed before them. But the possibilities are consequently all the greater—the prospect of providing the necessary background of fact and technique and feelings which will make this dream of the future a throbbing reality in human purpose. If the coming generation can be equipped for the performance of its social functions in the light of the opportunity in human organization, the future of the world is bright with rich possibilities. The obstacles that stand between us and the realization of men's possibilities are those of social attitudes and social and political management.

Of the great burdens of humanity, pestilence, poverty, war, and famine, two have been driven back into their caves. Poverty and war still stalk abroad, resisting the nets thrown around them. But there is no longer a valid excuse for poverty since the forces of nature have been subdued. The lingering brutality of war is a surviving witness reminding the human parvenu of his primitive origins. The stream of scientific invention will roll on, in all human probability, and if the devices of social invention are able to keep pace with the scientific organization of nature, the new world may be a fairyland of human achievement. The burdens of hunger, disease, toil, fear may be lifted, the book of leisure may be opened, and treasures of human appreciation and enjoyment may be made available to the mass of mankind.[1]

This is true not only of the mechanical contrivances which minister to our enjoyment of life in many ways, but also of the inner life of the personality, so long filled with vile broods of haunting fears and doubts and dreads. Science and social arrangement will conquer these jungles also, and open them to the sunlight of happiness, hitherto unattainable to many. Miracles have already been wrought, and others are on the

[1] See National Resources Committee, *Technological Trends and National Policy* (1937); Report of the Hoover Committee on Recent Social Trends (1933).

way. Beyond any question of doubt, science will bring life and light and healing on its wings.

In moments of industrial insecurity and bitter distress, the possibility of an infinitely richer and finer life for the mass of mankind may seem a mocking mirage. But the continuance of our ancient burdens can be avoided if the faculty of social and political contrivance is utilized as it might be by a generation prepared for entering into the kingdom. If there is affliction and bitter distress, it is because we will not reach out and take the gift of the gods in our day. There is food, shelter, clothing, adornment, relief from physical and mental disease, leisure for the appreciation, enjoyment, expression of the human personality in richest form for the entire population, if we are prepared to shape our social, economic, and political arrangements toward that end.

Educational and cultural opportunities are indispensable for the mass of the community, and that not merely in so-called "formal school education," but continuing through adult life. Theoretically everyone has the opportunity for an education—obligatory to a certain age—but practically the economic situation eliminates many who might well take the higher training. It is of vital importance not only for purposes of national morale, but of national inventiveness and ability, that the gates of opportunity shall be open to all who wish to enter and possess the necessary qualifications. No nation is rich enough to throw away these priceless assets coming up from the population.

One of the greatest weaknesses of what is termed "education" is that it puts a terminal point to study at graduation, as if education ended with a formal course, whereas it is just beginning. If the formulas of education close the chapter with graduation of one sort or another, minds are shut down at the very time when they might be opened out. Evidently the type of opportunity offered to adults will be widely

ASSUMPTIONS AND PROGRAM

different from that for the less mature. To this gigantic task of adult education much attention may profitably be directed in order that the thinking and learning process may be continuously at work, not merely in special branches of activity, but throughout the larger interrelations of social life.

No nation has made bolder experiments in the direction of mass education than the United States, but even here there are wide ranges untouched by adequate educational advantages, and the quality of education still leaves much to be desired and attained.[1]

This is not the occasion to point out the defects and possibilities of the American educational system. But there can be little question that great strides will be made in the coming generation both in the extent and in the content of educational facilities. These advances will include the oft-promised, democratic basis of education—long set down as indispensable to the operation of democratic institutions, but long lagging far behind in actual practice in many sections of modern states.

This section of the program of validation of the democratic assumptions cannot be written down in completed and final form, never to be changed. On the contrary, the assumption of the perfectibility of humanity involves the unending readjustment of the conditions of human living to the highest possible level at any given time. This level is not to be determined by a special few, with views colored by indifference to others or by special consideration for themselves, but as a part of a community program, determined by and for the common good of the commonwealth. The production and distribution of food, shelter, clothing, health, recreation, education, security in person and subsistence, and cultural advantages should be limited only by the given

[1] See Charles H. Judd, *Problems of Education in the United States* (1933); my *Civic Education in the United States* (1934).

level of technique, organization, and national resources. The test is not merely the quantity of goods and services available, but the spirit in which the decision is made, and the realization by the community of its responsibility for its own welfare. The "door of hope" is not closed upon any group in the community, but left open for all the members of the democratic society of which they are a part.

The torch of future attainment has been and still is the symbol of democratic aspiration for higher material and spiritual recognition of the mass of mankind. Most of the time, most of the way, in the history of the human race, the mass of men have been slaves—slaves of ignorance, of fear, of status, of custom. The democratic vocabulary has no place either for slave or for master; but for fellowship, fraternity, cooperation in the long struggle for higher standards of living and higher levels of personality.

3. *Mass Gains and the Many*

In order to bring about the distribution of the gains of the commonwealth, which are essentially mass gains, it is necessary to know what these gains are. It is important to survey existing resources accurately, that the gains in our assets be systematically reviewed from time to time and appropriate measures devised to ensure any necessary adjustments.

It is important for any commonwealth to consider systematically in the light of the given productivity of the nation the possible living standards, as for example:

a. Whether higher levels of education are possible.

b. Whether better levels of housing are possible.

c. Whether higher levels of medical care are possible.

d. Whether wider ranges of recreation are possible.

e. Whether higher standards of security in our cultural surroundings are possible.

ASSUMPTIONS AND PROGRAM

f. Whether the burdens of industrial depression and other national crises are fairly distributed and how injustice may be remedied.

g. Whether rewards to individuals or groups are excessive or inadequate and if so how they may be modified.

It is possible to make an analysis of the productive capacity of a nation and of the modes of further expanding the volume of production of commodities and services. Such a survey would present the volume of productivity as it is, and a picture of production as it might be with its possibilities more fully utilized.[1] This development is not so simple as it might seem, since it involves the calculation of various factors of production in relation to each other. Nor are all of the satisfactions that enter into a social equilibrium susceptible of analysis by the statistician. These factors must be determined in another way.

Over against this, there may be set a survey of the patterns of consumption—revealed by inspection of representative budgets or other modes of determining consumption, and their advance with advancing income.

When this work is completed at any given time, it would show, some experts declare:

(*a*) the actual production pattern over against the actual consumption pattern, and

(*b*) the idealized production pattern over against the idealized consumption pattern.

In the light of these estimates it might be possible to indicate new patterns and mark out new standards of living, within the new range of national production. This

---

[1] See National Resources Committee, *Patterns of Resource Use*, (1939); N. F. Hall, *Preliminary Investigation into Measures of a National or International Character on Raising the Standard of Living* (League of Nations Publications, 1938); "20th Century Economic Policy," *Planning*, a broadsheet issued by PEP (1938), No. 130.

might be made the basis of a national policy directed toward expanding the national income and ensuring that the possibilities of life within the given economy are realized in practice.

If experts declare the minimum essentials of living and if production figures indicate that these standards are obtainable, then the next step is to make these possibilities effective in the lives of men by such measures as may seem feasible.

What this eventually involves is a scrutiny of the national income with a view to observing its distribution, the priorities in its allocation, and its possibilities of expansion. This would reveal what it is, if anything, that takes precedence over the minimum fair essentials of human living; what it is that is more important than food, shelter, clothing, care, hygiene, security, education.

This rests, of course, on the assumption that the gains of a nation are essentially mass gains and should be diffused throughout the community, and that the community itself should be the final judge of the equity of the distribution of values in the nation.

In the United States, for example, this might involve the development of a minimum American standard of living, guaranteed by America as to certain fundamentals. It goes without saying that such a standard would be subject to review and revision from time to time, as significant changes occurred in the productive mechanism of the nation, and raised or lowered the productive capacity of the community.[1]

Above this minimum standard would be, of course, a broad variety of differentials in standards over and above the basic minima. The standard itself would rise constantly in a

---

[1] See National Resources Committee, *Consumer Incomes in the United States* (1938), and *Consumer Expenditures in U. S.* (1939).

ASSUMPTIONS AND PROGRAM

developing technical civilization and important surpluses would be absorbed in this rising standard of life.

The mechanical contrivances of democracy must give assurance that the gains of civilization shall be equitably distributed, including here the material goods and the nonmaterial values as well. The means of effecting this result are subordinate to the ends in view. The basic understanding is the seed, the root, the life from which the means spring and upon which they must depend. It is the special task of the system of democracy to scrutinize the gains of civilization and their diffusion, and to set up the ways and means within the limits of intelligence by which these gains may be translated into terms of democratic human living.

Whether this involves absolutely free and unrestricted competition, or controlled competition, or monopoly, or semi-governmentalization, or others of an innumerable variety of alternative contrivances for the purpose of enhancing the values of social life is relatively immaterial in comparison with the general principle.[1]

In general theory, democracy has no inherent and necessary relationship with any special form of economic production or distribution, although the accident of historical evolution may bring about special connections. Economic devices are not ends for democracy but means, subordinate to the larger framework of understanding in which they are set—namely, that the gains of a nation are essentially national gains and the assets of the nation. To say that men are limited to one of two systems of economics worked out a century ago under special conditions long since out of date is a gigantic misrepresentation of the possibilities of democratic rule.

Nor is democracy restricted to a special set of historic mechanisms arising out of special historical conditions. There

[1] See my *Role of Politics in Social Change*, Chap. II.

are wide ranges of alternatives from among which the system of democracy may choose as it goes along during the next generation. The defenders of outworn procedures, economic or governmental, may in good faith identify machinery of particular types with the spirit of democracy, but in the large their position is indefensible. The longer outlived mechanisms are defended, the greater is the practical danger that maladjustment and inaction may lead to the overthrow of democratic spirit and institutions alike, in a storm of violence and the personalism of authority. The meaning of mechanisms is found in their context, by and large.

Not every one that crieth Lord, Lord, shall enter into the kingdom; and not everyone that crieth Liberty is following the road that leads there. Equity may be twisted into defense of privilege instead of justice; equality before the law may become inequality measured by capacity to engage counsel; liberty of contract may become the mask for exploitation of the weak.

Tradition and symbolism have a legitimate place in every social system. But in the main, democracy cannot live upon tradition alone; it must adapt itself to changing conditions revealed by new steps in technology and social organization. Social interests constantly seek to "vest" themselves and become entrenched in the order of social values after their real value has gone or is on the decline. Under these circumstances, rights may become wrongs and the dead hand of the past may restrict the life of the present and the unfolding possibilities of the future.

It cannot be too strongly stated that one of the primary methods of validating the assumption that the gains of civilization are essentially mass gains and should be distributed throughout the community as rapidly as possible is the *deliberate, continuing, systematic analysis of civilization's gains in a commonwealth, the mode and range of their*

ASSUMPTIONS AND PROGRAM

distribution, the enlargement of national income and the consequent adjustment of mass gains to total gains. The underlying principle is more important than the particular mechanisms or methods adopted.

A wide range of differentials is not precluded by such a policy. But the relation of differentials in reward to differentials in capacity must be faced openly, and the necessary adjustments must be made from time to time. If the process is continuous, the necessary modifications may be made with a minimum loss of morale and efficiency. In such a process violence, hypocrisy, chicanery are least useful, whereas collection and analysis of basic data, interpretation of them, and foresight in planning are of the highest value. And, I may add, decision and resolution in action.

If suggested methods of validating the assumption that the gains of commonwealths are essentially mass gains to be shared by the commonwealth seem inadequate or inappropriate, it may be pointed out that the important consideration at this moment is not the elaboration of detail but the assertion of the general principle. The recognition of the responsibility of the commonwealth for the guaranty of social justice in the distribution of common gains is of overwhelming importance for the life and vigor of democracy in our day. Not only has the ancient question, Am I my brother's keeper? been ignored in many instances in the nineteenth and twentieth centuries, but the actual answer has often been, no. No, as far as a democratic program has been concerned. No, in the declaration that the real responsibility for the distribution of common gains lay in the automatic process of production and not in any organization of democratic society.

From time to time aristocratic, oligarchical, plutocratic influences have been able to determine a governmental policy of ignoring the mass welfare. It was indeed maintained at times, not only that democracy had no concern with a positive type of social policy, but that indifference or neutrality was itself the very essence of democracy—its peculiar and distinguishing characteristic.

This was never, however, a doctrine squaring with the general theory of democratic association. It represented a phase of development in which the machinery of government was captured by undemocratic influences or by those restricting their interpretation of democracy to a narrow and untenable line of activity or inactivity.

We are passing out of this period, and in the oncoming epoch it may safely be predicted that democratic societies will assume responsibility for the guaranty of the commonwealth enjoyment of commonwealth gains. Democratic theory demands this course, and democratic machinery is more readily adapted to this purpose than any other yet devised.

4. *The Consent of the Governed*

It is essential that there be a body of understandings and of institutions through which the mass may express itself and formulate basic decisions.

Mass rule requires understandings both as to how things are to be done, and specific mechanisms for action. But the understandings are as important as the means through which the understandings work, and often of more permanent and widespread significance. Psychologically, of course, a mechanism or procedure is really an understanding, an attitude. The failure to grasp the meanings and significance of understandings has often led to overemphasis on mechanisms of one type or another, and indeed to placing the mere machinery of mass rule in a position of greater importance than its real purpose—to the use of the machinery to defeat the general understanding out of which it came into existence and for which it was designed.

ASSUMPTIONS AND PROGRAM

a. THE ELECTORAL MECHANISM

A basic factor in popular rule is that the persons who determine the policies of the commonwealth shall be responsible to the community through some workable contrivance. The most common device for this purpose is the electoral process, which is based on general suffrage and free and uncontrolled pollings, preceded by free discussion of the personalities and principles at issue.

The frequency and type of elections, the nature and forms of officials selected, the directness or indirectness of choice, the relations between elective and non-elective personnel—all these differ widely in different systems and from period to period. Variations in organization correspond to historical variations in the experience of special countries such as England, the United States, Sweden, and France, but the common understanding is essentially the same, underneath the surface differences in structure and in division of function. The variations are all subordinate to the main question—whether the instrumentality is effective in enabling the mass to exercise its control over basic policies in the state. Beyond that, the cultural level of the given community and the type and form of its political experience and habituation will determine the actual use of particular electoral mechanisms.

The electoral method of presenting community choices has been subjected to severe criticism from many different points of view.

(1) It has been charged that the counting machinery is inexact in that it may be controlled by fraud, bribery, intimidation, violence, duress of various forms which are illegitimate, but found in actual practice.

(2) It is charged that elections may be swayed by low-level arts of demagogical persuasion of the most blatant type.

(3) It is charged that the electoral result may be determined by the excited pressure of special-interest groups in fact constituting a minority.

(4) It may be charged that the outcome of elections generally is clearly unrepresentative of the common intelligence, interest or will.

(5) And finally the conclusion may be drawn that the voting process is on the whole so unreliable as to be inferior to the determination of the national will or interest by a group of self-selected and nonresponsible officials.

The force of many of the charges in particular instances may readily be conceded, and they have been carefully canvassed by democratic leaders. But the alternative of irresponsibility gives the skeptic as to elections pause. How do the Few who make the decisions come into the position they hold? How can we be sure that they will understand the common interest or possess the self-restraint to render verdicts accordingly? How can we ensure a line of Superiors who will continue to render just judgment upon themselves and others? What remedy will there be if the Few betray the interest of the Many?

Propaganda and histrionics may bear the load for a time, counting smiles and hurrahs instead of votes. But rival propaganda machines must be rigidly repressed, and contending hurrahs must not be permitted a free field. Force may be the answer for a time, but not forever.

Is any form of assent in non-democratic situations to be required or institutionalized at all? In any system it is difficult to avoid the gathering of some form of conference, council, experts or wise men around the throne of the leader, summoned for the occasion or appointed for a longer period of time. In these groupings it is probable that the voting technique will arise,[1] if the number of councilors is above

[1] On the history of the voting technique, see *Encyclopedia of the Social Sciences.*

ASSUMPTIONS AND PROGRAM

a very few—as in parties of the type set up in Italy, Germany, and Russia. Here the despised voting method springs up again after being thrown out as invalid for purposes of community employment. But if the vote really is significant and not merely a camouflage of intimidation, the evils charged against the democratic ballot are again in evidence.

A factor of deep meaning in the validation of the electoral process is that of open channels of intercommunication. Free speech, freedom of assembly and association, free press, freedom of the air, freedom in other ways and means of interchange of ideas are a prime requisite of democratic government. Without this the process of popular choice of personnel or policy becomes an empty shell. With this it is possible to offset a considerable amount of bribery, duress, cheating in the count, all of which may be futile if the other ways are left open. If the bulk of the community is unable to arrive at an understanding upon such procedure, the process of popular consent is for the time incapable of operation, and violence will take the place of orderly ballotage. Not all the laws of order adopted by one generation can bind another, if the latter does not wish to be bound, if it prefers blood to persuasion. Even a relatively small minority may compel the lover of peace to defend himself in battle. The state of nature in the old phrase becomes a state of war. One man with a gun may break up a meeting, but not forever, unless the group wishes to shoot instead of talk.

What reason is there to suppose that the majority will be representative of the wisdom of the community? Obviously there is no special sanctity in a majority of one over a competing minority. Indeed, many elections are determined by a plurality in contests where there are several rival candidates. What happens in a voting system is the existence of a general understanding that the electoral process is to be the framework of general decision upon community policy. The tacit agreement is that a count is to be taken as decisive in the given instance.

This is, indeed, only another illustration of the truth that the validation of the democratic process often depends more upon general understandings than upon specific mechanisms. Understandings are harder to break than laws.

The electoral process as such is not a panacea for all political ills. It can only facilitate the exercise of qualities found in the electoral area. It can only utilize material available for the selective process. It presupposes the existence of habits of mind and habits of action adapted to this type of procedure. If men care to fight rather than to discuss; if they are unwilling to abide by an electoral decision; if the condition of ignorance of facts and misunderstanding of situations, or unsound judgment regarding facts and situations, or selfish interest in interpretation of facts and situations predominates, then the institution breaks down, and the selective process will not operate effectively. The so-called "election" then becomes an outright sham, or works only haltingly and ineffectively.[1]

It may be said that any balloting process with its emphasis on relative ratings, on balancing of personnel or policy, will tend to develop useful qualities of judgment in a community. The mere fact of choice is a concession to consent, however weak the gesture may be, and however much chicanery and force and fraud may influence the process and the result. The point of interest in these situations is whether there is a trend in the development of capacity for popular judgment and decisionism. A series of pseudo-votings with a continuation of force, fraud, corruption, intimidation of various sorts tends to crystallize the idea that the selective

---

[1] See John Stuart Mill, *Representative Government* (1861), Chap. IV, on the conditions underlying a representative system.

ASSUMPTIONS AND PROGRAM

process is futile and to discredit it with the community. This has happened from time to time and from place to place.

The first index of this condition is the suspension of freedom of the press, freedom of speech, and the right of association and assembly. Without these any election is a fraud. Not every choice called an "election" is correctly so labeled. Where there is no freedom of speech, of press, of assembly and organization, where force and intimidation are at hand or standing in the background, the action of the electors is in no sense an electoral choice. It measures not voting, but the intimidating power of those in authority, who, if they were sure of their thrones, would welcome the free expression of popular allegiance, indicated by the free popular vote of the given community.

It is chiefly in short-run periods that the electoral process shows its defects most clearly. When longer stretches of time are taken, it is more likely that electoral eccentricities are smoothed out. It is sometimes said in America that the life of a political machine does not exceed ten years. It may also be pointed out that electoral irregularities are more likely to occur when there is relatively little interest in the choices to be made by the voters. The factors of fraud and venality are less weighty in times of widespread general interest on the part of the electorate. Press and propaganda may carry weight, and the radio and the spoken word are also extremely influential.

The voting process per se has no validity unless it is re-enforced by a democratic way of life and a democratic practice of free choice. In theory, the voting process recognizes the dignity of citizens, consults their consent, assumes their willingness and capacity to accept responsibility for the basic policy of the commonwealth.

If it is said that this imposes too great a strain on human nature, exaggerates the capacity and good will of men, then the search must be made for an alternative and superior principle of selectivity and consent.[1] Notwithstanding the many weaknesses of the electoral method, no better system of obtaining popular consent to the government has been found.

The most obvious alternative is that of force—a process implying the breakdown of consent and persuasion. An election may seem irrational, but it is reason itself compared with civil war, with the substitution of death for argument. There is much wisdom in the old saying, "We count heads to save breaking them."

The practical problem of electoral processes is that of determining the field of electoral decision, of soundly setting the wisest metes and bounds within which electoral choice shall be employed. Not all measures can be decided by elections, obviously; not all officials and policies can be voted upon, for this would mean the end of government.

The area of electionism becomes a question for determination in each community where democratic association is accepted. Political prudence will dictate the range of consultation and consent necessary for purposes of the common control of common affairs. This range will vary from time to time and from place to place with varying conditions and situations. The wisdom with which such lines are drawn will be a searching test of the judgment and capacity of the community for popular rule. In this field as in other political areas, the principle of moderation is often a condition of survival. In the United States, for example, the national governmental organization exhibits a wise limitation of the electoral process to basic questions, whereas in the localities the elector is often burdened with a long and impossible "jungle ballot," in which he flounders.

In our time the protest against the electoral procedure arises chiefly from the insecurity of those who fear a free

---

[1] See Lippmann's critical analysis of the public in his *Public Opinion* (1922).

ASSUMPTIONS AND PROGRAM

popular verdict, and hence prefer the use of terror and intimidation. They retain the voting but not the election, endeavoring to keep the symbol of consent without its real inner meaning. The moral value of expressed and authentic popular consent is enormous in any modern state, and for this good reason it must be given lip service, if no other. Chicanery is the compromise between free choice and the open terror as a means of obtaining popular support for a government.

If we were to pose the question, "Is the vote on its way out or on its way back and in?" I should venture to predict that the vote is here to stay, as a means of measuring popular attitudes and interests. The straw vote, the sample vote, the representative sample are illustrations of the keen interest with which observers follow the indices of general assent and dissent.

If we assume, however, that a few are to rule without popular responsibility how shall they be chosen?

The doctrine that the elite is constantly "in circulation" is not very helpful at this point, since the present elite may fail to recognize and to give way to the oncoming elite quickly enough to avert disastrous consequences to the peace and order of the community.

For a short time, in periods of great tension, in mutual fear of external attack, it is possible for a few to maintain a fairly solid front, but there can be no guaranty that this will endure. The characteristic weakness of the few has been, as pointed out by Montesquieu, jealousy and rivalry. One faction may appeal to the mass as against the other; one faction may set up a strong man as against another; one faction may fear and attempt the annihilation of another. Hitler's bloody purge of June 30, 1934, and Russia's recent trials are only modern illustrations of what has happened innumerable times in the history of the anxious elites who could not trust each other—or perhaps trusted too fondly, as in Machiavelli's case of the leader who invited his rivals to a peace party which ended in the death of all the undesirables. The Soviets have found it necessary to rid themselves one by one of many of their greatest leaders holding high position and immense prestige. We do not yet know the inner history of these astounding episodes, but we do know the external fact of inner jealousy and rival ambition.

The loss of hereditary distinctions as a mark of nobility and the decline of wealth as an index make the status of an autocracy extremely dubious. Military prestige is always uncertain, in that no one knows when or where it will spring up, often at some inconvenient point, upsetting the balance of the comfortable occupants of the bowers of authority.

Once it is accepted that the few are to rule without legal responsibility to the rest of the state, and further that neither birth, wealth, electoral choice, nor standardized merit shall govern the line of successions, what shall be the means by which the allegiance of the bulk of the community is held in line for the support of the superior? How shall stability be insured? Even Plato was driven to say that he would start his ideal state with "one royal lie," namely, that the various classes had been born as they were. But in modern times this is not an adequate answer, unless the biologists produce new evidence. And there are lie detectors, even.

In modern terminology this is a large-scale problem of morale—of the maintenance of such a driving form of esprit that the community will produce, will fight and work, will be happy, and above all will accept the sway of the aristocracy as one of the major facts of life. The alternative presented is a dark picture of malaise, discontent, and actual or threatened revolution. And if the institutional channels of responsibility are clogged, the only way of action will be the channel of force.

ASSUMPTIONS AND PROGRAM

With this in mind, many aristocracies have studied the problem of pleasing those over whom they rule, of charming those whom they command so that they will obey, of combining the club and the charm in the most acceptable manner. In a sense, their tenure of office depends upon the outcome of a perpetual play. The mass of the inferiors do not vote, but they cast an informal ballot expressing their attitude toward the superior power. These ballots are not counted directly, but are reckoned in terms of crowds, hurrahs, applause, readiness to serve, and the absence of resistances and revolts. One hiss may count as much as the loss of a seat in the legislative body; one boo may sound like a revolt. There is need of a meter to measure the volume, the length, and the tone of applause in autocracies.

The appeal may always be made to the higher levels of statesmanship shown by achievement. The Few may appear as the continuing benefactors of the community of which they are the heads. More territory, more loaves and fishes, and more expanding sentiments of group prestige may be the fruits of their rule; and this may be appropriately presented as a justification. Or inferior achievements may be magnified until they seem important.

All this is, however, an appeal from ourselves to them, from the minority to the majority, as if they were the competent judges of what is good. Hence it contains within itself the seeds of some form of popular responsibility—to be avoided in the most complete form of superiority which assumes not merely superior power but superior competence in judgment of community affairs, and which avoids institutionalized responsibility.

The electoral device, however, none of the modern despotisms is willing to abandon wholly. All retain it in one form or another. It may reasonably be asked, Why do the modern tyrants, styling themselves leaders, play with the electoral system in their organization after repudiating it as a useless device of outworn democracy? Mussolini once said, by way of illustration, that the people might vote until sick at the stomach, but the inner circle would determine policy. In general, he protested against what began to be termed "electionistic" tendencies, meaning thereby too great emphasis on electoral devices. The answer may be, from one point of view, that the use of elections is merely a device of a transition period, and that the machinery of counting will be abolished in the fulness of time and with the perfection of the system. Or, from another point of view, it may be said that the electoral device is useful in creating a feeling of popular participation in the government, as a means for improvement of general morale, although in fact the important decisions are made in another fashion. Elections from this point of view are morale mechanisms rather than modes of selection of personnel or determination of broad policies.[1] Also they may be looked upon as warnings to outside powers that the autocracy is unified 100 per cent.

It is unlikely that bullets and battles will in the long run supplant the more tranquil and more accurate polling of the electors as a mode of ascertaining the general understandings and registering community consent to a type of governance.

b. COMMON COUNSEL

The charge against the validity of the process of consent is further extended to a condemnation of the institution of discussion through agencies of conference in representative and parliamentary organization.[2] Representative govern-

---

[1] See Gaetano Salvemini, "Totalitarian 'Elections' in Italy Today," *Social Research*, February, 1937, pp. 108*ff*., for a discussion of voting in Fascist Italy.

[2] Among the critics of parliamentarism is Hilaire Belloc; see his *The House of Commons and Monarchy* (1920). See also Ralph Adams Cram, *The Nemesis of Mediocrity* (1917), pp. 24*ff*.; Émile Faguet, *The Cult of Incompetence* (1911), Chap. IV; Wilhelm Hasbach, *Die moderne Demokratie* (1912), pp. 580 and 588*ff*.; Adolf Hit-

ASSUMPTIONS AND PROGRAM

ments are really unrepresentative, it is contended, and in any case they are incompetent in the field of policy determination. Government "by talk," government by adjustment, compromise, conciliation is out of date in the modern world, it is maintained. The community intelligence is not really recruited and the action of representative bodies is slow, incompetent, timid, and confused. The remedy is the destruction of popular representation as a factor in emerging forms of government, and the substitution of "leaders" who reflect and represent the general interest.

The organization of the conciliar function is one of the very oldest and most fundamental of human institutions.[1] The end sought in these conferences is the union of wisdom and will—the combination of intelligence and morale. In some types of conference wisdom predominates, and in others the factor of consent. In some they are combined.

Representative bodies of a public and formal type attempt the combination of group thinking and group solidarity of sentiment. Obviously a precondition of their success is a willingness on the part of the bulk of the group to deliberate and to effect an agreement, or to accept an agreement when reached, even if not wholly satisfactory. If this feeling is not present, the assembly may, of course, become an arena of battle rather than a concourse of consideration. The old

---

ler, *Mein Kampf* (Reynal and Hitchcock translation, 1939); William E. H. Lecky, *op. cit.*, see particularly Vol. I, pp. 142*ff.*; William S. Lilly, *First Principles in Politics* (1899), pp. 140*ff.*, and Chap. VI; A. M. Ludovici, *The False Assumptions of Democracy* (1921), pp. 90*ff.*; Henry Sumner Maine, *Popular Government* (1886); H. L. Mencken, *Notes on Democracy* (1926), see particularly pp. 122*ff.*; Vilfredo Pareto, *Mind and Society* (1934), particularly Vol. IV, pars. 2237-2278, also Vol. II, p. 558 and Vol. III, pp. 1157*ff.*; Carl Schmitt, *Die geistesgeschichtliche Lage des heutigen Parlamentarismus* (1923); Oswald Spengler, *The Decline of the West* (1926-1928), particularly Vol. I, pp. 415*ff.*

[1] See William C. MacLeod, *The Origin and History of Politics* (1931); for general bibliography on the history of parliamentary institutions see article on "Legislative Assemblies" in *Encyclopedia of the Social Sciences* Vol. IX, pp. 395-398.

THE NEW DEMOCRACY

Austro-Hungarian Parliament and the German Reichstag of 1932 present striking examples of this.[1]

The units and types of representation may vary widely within a range of understanding and institutions resting upon efforts to validate the mass decision on basic questions of social policy. Whether territory is a basis, or population, or occupation, or function, or whether the vote is proportional or plural, or whether there are two houses or three or one is not indicated by the formula of democracy; and there may be wide ranges of difference and even eccentricity within this field. Understanding and good faith are more important here than the detail of the special form of implementing the popular assent to policy. In manipulation of the mechanism, indeed, the spirit of the understanding may be lost, and an institution become a prison of popular hope.

It is historically possible to find all manner of methods of organizing the popular will, from mass assembly on the hills of some Swiss commune to complicated and indirect forms of effecting an ultimate decision. The future may develop many more new and perhaps puzzling forms of popular choice with the increasing precision of quantification. From the broader point of view these are details, important details but always subordinate to the question of the organization of assent.

No governments really act without taking counsel, however autocratic they may appear on the surface. Even within the narrow circle of military law there are courts and councils and procedures. It is an illusion to suppose that the Superior or even the Despot takes no counsel, engages in no "talk," develops and encourages no discussion. Within the inner walls, the parliamentary process goes on, modified to suit the special circumstances of the case. Interpreters

[1] See Hitler's comment in *Mein Kampf*, pp. 83*ff*.

ASSUMPTIONS AND PROGRAM

of interests come and go, stating their case as best they may, staking perhaps life, liberty, and the pursuit of happiness on their counsel and their voice or vote. Where do the lines of responsibility run, under such conditions? In early times, to blood and soil and arms perhaps. In later days, they run, who knows where? There may be no debates as in open parliaments, but behind the door there is discussion and sometimes concussion, when patience is replaced by violence.

It is a very naïve conclusion that under the rule of the Superior all the troubles attributed to electoral processes or to "talk" (discussion) magically disappear, leaving only a silent, crystal-clear pool of intelligence and decision. Only the credulous can believe that all selfish, conflicting, noisy interests vanish, leaving only pure intelligence and pure unity.

The truth is that in every government that does not have an open parliament there is a *Secret Parliament*, a shadowy group coming and going behind the scenes. Individuals and groups, cliques and factions, favorites, male and female, struggle for the ascendancy. The salon or even the bedchamber becomes the legislative hall, where affairs of state are settled by such wisdom and will as are there convoked.

Or there may be formal councils of state appointed by the Most High and responsible to him alone. But every ruler must have men who represent the wisdom of the community and its will as well; for he is conditioned by the social and economic and political elements out of which he comes, and which he can use only according to their own qualities. The ruler is greatest when he uses his arbitrary power least and when his faculties of consultation are not forgotten.

Although it is easy to jibe at the futilities of modern responsible representative bodies, the irresponsible representatives are not automatically transformed into exemplars of wisdom and virtue by the hand of history. The colors of

THE NEW DEMOCRACY

Shame and Mirth are needed to depict many of the scenes of the Secret Parliaments where the Great Decisions of the Most High were reached.[1] Fortunately for mankind no verbatim reports are available for many of them, or modern cinema reproductions of such Councils.

Nor is there any assurance that five men or even one will be able to decide more quickly or act more vigorously than a larger number. Indecision is often a curse of individuals of small as well as of larger groups; and the fact that one sits on a throne or wears a crown is not a guaranty that he or his little group of private councilors will reach a wise or a swift conclusion in moments of community tension when action is urgent. Even generals may find difficulty in making up their military minds. Lincoln once wrote to General McClellan asking that he be allowed to use the army himself if the General did not intend to employ it; military history is full of the deeds of those who dallied when they might have moved and won. They were not embarrassed by lack of authority, but by lack of intelligence or will to use it.

It is clear that the forms of representation must always be open to reconsideration under changing circumstances, and that twentieth-century representative institutions may be widely different from those adapted to the seventeenth century or the nineteenth. I am not impressed with the credentials of those who profess to have discovered a permanent system of organizing the conciliar functions of the state.

For the future, several modifying factors not discussed in detail here will require serious consideration. Among these are

[1] See Maurice Paléologue, *An Ambassador's Memoirs* (3 vols., trans. 1923–1925); *Guillaume II et Nicolas II* (1935); V. N. Kokovtsov, *Out of My Past: Memoirs* (trans. 1935); Theodor Wolff, *The Eve of 1914* (trans. 1936).

ASSUMPTIONS AND PROGRAM

(1) Concentration of conciliar bodies on broad questions of public policy with the avoidance of over-detail.

(2) The relation of the executive and the administration to councils.

(3) Reconsideration of the units upon which councils of state are based, with reference to the new forms of association emerging in modern society.

(4) Reconsideration of the bicameral principle on various levels in the light of newly developing conditions, with a view to clearing the confusion of councils.

(5) Consideration of measures for strengthening councils by various devices and procedures, designed to sharpen their responsibilities and powers of general review and appraisal of executive activities, and by closer attention to the adequate organization of controversy in discussion of commonwealth policies.

The process of conscious lawmaking is relatively new in the history of the world, and has developed in the last century in the midst of a whirlwind of social change. Most of the time in human history laws were not deliberately made, but were in large measure inherited customs and traditions which were accepted and applied, modified to be sure in the course of their application. Large-scale lawmaking is a distinctly modern phenomenon. In the midst of an economic revolution, a scientific revolution, a technical revolution in the means of communication, legislative bodies are groping their way toward insight and action appropriate to the problems of our day.

Our modern problem is not that of the destruction or sabotaging of representative deliberative bodies, but of strengthening and developing them in the light of our emerging conditions. Democratic associations will naturally attempt to adapt them to the fundamental assumptions of democracy, but the conciliar function is a problem for all governments of whatever type in our day—a problem for Soviets, for Nazis, for Nippon, and for Turkey. A large and imposing array of useful legislation has been enacted during recent years by legislative bodies, and it is reasonable to assume that this process will continue for an indefinite period as legislative processes meet the demands of our time for the formulation of effective rules of the game under changing conditions.

The difficulties of effective legislative action arising from the vastness and complexity of modern society are not, as some seem to suppose, inherently insuperable, but are capable of solution by adequate organization of the legislative process. The problems of a legislative body are twofold:

(1) Formulation of general lines of public policy, including fiscal policy.

(2) The general supervision of the administration of policies laid down and of the general character and type of administration, including fiscal administration.

The successful performance of the first function rests upon limitation of the field to very broad questions of policy which may be thoroughly discussed, and it also involves the avoidance of detailed legislation and appropriation. The most complex of social and economic situations may be reduced to a relatively few outstanding questions, the decision of which determines the policy of the commonwealth for the time.

This is true of any association or organization, placed in the position of policy determination, and faced with the focussing of its attention on the strategic situations before it. Absorption in the detail of any one policy or in the formulation of too large a number of policies interferes with the smooth operation of the over-all function of political control, and really defeats itself by bogging down. Fixing the minutiae of legislation may seem like the exercise of power on the part of lawmakers, but it is really the opposite, for it absorbs the interest and time that should go to the judgment of larger problems of the state, and to the effective supervision of the general character and conduct of the administration. What individual members may gain, the legislative body as a whole loses.

Supervision of the public policy through inquiry, question, mandate, and action is also one of the primary functions of the legislative body. If effectively organized and utilized, this supervisory power is capable of providing leadership for the common good. It gives the necessary review and appraisal of the activities of officialdom, and correction from time to time as need indicates, either by turning the spotlight of public interest on special situations—Teapot Domes—or by drastic action in validating declared legislative program.

The organization of controversy in a democratic community is a vitally important element in the success of its operations. A legislative body may lead the commonwealth in this direction by its own debates and discussions, but it may also assist the process by the collection and analysis of data and by the encouragement of sharp discussion upon issues clearly joined. Many parliamentary and congressional commissions and committees have contributed greatly to the enrichment of public information and analysis and to the statement of the various aspects of the problem under consideration. To the extent that such inquiries are partisan and unfair, they are inadequate, but on the other hand there are many examples of inquiry in which the different sides of the question are adequately stated and full opportunity given for the formulation of different policies.

The important point in all this is, first, the recognition of the values of public discussion on the basis of adequate data and analysis, and, second, the disposition to find a solution through peaceful consent rather than by division and violence.

THE NEW DEMOCRACY

From time to time the action of legislative bodies is criticized because it is influenced by pressure groups of one sort and another—agricultural, labor, industrial, and social. This view, however, reflects a naïve conception of the political process among mankind. What type of human association is it in which there are no pressures and counterpressures for group action of one type and another? It is indeed these very pressures of individuals and interests that call for the balancing function of the state. If all interests and pressures settled themselves automatically, there would be no need for government at all. The stars would move in their courses without any central control at all.

The appearance of these social and economic interests is an inevitable phenomenon of social organization and control. In any form of government, whether that of the Many, the Few, or the One, these or like pressures will exist and will be reflected in one form or another. The interests may be less obvious and less public, but their activity will be observed by anyone familiar with the operations of the governing process.

Behind the formal social legislation in a democracy there is a large body of non-political representative bodies of many types operating as a part of the democratic process. These groups are not repressed, intimidated, or controlled by the state, but their activity is encouraged in the interest of sound formulation of public policy—in the interest of encouragement of the process of common consent to the broad trends of the nation. Some of these groups are able from time to time to dictate to the government their programs, but on the whole one is likely to be balanced by others, and the net contribution is that of a broader discussion of legislative policies.

The clearing house of individual and group interests in a democracy is the party system,[1] which takes on the function

[1] For bibliography of studies of party systems see *Encyclopedia of Social Sciences*, article on "Political Parties," Vol. XI, pp. 636ff. See Charles E. Merriam and Harold

of aiding in the organization of general opinion. Competing forms of policy are filtered through factions into party policy and through parties into political policy. The rivalry of interests and individuals is thus given an arena of conflict, an organization of controversy, which may be carried on without resort to civil war. Parties not only presuppose a certain solidarity of national interest, but they tend to induce such a solidarity by the nature of their operations. Thus in America the last bond to break of the bonds uniting the North and the South was the party bond, which hung tenaciously until the end.

C. PUBLIC ADMINISTRATION

The organization of public administration is of far-reaching significance in the system of democracy. The body of practices and principles gradually accumulating in this field, the growth of technical skills developing in modern times, the advance from the domain of art to the edge of science—all these point to the emergence of administration as a more significant factor in the realm of government than ever before. We may reasonably anticipate

(1) Devotion of legislation to the statement of broad general principles, and the supervision of their administration.

(2) Administrative initiative in the presentation of policies from the point of view of the actual practitioner and from the point of view of the scientist developing the products of his research.

(3) Administrative management of general policies.

It will also be found that one of the greatest guaranties of daily liberty and security is the presence of a facile administration, skilled in the adjustment of broad rules to the

---

F. Gosnell, *American Party System* (1939). Two more recent studies of parties in America are Peter H. Odegard and E. Allen Helms, *American Politics* (1938), and Charles W. McKenzie, *Party Government in the United States* (1938), see classified bibliography pp. 565*ff*.

specific problems of individual life, and avoiding the inflexibilities of bureaucracy.

We may anticipate that administration will increasingly possess some of the insight and authority of scientific intelligence and some of the prestige of the art of human relations and management.

If the spirit of science and the spirit of democracy enter into administration, many of the historic evils of officialism will tend to disappear. Administration as the tool of the Superior for the Superior will be transformed into administration for the mass—as a road to general welfare.

Modern scientific administration must be sharply differentiated from the inflexibility and legalism of the older forms of official organization recruited from a special class, and directed by an autocratic will.

More revolutionary than the changes precipitated by violent overturns accompanied by blood and fire is the quiet revolution going on in the nature of public administration, in the transition from arbitrary and rigid inflexibility to modern personnel with scientific equipment, with objective determination of standards and their application. No war has been fought to establish better administration. Technology, science, training have quietly taken their places in branch after branch of the public service as doctors, engineers, teachers, welfare workers, technicians in industry, agriculture, labor, geology, botany, chemistry, etc., have filtered into the administration. Partisan and personal administration still survive over great areas of service and will not disappear at once, but they are on their way out; and when they have gone they will not be missed. No monuments will be erected to them.

Furthermore, in the field of administration the recruitment of personnel and their continuity are far better established than elsewhere. By the application of now known methods it

ASSUMPTIONS AND PROGRAM

is possible to set up, on any one of several models, a competent and stable body of personnel operating under procedures that are reasonably satisfactory for public purposes.

That corruption, incompetence, or favoritism may enter into such a service is, of course, not excluded, but in the main public administration may with reasonable precaution be made effective from the point of view of the community and in keeping with democratic ideals of recruitment.

In close connection with public administration may be observed the emergence of the modern type of executive who combines the direction of public administration with leadership—a phenomenon of business, labor, and government alike. The outstanding political example of this development is found in the presidency of the United States.

The growth of the modern "executive" in many different social groups is not due merely to the desire of some persons for wider authority, but to the general appreciation of the facility with which the executive may take an over-all view of a set of complicated and conflicting situations which has brought him to the fore. He may, to be sure, become temporarily Czar in fact as well as in name, but this is accidental to his position and not the essence of his authority. In a period of extraordinary division of labor of all sorts, and of extraordinary rapidity of change, the overhead view of the general coordinator has become of unusual significance, and to this may be attributed the rise of the persons who fill this function in the modern social process.

That there are dangers in the possession of such authority is evident. What is not always equally evident, although equally important, is that there are greater dangers in lack of such power, in inability to act in critical situations. Inaction may ruin a state as well as a man.

The strengthening of public administration and the emergence of the executive leader constitute by far the most striking feature of recent political development, and mark a new era in the organization of mass government. Administrative initiative, executive unity and insight, coupled with policy-determining legislative action and popular control in the last analysis, make possible a policy of intelligent action even in times of most difficult adaptation to swiftly changing conditions of war or of peace.

Modern governments have addressed themselves to the problem of setting administration in the most favorable national position, and this inquiry and experiment has included societies of all descriptions.[1]

The reorganization of the executive is indeed one of the notable phenomena of the time. Impetus has been given to this undertaking by the increased interest in the efficiency of large-scale organizations both public and private, by the prolonged crisis of the late war, by the postwar pressure for widespread social services now undertaken by all governments, and by measures for various forms of economic stabilization.

These factors taken together have brought about a general movement in the direction of sharpening of the tools of management and definitizing the position of the executive in organizations of all types.

In the report presented by President Roosevelt's Committee on Administrative Management (1937) an outline of administrative organization was prepared. This included as over-all agencies.

---

[1] See excellent summary in the proceedings of the International Institute of Administrative Sciences, Warsaw, 1937; see also Lindsay Rogers, *Crisis Government* (1934); Léon Blum, *La Réforme gouvernmentale* (1918); Carl J. Friedrich, *Constitutional Government and Politics* (1937); L. D. White, *Introduction to the Study of Public Administration* (2d ed. 1939); Zoltan von Magyary, *The Chief Executive and His Auxiliary Agencies* (1938); Studd Lectures on Industrial and Business Management (1938); Luther Gulick and L. Urwick, *Papers on the Science of Administration* (1937).

ASSUMPTIONS AND PROGRAM

(1) Fiscal management
(2) Personnel management
(3) Planning management

under the immediate direction of the President.[1]

The significance of the executive in modern democracy was emphasized and the need of machinery necessary to make democracy work under modern conditions.

> Intelligence, vision, fairness, firmness and flexibility are required in an assembled, competent, strong organization of democracy. To falter at this point is fatal. A weak administration can neither advance nor retreat successfully—it can only muddle. Those who waver at the sight of needed power are false friends of modern democracy. Strong executive leadership is essential to democratic government today. Our choice is not between power and no power, but between responsible and capable popular government and irresponsible autocracy.[2]

The modern problem is that of a unified and intelligent action—a program in which delay may be the unpardonable sin, as fatal as ignorance or betrayal of the general interest.

When government was regarded as an enemy, weakness was the strategy of the hour; but when government is the friend of the commonwealth, the reverse becomes the strategy of a new time.

These administrative procedures are, of course, the property of a wide range of political systems and might be found under the rule of the Few as well as of the Many, theoretically, assuming that a fair degree of neutrality is developed under a regime. But what emerges in the rule of the Few is usually caste rule, class law for the higher, lower, and middle-justice groups; and what is termed "equality before the law" is ignored. Each class may then receive whatever "justice," whatever "equality" it is fit for—in the judgment of the Superior. Even under a democratic

---
[1] See this report and accompanying documents.
[2] *Ibid.*, p. 53.

system, wide disparity of wealth subjects the doctrine of equality before the law to the very gravest strains.

Whatever may have been the case in prescientific and preeducational periods, at the present time there is every reason to believe that the mass is able to set up instruments of social intelligence surpassing those of any other period in the history of the race, and to interpret their findings, conclusions, and recommendations in its own interest through a period of time. Intelligence organized through scientific social research and embodied in public administration is already set up in important democratic states, of which Sweden affords a striking illustration.

It is not important for the mass of the community to know and identify each individual leader in the domain of science or of administration, but only to identify and support the scientific, administrative procedure as an institution under popular auspices and control. Beyond this the mass of the community must be able to act upon conflicting and competing proposals for social justice and order in the light of the community's organized intelligence; and it must be capable of identifying personalities in the role of leadership of the type considered in the procedures of popular assent. That this is possible has already been amply demonstrated in modern times in the experience of England and the United States and many other states in the twentieth century under the most difficult situations in times of peace and of war.

What is happening is the rise of a scientific-administrative group, broadly recruited from all classes, and possessed of the principles and skills upon which common policies may be based. They are at the service of the commonwealth which establishes them. They are ultimately responsible to the community which sets the broad lines of their support, their activities, and their personnel, and passes judgment in last

ASSUMPTIONS AND PROGRAM

analysis upon their conclusions. They are means by which the people's ends are reached.

Contrary to the general view, the defence of human liberty depends in large measure on public administration. The judicial agencies play their proper part in the protection of private rights, but with increasing difficulty in view of the slowness of procedure in a fast-moving society, and in view of the complexity and rigidity of technical rules.

In a large and increasing measure, administrative agencies supply the diffusion of power upon which the growth and play of individual initiative rely for their protection and stimulation. The degree of adaptability within the administration itself, the extent to which it is able to comprehend, sympathize with, and incorporate the popular attitudes—these are factors that will be effective in determining the scope of free play of activities of the citizen in the period ahead of us.

The real gulf often found yawning between the citizen and the technical administrator is partly an emotional one, due to the fact that the graces and arts of administration have not been rated so highly as its skills and techniques.

Important changes are impending in the United States and elsewhere in the field of administration. There is involved the progressive development of new procedures and processes adapted to the changing technology and psychology of our time, drawing in and utilizing the skills of the old-time official, the new arts of the engineer, the physician, the technician, the welfare worker, the businessman in a new form of understanding and competence.

There is reason to anticipate that the new administrators will develop the flexibility, the adaptability, the creative interest, the graciousness and human *savoir faire* that characterize the superior forms of administration, public and private.

THE NEW DEMOCRACY

Administration plays as large a role in government as adjudication. In administrative management there are developed types of competence upon which wisdom in decision is conditioned, a professional attitude of objectivity and fairness of far-reaching importance, and an over-all point of view and attitude of deepest meaning in the life of the commonwealth.

It is important that, in the transition period leading to the surrender of public administration by spoilsmen, mediating non-governmental agencies should contribute what they can, not only to the adoption of administrative standards and to the professionalizing of officialdom, not only to the stimulation of interest in invention, growth, development in official groups, but also to its humanizing. To this end easy interchange of information, of experience, the free flow of ideas and ideals, mobility of personnel, facility in conference and consultation, and emphasis on the strategy of administration as well as its technical efficiency are important.[1]

The techniques and procedures of adjudicating bodies known as "courts" are technically not parts of the policy-determining body of the state. They are set up as independent agencies. In a static society when rules laid down in advance can be administered in accordance with accepted principles and procedures, the adjudicating group functions with greatest ease and success. In times of rapid change, the difficulty is greater, inasmuch as the understandings of the time are less well developed and recognized.

In a democratic association, as indeed in other forms of political organization, the primary function of the courts is not that of policy determination, but of policy application in specific instances. In operating with the specialized technique of adjudication, however, it is inevitable that the

---

[1] See *National Governmental Organizations* (1938), p. 2, for a description of the activities of the Public Administration Clearing House.

ASSUMPTIONS AND PROGRAM

interpretation of the law, common, statutory, or constitutional, leads to the possible broadening or narrowing of the law itself. In the United States this has constituted a problem of major importance, but not by and large in democracies generally.

Another problem of significance is found in the relation between the quasi-judicial or other related activities of administrative agencies and the regular judicial procedure. In dealing with the new frontiers of governmental regulation, this may become a serious perplexity, as in the United States, but in the main it has not been one of the characteristic problems of democratic association broadly considered.

In this connection it is important to emphasize the importance of continuing consideration of the decentralization of administrative agencies.[1] Centralization of political control and management and decentralization of types of administration are not conflicting in tendency, but supplementary. Broad rules and broad decisions and directions may well be made centrally, but there must still be a wide range of activities and decisions which may advantageously be made locally.

Congestion and delay are political sins that are perhaps more common than arbitrariness and oppressive conduct. In some circumstances in the modern swiftly moving world, delay and non-delegation are the cardinal sins. They may not interfere technically with either liberty or justice, but they obstruct progress and productivity.

A new bill of rights might include the right to speedy decisions by competent persons upon questions of administrative significance bearing on the daily life and business of the citizen.

[1] See National Resources Committee, *Regional Factors in National Planning* (1935).

THE NEW DEMOCRACY

d. DEMOCRACY AND DECISIONISM

It is charged from time to time that the democratic form of political association is incapable of dealing effectively either with the problems of legislation or of administration, or with the general direction of public policy, whether executive or legislative or on the boundary line. The effort to procure popular consent and support, whether in legislation, personnel, or general policy, is alleged to be fatal to the prospects of democratic societies in the modern struggle for survival. This doctrine is now advanced by the autocrats in their struggle for national and personal prestige.[1]

It is confidently asserted by its critics that democracy is unable

(1) To meet with speed and force the crises arising in international relations, as in war and diplomacy.

(2) To meet effectively the necessity for economic stabilization in the modern state.

To obtain a clear picture of the first of these questions we may recall that one of the problems of the nineteenth century was the reconciliation of democracy with the military forces of the nation,[2] how to constitutionalize the army in some form and to bring it under control of the policy-determining agencies of the government. In America this principle was early stated as that of the subordination of the military to the civil authority of the people.

---

[1] See Part II for fuller elaboration of these doctrines.
[2] See the important discussions of this struggle in J. S. Omond, *Parliament and the Army* (1933); Alfred Vagts, *History of Militarism* (1937); Frederick Maurice, *Governments and War* (1928); George Fielding Elliot, *The Ramparts We Watch* (1938); Silas Bent McKinley, *Democracy and Military Power* (1934); Basil Henry Liddell Hart, *The Re-making of Modern Armies* (1927), *Europe in Arms* (1937), *Paris, or the Future of War* (1925); Ernst Rudolf Huber, *Heer und Staat in der deutsche Geschichte* (1938); P. Schmitthenner, *Politik und Kriegführung in der neueren Geschichte* (1937); Reinhard Höhn, *Verfassungskampf und Heereseid* (1938).

ASSUMPTIONS AND PROGRAM

In earlier times the armed forces of the commonwealth were looked upon as the instruments of autocracy in somewhat the same fashion as public administration was regarded as the tool of absolutism, and the liberals often tended toward non-recognition of the military as a part of the public equipment or at least toward the neglect of these agencies of national policy. In general, the processes of peaceful persuasion were preferred and encouraged, as against the methods of violence and coercion, and the use of armed force was not seen to be, under certain situations, an indispensable instrument of democratic defence. In the United States, however, the events of the Civil War served to make this relationship clearer, and a democratic army was organized and operated over a considerable period of time. In the World War the significance of military forces under the general direction of the nation was recognized and definite action taken in this direction, by the French, the British, and finally by the Americans.

The history of British experience is highly instructive. The relations between the civil and the military in England, as described by an English military historian,[1] point to the extremes to which Parliament went in Great Britain following its experience with military government in the "Glorious Revolution." Parliament on the one hand limited the size of the Army, and on the other engaged in a policy requiring a large one. It failed to centralize the army command, starved it in munitions, and failed to give it adequate housing. This unintelligent military policy Liddell Hart ascribes to an Anglo-Saxon zealousness for religious and political liberty, and a corresponding fear of militarism.

Yet [says Hart] by their lack of interest in military questions they do in fact relinquish any check on a policy which affects the security of their

[1] Omond, *op. cit.*

lives and livelihoods to an even greater extent. For, when war bursts upon the nation, it is the ordinary citizens who pay the toll, either with their lives or from their pockets. Only by taking an active interest in the broad aspects of national defence, and so regaining control of their military conscience, can they avoid being driven like sheep to the shearer and the slaughterhouse as in the last war.[1]

The struggle of the various German states with the problems of militarism and democracy is recounted down to 1850 in some detail in the treatise by Höhn,[2] and for the whole period down to the present day by Huber.[2] In these encounters there is evident the struggle for a policy of democratic control over the military arm of the state and the resistance to such control by the military leaders in many instances. Bismarck, for example, was able to break through and direct military policy, whereas the Kaiser was less successful.

In France, however, the Republic was successful in building an army of first-rate ability, yet under democratic supervision and direction in the main. Clemenceau in France and Lloyd George in England were able through force of personality to hold the reins of control during the periods of greatest tension in the recent war.

Assuming that speed is of the essence of strength, which is sometimes not true, there is nothing to inhibit a democratic organization from action. In the World War it was found possible to advance at times with great celerity, in granting both money and authority to various officials at strategic moments. In France and England, it was possible to organize an effective fighting machine. American military preparations and movements went forward as rapidly as any like movements in Germany or Russia; and there was no insuperable difficulty in reaching important decisions when they were urgent, as in 1917 on the question of conscription and on the transfer of troops to France.

[1] Liddell Hart, *Paris, or the Future of War* (1925), pp. 17-18.
[2] *Op. cit.*

ASSUMPTIONS AND PROGRAM

With the strong emphasis in modern times upon nationalism and upon mass psychology, with universal military and educational training, it is clear that the rapport between the military and the civil command becomes increasingly important. But with our increasing division and subdivision of labor, the military commander tends to fall into some one of the categories of specialization, whereas the over-all function falls to the political leader. The general has his hands full with the highly specialized organization of violence, whereas the weaving together of the strands of national will and interest becomes also a highly specialized function for which the trained statesman is particularly competent.

In military relations it occasionally happens that there arises a general who is both a military commander and a statesman as well: a Caesar or a Napoleon. But more commonly the war movement involves the severance of military command on the one hand from civilian or non-military authority on the other. Those concerned with the organization of violence are seldom equally well equipped to deal effectively with the organization of popular morale or with the interpretation of popular interest and will. It cannot be said that the union of high military command and of civil authority was well worked out in the recent war by Germany, Austria, or Russia.

Furthermore, decisiveness is not always a characteristic of an individual mind, for there are many persons who are able to arrive at an important conclusion only after long delay and much oscillation between opposite courses of conduct. There is no reason to suppose that one man, legally vested with wide-ranging powers, will be able to pull himself together and make a series of vital decisions with great speed and accuracy. A particular man, at a particular tension moment, with a united community will behind him, may act in this fashion; but so may a particular legislative body at a particular time and with a unified community behind it. Decisionism is as much a matter of special social tension and unity of community purpose at a particular time, as it is of particular forms of organization.

Unless there is a mechanism for providing continuity—a mechanism generally accepted as adequate—the loss of the leader will very seriously embarrass the whole operation of the state, in the absence of any special mechanism generally accepted. And precisely here, in the choice of the new leader, lies the possibility of serious disorganization of the unity and continuity of command.

The more we claim for the occasional figure who may be either a great general with a flair for statesmanship, or a great statesman with a flair for military affairs, the greater the gap caused by the loss of such a general or statesman, and the greater the disorganization caused by his disappearance from the scene without adequate provision for a successor.

In the democratic society on the other hand the apparatus of selection is ready at hand, set up for action, with recognized standards and recognized methods of applying them to the choice of a political head or a head of organized violence.

Students of government recognize that the interplay of influence between the "frocks" and the "brass hats," the political and the military authorities, is under any governmental system a problem of the very first magnitude. These boundary lines have never been adequately explored thus far. It is naïve to suppose that the difficulty is completely avoided by the elevation of one man or a small group of men to nominally supreme command. The jurists may call this the "authoritarian," but the historian may say "futilitarian."

ASSUMPTIONS AND PROGRAM

Unity does not lie merely in the legal formula of command, but in coordination of administrative agencies, in the relation of these agencies to national policy.

In the United States the Executive was from the beginning the commander in chief of the military and naval forces of the nation, as well as the chief civilian administrator, and a participant in the legislative power through his power to recommend measures of national concern and through his veto. But in this case the continuity of succession is assured through clearly defined channels, flowing from the free expression of the national will through the electorate. This combination of authority based upon national consent and mandate operated successfully in the great military crisis of the Civil War under Lincoln,[1] and again in the recent World War under Wilson.

The prime ministers of England and of France are likewise able to make the necessary union of forces, as was clearly seen in the case of Lloyd George in England and Clemenceau in France, under extraordinarily difficult conditions.

The central problem is: What are the relative merits of different methods of organizing consent and force? It is possible to speak of war as involving two problems—one is that of technical civilian and military organization, the other is a civilian-military and political relation. If a military machine is to be efficient, its branches must be co-ordinated, its controls centralized and adequately geared in with civilian administrative agencies.

World War experience, critics declare, shows the conservatism of the military, its inflexibility and unwillingness to take a new step. Lloyd George's memoirs point to a rigidity and lack of pliability and imagination

[1] See Maurice *op. cit.*, for acute discussion of our Civil War and of modern organization for war.

in the army leaders. He asserts, with some heat, that on many, even most, of the matters in dispute, the civilians were more correct than the army leaders. France had a similar experience during the World War. Pressure by parliament and the president of the republic was responsible for the adoption of the latest in techniques and munitions.[1] The general conclusion to be drawn from these facts is that in peace time there is a tendency for the civil arm to sabotage, or, worse, to pay no attention whatsoever to the military establishment, the result being unpreparedness in time of war. During war, on the other hand, when the civil arm has already recognized the crisis, the influence of the civil over the military is generally of a valuable character, since the rigidity of military thinking is compensated for by the discussion and pressures of parliaments, cabinet ministers, and civilians generally.

The inefficiency that resulted from the lack of rapport between the civil and the military in democracies took a different form in such a militarist monarchy as Imperial Germany. "The German military machine brooked no interference from politicians. The general and politicians were on a parity in dealing with the Kaiser. The Kaiser was the war and the political chief."[2]

---

[1] See Léon Blum, *La Réforme gouvernmentale* (1918).

[2] Lindsay Rogers, "The War Machines Examined," *Southern Review*, 3: 673.

"And it was precisely this [says Rogers] which was a decisive factor in bringing about the allied victory. Possibly a superman might have performed the dual role successfully. William II did not. In disputes he sided with his military and naval advisers, and they were incompetent on matters that involved issues wider than technical operations. The Kaiser did not know that. Of all the commanders on either side, Ludendorff possibly came closest to greatness. But he was blind politically. He had no conception of the mentality of his enemies. Even more disastrously he molded to his will successive German governments. When the break came, he outdid the politicians in his desires for peace, and then blamed them—and the civilian population—for stabbing the army in the back."

ASSUMPTIONS AND PROGRAM

Lloyd George declared in his memoirs:

No one can doubt that the cause of Germany's defeat lay in the usurpation of political powers by the military leaders. Bismarck had had almost exactly the same trouble in 1870 and 1866, but with a great effort had checked this attempted usurpation. Bethmann Hollweg could not; in fact it was their political system that failed the Germans. The same attempt was made by a military clique here (in England) but it did not succeed. Our political system did not fail us.[1]

It is a serious question [continues Rogers] whether, in the totalitarian regimes, a similar concentration of authority will not invite disaster.

The advantages of democratic control over the military is its flexibility, Captain Liddel Hart asserts;

. . . politicians and business men are always at war—in competition with each other. They have constant practice in conflict, and increasing experience of its psychological conditions. Soldiering, by contrast, is a sheltered occupation, save in war. The higher a man rises in the profession the less he is called on to contend with opposition, and the more immune he becomes even from criticism. The ease with which the will of the superior prevails inside an army becomes a handicap in preparation for dealing with a hostile army. Always revolving between the poles of authority and obedience, the soldier gains little or no psychological experience as a fighter. His training tends to suppress rather than to develop the combative qualities. Exercise in mimic war, regulated by umpires, cannot compare with the exacting tests of the political or the business field.[1]

The weakness of democracy for war [says Hart] was also its strength. Inefficiency was the price paid by the democracies for their political system. Vitality was the value they derived from it. They were more likely to bend, but less likely to break—because they had elasticity and because they could break the grip of a dead hand on the helm.[1]

Democracy preserves many war potentials [says Vagts] such as initiative in business and on the battlefield, and taps many deep sources of energy, intellectual and nervous, as well as economic, which may quite conceivably fail authoritarian governments. It has yet to be demonstrated that Fascism makes better tanks and planes, or more ingenious and valorous use of them than democracy.[2]

[1] *Ibid.*
[2] Alfred Vagts, *op. cit.* Even the military theorists of Italy and Germany are aware of the demands which will be made upon the soldier in a future war. General Von Seeckt is quoted by Vagts as having said that the war of the future will require that the soldier possess an "autonomous personality." An Italian colonel remarks

THE NEW DEMOCRACY

One of the perennial problems of politics is that of the ways and means of relating the organization of violence to the organization of consent in some form from which morale and military unity emerge in happy unison. Rational control over violence has always been the *bête noire* of all modern governments, whether democratic or otherwise. The old "Mirrors of Princes" did not contain the answer; nor do the modern manuals of politics contain the precise prescription of the modus operandi in this relationship.

that conditions of modern war will "render the leader invisible and often miles away from his troops," and that "obedience must exist in interpreting with open eyes the ideas of the commander." Vagts asks in conclusion, "Can Fascism, with its general militaristic tendency to over-govern men and materials, produce this individualistic soldier? Is it possible to regiment the individual in almost every sphere, and leave him the feeling of freedom needed for war purposes?" (p. 473).

And American military theorists, Dupuy and Eliot, also speak of the increased responsibility placed upon the individual soldier in modern war. "There will be less standing shoulder to shoulder, supported by comrades on either hand, inspired by the sight and example of trusted leaders; a tank driver or an airplane pilot is very much on his own, must find within himself the powers that he needs to face the grim issue of battle." [R. Ernest Dupuy and George Fielding Eliot, *If War Comes* (1937).] And Eliot makes the point in greater detail: "[In the war of the future] . . . isolated action by small groups will be the rule rather than the exception. Improvement in the fire power of the defence, coupled with the tremendous improvements in aviation, force attacking infantry to spread out more, to take great advantage of cover, to use every accident of cover, to use every accident of terrain; operations at night, or under cover of artificial fog, will be frequent. All these conditions impose the greatest responsibility on the leaders of small groups, the non-commissioned officer, and even on the individual private soldiers." (George Fielding Eliot, "Men-at-arms," *New Republic*, p. 184, Mar. 23, 1938.)

"The war of the future may be a war of movement brought about by mechanization and the development of the air arm. For such a war of movement, of surprise, of swiftly changing situation, the machine army is ill adapted. The machine trained soldier, officer or man, will come upon too many surprises, too many situations to which the answer is not to be found in the books. If he has not the individual resources within himself to deal with those situations, if he has not lived and thought and acted independently, and in an atmosphere of freedom and individual competition whether in sport or in labor, he will not be equal to the terrible demands that modern war will make upon him." (*Ibid; cf.* "The Assassination of Initiative" in *Infantry Journal*, October, 1938.)

Liddell Hart also joins in this opinion. "We must recognize that so long as men fought in close formations, from the Spartan phalanx of spears down to the serried

ASSUMPTIONS AND PROGRAM

In any case it cannot be doubted that the French democracy has been able to set up a powerful democratic army, that the United States and the British possess navies of parts, and that from time to time they have even been able to unite their war forces with their political controls, or, even more difficult, to unite the Franco-English military-political controls in formidable fashion.

The problem of civil-military relationships is not solely one of the democracies, but a continuing problem of all

---

lines of Frederick's grenadiers—wherein each man must move in dovetailed uniformity with his neighbors to ensure cohesion, there was a military value in a discipline and drill that turned men into machines. . . . Today the revolutionary changes in warfare point the urgent need of a fresh change in discipline. The increasingly mechanical nature of weapons demands the intellectual development of the men who handle them—at any rate of those who act individually or in little groups. When battle was waged essentially between physical bodies there was a value in turning men into machines. Now that battle is being waged more and more between machines the object of military training should be to produce men who will be masters of the machine—by developing their mental powers. (*Europe in Arms*, pp. 166*ff*.)

Democracy, these writers maintain, tends to preserve these qualities of initiative and independence now apparently essential both for effective modern military leadership and rank-and-file military action. It was observed in the World War that the French soldiery tended to be more resourceful in the absence of leaders than the German, they allege.

Of the consequences of the regimentation and militarization of every-day life in dictatorships Eliot concludes: "If during his formative years a youth has been subject to rigorous regulation of his every activity—in his school, his work, his sport, his daily life; if he has lived in an atmosphere where any sign of independence of thought or conduct brings immediate punishment, whether as anti-social, or counter-revolutionary, or 'deviation from the party line'; if he has in consequence lived with fear from his first dawning thoughts, and learned to depend upon a higher power for regulation of his activities rather than daring to think for himself, he will not suddenly, with the donning of a soldier's uniform, throw off the carefully inculcated habits of twenty years and become the sort of soldier that modern war demands." ("Men-at-Arms," *op. cit.*)

See also the interesting discussion of military efficiency in democracy and dictatorship in the most recent work of Liddell Hart, *Through The Fog of War* (1938).

Not only the military theorists of democracy have recognized the dangers for military and civilian morale of autocracy and its suppression of freedom of thought, but a keen contemporary German military psychologist, Karl Pintschovius, has emphasized these dangers in a general treatise on morale in modern war (*Die seelische Widerstandskraft im modernen Kriege*, 1936).

political associations—a problem of the reconciliation of policy and strategy, of statesman and soldier. Von Clausewitz, one of the founders of military art, was not unmindful of this problem when he wrote:

> Experience in general also teaches us that notwithstanding the multifarious branches and scientific character of military art in the present day, still the leading outlines of a War are always determined by the Cabinet, that is, if we would use technical language, by a political not a military organ.
> This is perfectly natural. None of the principal plans which are required for a War can be made without an insight into the political relations; and, in reality, when people speak, as they often do, of the prejudicial influence of policy on the conduct of a War, they say in reality something very different to what they intend. It is not this influence but the policy itself which should be found fault with. If the policy is right, that is, if it succeeds in hitting the object, then it can only act with advantage on the War. If this influence of policy causes a divergence from the object, the cause is only to be looked for in a mistaken policy.[1]

Or, I might add, in a mistaken military position.

Nor can it be successfully maintained that in the field of diplomatic action democracy is handicapped by its special form of political association. Great individual diplomats may arise under any system of government, the Metternichs, the Talleyrands, the Cannings, the Disraelis, the Franklins, the Benes, and by their extraordinary facility in the negotiation of national relations may substantially advance the interests of their states. This special form of genius is not, however, the product of any special form of political organization. The great diplomat may indeed prove an embarrassment to his political lord, as in the cases of Richelieu and of Bismarck. Under an autocratic system, the great diplomat must not be too triumphant, otherwise he may overshadow his master and imperil his own position.

There are those who seem to think that the conduct of international affairs consists chiefly in the making of swift

---

[1] Carl von Clausewitz, *On War* (trans. 1911), Vol. III, Book VIII, p. 126.

ASSUMPTIONS AND PROGRAM

and strong decisions, without any consultation or conference with others, and that therefore democracies are seriously handicapped in dealing with dictators or despots of sundry types.

Diplomacy is not a short dash. Most of the time it is a long race, or more accurately perhaps it is a long journey over an unending way. Diplomacy requires qualities of understanding, appreciation, patience, talents in contact, conference, concession, adjustment, understanding of the balance between several complicated sets of internal forces and external forces. Strength in international relations is not merely speed, but wisdom.

A diplomat is not an autocrat. What he can dictate, he will not discuss. It is only when there is something to consider carefully that he becomes evident and important.

Diplomacy is in part a game of poker, where bluffing is important, but it is also in many respects a game of chess. The autocrat in dealing with other nations is never entirely solo—he must deal with his army, with his bankers, with his propagandists, with a range of special interests affected by what he may do. Without them, his swift decisionism may ruin his country—and himself. Theoretically, of course, he might act with complete arbitrariness—once—but in brutal reality he must restrict himself to a relatively narrow set of alternatives.

Under a democratic parliamentary system, it is entirely possible to conduct diplomatic affairs with such strength and speed as are indicated by the situation. There is no reason to suppose that the decisions of Hitler and Mussolini are any swifter in kind than those of Disraeli, Lloyd George, or Roosevelt. The diplomacy of the great democracies such as France, England, Sweden has been by and large more effective than that of any of their undemocratic contemporaries.

THE NEW DEMOCRACY

The assumption that democracies are incapable of international action, or effective action in dealing with autocracies, is a survival of the ancient scorn of the Few for the Many. Or it is derived from the conclusion that discussion is not consistent with decision, and that democracies based on discussion and consent are impotent. This illusion has filled many cemeteries and may fill more of them in the future.

The gospel that governments derive their just powers from force is not a doctrine of continuity—for when reason and persuasion and consent are thrown out, there is no moral reason why force should not be used by anyone.

We cannot of course deny that a highwayman may take a purse, or that an international aggressor may snatch something in the face of unheeded protests. But beyond Al Capone there was Alcatraz, and beyond Napoleon, St. Helena. There are G Men locally; and there are limits beyond which it is not even clever to defy international law and the comity of nations.

The bland assumption that democratic states *will* not fight because they do not *wish* to fight is fallacious in the extreme. It is the open road to war. The organization of consent is superior to the organization of violence, but it is also capable of effectively organizing force. And it will make its strength felt however rude the terms of conflict may be. We cannot of course predict the outcome, but we reject the adolescent view that there will be "no trouble."

Will it be seriously maintained that the organization of the jural order of the world is to be reached by clashing and competing measures alone? If so, we must wait the establishment of another Roman Empire or world empire indeed, with one system of order, justice, and law.

If all the fifty-odd nations of the world simultaneously repudiate the principles of international law, and proclaim

ASSUMPTIONS AND PROGRAM

the sacredness of violence, who would be the gainer in such a world? The logic of fifty systems of violence would itself lead around once more to the beginnings of conference, persuasion, international agreement, and consent. Even violence cannot always be violent; it must alternate violence with reason and fraud with good faith. Violence is most useful not in a world of violence universally acknowledged as a rule of life, but rather in a world where some operate on the principle of violence and others on that of persuasion and reason.

Violence in this sense is not a rule of uniform action, but a rule of differential exception. It needs partial acceptance to make it effective, or at least the cloak of hypocrisy to veil its otherwise undisguised intentions.

e. PLAN MAKING[1]

But it is also freely asserted that a democratic form of association is incapable of dealing with the direction of the social and economic forces now disturbing the internal life of modern states—with industrial stabilization, unemployment, insecurity, with stimulation of productivity and national income. Democracy, it is maintained, is unadapted to dealing vigorously and effectively with these problems. It must yield to the superior facility with which the sword settles such intricacies, or the "I will" of the autocrat, or the guidance of some group going under the name of the elite.

This assumes what it starts out to prove—the inflexibility of democratic institutions and their incapacity for dealing with larger problems of state. If we assume this, of course it is thus assumed, and the argument may procede without interruption. But the assumption may be examined in the light of democratic theory and experience.

[1] See Henry Bunbury, *Governmental Planning Machinery* (1938).

THE NEW DEMOCRACY

At this point it is important to direct attention to some of the developing techniques of modern democracy through which the commonwealth is able to deal with its emerging economic and social problems.

Democracy in the future may take more initiative in planning, in looking at proposed policies as a whole, and in intelligent efforts to indicate a course for the future. In the end, the determination of national plans will and should be made by those authorized to make political decisions, but alternative suggestions may well come out of administration.

With respect to particular sections of policy much planning has been done already. The next step is to examine policies as a whole, in their interrelation, and chart a course of action accordingly.[1]

A planning agency may well be made a central point in the coming development of public administration, serving as advisor to those who make the ultimate decisions regarding the policy of the state.

The validation of the democratic mechanism calls for an agency to deal with (1) the collection and analysis of basic data regarding our national resources, natural and human; and (2) the development of forward-looking national policy based upon these data and their implications.[2]

The mechanism of plan-making and planning is experimental and clearly there may be many different forms adapted to different situations. Two main types have emerged recently—the economic council, developed in France and England (earlier in Germany), designed to include representatives of various economic interests; and the planning agency, not primarily representative in composition. The first type, the economic council, is set up as a form

---

[1] *Ibid.*

[2] See my *Role of Politics in Social Change*, Chap. V, on "Strategic Controls and Planning."

ASSUMPTIONS AND PROGRAM

of representation of different interests assembling for purposes of interchange of views and of formulation of policies. The French Council contains sixty-six members distributed among the general public and consumers, production (including management, labor, and professional workers), capital (ownership in land, industry, trade, finance, and banking). The English Council consists of some twenty-four members, four ministers ex-officio and some twenty non-official members selected by the Prime Minister.[1]

The other type is not intended to be primarily representative in character, but inclusive of various official and non-official elements in the state.

In the United States the National Resources Committee, an outgrowth of President Hoover's Committee on Recent Social Trends, has been used as an advisory planning agency, dealing with the highest and best use of national resources, both natural and human.[2] The committee has acted as an advisory agency to the President. It was composed of five Cabinet Members, the Emergency Relief Administrator, and four others—all chosen by the President. Comprehensive reports have been made dealing with land resources, water resources, mineral and energy resources; with urban communities; with population; with scientific research in government; with the long-time planning of public works; with the analysis of consumers' expenditures and consumers' income; with tentative patterns of resources use; with regional, state, and local planning problems and results. This committee served as a clearing house of planning activities in the United States, local, state, national, and unofficial as well; and dealt with the strategic and long-time problems of planning of national resources. It was given no executive

---

[1] See H. J. Laski, *Parliamentary Government in England* (1938), 221*ff*.

[2] See annual reports of National Resources Committee, and series of publications covering activities of committee since its establishment in 1933.

or legislative powers whatever, serving solely as an advisory group for the assembly and analysis of data and for the consideration of the interrelation of fundamental and long-time national policies.

It cannot be overlooked that there are numerous *ad hoc* planning committees and commissions, and other agencies engaged in the task of developing long-range plans for national development in England, Sweden, and elsewhere. In this general field there are also private planning associations, such as PEP (Political and Economic Planning) in England. Of these PEP is a notable example of plan making under private auspices.[1]

In such types of states, such as Russia, Germany, and Italy, central agencies for national control of quite a different type have been organized, either with the expressed design of socialization of industry or of subordinating all interests to the demand for military efficiency. In none of these cases is the organization of plan making and planning intended to function as in a democratic political association.

The details of planning organization are naturally the subject of wide difference of opinion. In general, it may be said, however, that the economic council has proved a failure or a disappointment and will probably continue so in view of the fact that it sets up what is in effect a rival parliament or legislature. The economic council roots in the earlier idea of a bicameral legislature made up of an industrial house and a political house cooperating in some joint pattern of action. In older Germany the economic council broke down, in England it rarely functions, and only in France does it appear to retain any vitality.

My own preference is for a national planning board appointed by the executive and responsible to him, serving

---

[1] See *Planning*, publication of PEP (Political and Economic Planning); and *Plan Age* of NESPA (National Economic and Social Planning Association).

ASSUMPTIONS AND PROGRAM

on an indeterminate tenure. Such an organization might act as a long-time planning agency for the coordination of various plans among departments or bureaus, and for the elaboration of further lines of long-time national policy in the larger sense of the term.[1]

It is apparent that such an organization should not be an "economic planning" board, since this defeats the whole purpose of broader integration of national policies.[2] Business planning alone, or agricultural planning alone, or welfare planning alone, or educational or scientific planning alone, is not adequate to meet the genuine needs of the situation in any long-time view. The value of planning in these special fields is evident, but somewhere these various separate plans must be brought together and considered in their interrelations, balanced against each other, and so organized that the different plans shall not work at cross purposes.

The weakness of business planning alone is soon revealed in a period of active operation. The difficulties may be summarized as follows:

(1) Business can secure effective cooperation only within the limits of an independent business enterprise. Different undertakings have no common authority to maintain a common program of action, and hence efforts in that direction may prove negative and wasteful rather than positively productive of advantage either socially or profit personally.[3]

---

[1] See National Planning Board, *Report*, 1934, and analysis of various forms of boards there described.

[2] See Bunbury, *op. cit.*

[3] See National Planning Board, *Reports*, 1933–1934, p. 21. For discussion of larger aspects of planning in the specifically economic field see F. A. von Hayek (and others), *Collectivist Economic Planning* (1935); Ludwig von Mises, *Socialism: An Economic and Sociological Analysis* (trans. J. Kahane, 1936); H. D. Dickinson, "The Economic Basis of Socialism," *Political Quarterly*, Vol. I (1930), pp. 561*ff.*; "Price Formation in a Socialist Community," *Economic Journal*, June 1933; "Freedom and Planning," *Manchester School*, IV (1933); T. E. Gregory, "An Economist Looks at Planning," *Manchester School*, IV (1933); Benjamin E. Lippin-

(2) Business planning aims at personal gain, which may or may not be nationally advantageous in a given instance, and may readily lead to wide discrepancies in the distribution of income, with repercussions again on consumption.

(3) Business cannot protect itself against the recurring hazards of the business cycle, and hence is forced to appeal to government itself from time to time for protection against evils it cannot control. The centralizing movement in industry is an effort to eliminate some of the hazards from which business cannot save itself. "Business planning has found no way to prevent the growth of factors that tend to make the business cycle more hazardous. Indeed, the hazard grows greater in large part because of business planning itself."[1]

Furthermore, the planning of great corporations and the systems in vogue among agricultural producers do not synchronize or harmonize, and in consequence there may be disastrous gaps between the economic situation of one and the other.

Consequently, it follows that when the government attempts planning in these fields it is attacking problems of enormous difficulty which no one has yet solved. It is not making inexpert attempts to do what business itself accomplishes satisfactorily. "So far as government succeeded in finding solutions it would be broadening and making safer the field of private enterprise."[2]

There has been an abundance of planning in the last generation—planning by industries each for itself, planning in agriculture, planning by scores of local and special agencies concerned with forward looking policies; but it is precisely

---

cott, editor, *On the Economic Theory of Socialism* (1938); Findlay Mackenzie, editor, *Planned Society* (1937). Barbara Wooton, *Plan or No Plan* (1935).

[1] National Resources Board, *Report*, Dec. 1, 1934, p. 82.
[2] *Ibid.*

ASSUMPTIONS AND PROGRAM

the problem of our time and indeed of any time to bring these unorganized systems together and at least relate them to each other in the national interest.

It may be alleged that the affairs of a nation are too intricate to make any useful planning possible. But the assumption that these complex affairs will operate automatically is belied by the facts of modern life. It is precisely because these automatisms do not work and cannot work that the countersuggestion comes forward insistently throughout the world.

Out of the very complexity of our technological organization, its swift rates of change, the delicacy of its interconnections, comes with resistless force the pressure for a central coordinating system which shall at least hold the parts in order and prevent their clash and collapse.

If by some happy lapse of memory the world should wake some morning to forget the slogans and ideologies of communism and of capitalism, the class struggle and political parties, we should confront the realities of technological change and the importance of rapid adaptation, the rise of a gigantic unsystem of terrific forces moving around us with incredible speed and force, and a need for the rationalization of this immense procession of evolving forces without central control. The inner logic of the situation would drive us to organize for the prevention of chaos, and to plan for the better ordering of social forces.

Various misapprehensions regarding the nature and tendencies of planning have misled many persons. Among these are the following:

(1) That all planning is centralized national planning developed at some fixed point of authority. In some tension situations this might be the case, but in democratic societies strategic planning is typically an enterprise in which many different levels of activity are involved. In the United States

and elsewhere there are town-planning agencies, county-planning agencies, state- and regional-planning agencies. There may be national planning and various types of local planning. There may be planning suggestion from public, private, and semipublic agencies of all sorts. Unquestionably there must be a central directive and a unified general system of guidance, but there are areas within this larger framework, there are circles of influence and activity within the greater circle, and all of these agencies may react upon each other without preventing the general concert of action which is to be attained.

(2) That planning involves a fixed and unchangeable system to be clamped down like a steel frame on soft flesh. Planning is a continuous process involving continuous readjustment and revision to meet changing situations as they arise. "The national life is like a moving wave in which a new equilibrium must constantly be found as it sweeps forward." This is true even of physical planning and even more applicable in the case of social planning.

(3) That all planning involves regimentation, using this term to mean arbitrary and autocratic action—the equivalent of oppression. First of all, liberty exists only in some ordered framework of operations and understandings. Without these understandings as to the protection of liberty and without their implementation there could be no domain of non-interference. In many operations of government this is fairly well understood, but not yet fully recognized in the areas called the "economic," where the idea of "natural liberty" still survives, long after it has been replaced by a more constructive idea in the political world. The truth is that the inner areas of spontaneity and creative impulse need to be protected by the general regulative system in order that they may attain their most complete development. In a very real sense we may and do plan for liberty

ASSUMPTIONS AND PROGRAM

of action as well as for restraint of action. Paradoxical as it may seem to some, the governmental system may cultivate individual initiative, growth, and development, instead of repressing and crushing it down and out.

It may readily be conceded that this has not always been the guiding star of all governments in all times and places, but there are brilliant illustrations of the possibilities in this direction; and in a period of more intelligent social direction, the range of possibility is greater than ever.

Wise planning deals with the "zoning of power," with the diffusion of initiative and responsibility most conducive to the welfare of the group at a given stage of its development. It is quite possible for the state to be legally, in the narrower sense of the term, omnipotent and irresistible, although in actual practice very wide areas of behavior are left wide open for local and individual initiative. This, indeed, is as true of industrial organization as it is of political or ecclesiastical for that matter. There is as much initiative in the French nation today as there ever was in the French feudality of centuries ago. There was as much liberty in the United States after the Constitution was adopted as there was in Rhode Island before that event.

The strategy of planning involves, then, the kind of prevision that contemplates zones or areas of independent initiative, both territorially, individually, and associationally, if there were such a word. Congestion and overcentralization are among the very gravest diseases of the body politic, and judgment and foresight are indispensable if they are to be averted. But this is not a pot that can be left to boil without attention; it must be carefully watched by experienced persons. The strength and direction of social change is the clue to the type of organization feasible at a given phase of development in a society.

THE NEW DEMOCRACY

The test of planning is not whether it may for the moment set up a new series of regulations, inevitable in a period of readjustment, but whether the new pattern taken as a whole opens the way for a wider range of human activity and happiness. The temporary outline of a form of order may be the task of a policeman, but the larger and more enduring pattern will be worked out with the aid of the planner.

In this task science, education, skillful administration, organized persuasion are far more effective than the sword or the gun. The swashbucklers are seldom the statesmen. And the warriors who really fight, as distinguished from those who know how to make gestures and declaim, are seldom social planners, although there have been some notable exceptions to this broad statement. Their very elaborate planning is designed for war.

An unwarranted assumption in the discussion of regimentation is that in the absence of governmental regulation there is no equivalent regulation by someone else. This is falsified by human experience, which shows that arbitrary and oppressive control of individuals has arisen again and again—is indeed the commonplace of human relations. To ignore this is to pass by one of the foundation principles of government. To break down petty forms of oppression exercised by one man over another has been historically one of the very great tasks of the political association. The emancipators may have utilized this power for their own selfish purposes, but they were able to function because the balance was in their favor—they gave more than they took. The order and justice of the national state was better than that of the feudal organization. The great lords were better received than the petty lordlets of the locality, and thus the King's Highway, the King's Justice, came to be accepted as deliverance rather than oppression, in the first stages of the

ASSUMPTIONS AND PROGRAM

larger area or unit of authority. It was in this mould that modern politics was cast.

Again and again the state has intervened to protect the weak against the strong, to restrict the regimentation of tenants by their landlords, of servants by their masters, of employees by their employers. In the Fourteenth Amendment, America guaranteed civil liberty to citizens as against their respective states. To assume that no group except the government has the urge or tendency to oppress individuals is to ignore the most obvious facts of human experience—to refuse to look at the monumental evidence showing the cruelty of man to man on every level of action and association.

Although many of the oppressions of the old land system have been eliminated from modern practice, some remain; and although the private regimentation seen in human slavery has been abolished, there remain wide areas of private regimentation in the swiftly changing industrial order. Here the tempo has been so fast that the usual trade customs and practices have been left behind in many cases, and the new rulers have been almost unrestricted in the exercise of vast powers over the lives and fortunes of workers. Employment, wages, working conditions, insurance were in private hands without the earlier responsibility for the serf or slave. Price fixing, production control, credits, and a long series of far-reaching powers were placed in the hands of individuals or small groups without any practical restraint upon them, and with the inevitable appearance of widespread oppression—not by government, but by private groups or persons.[1]

In many ways of life, the choice is not between regimentation and no regimentation, but between public control and

[1] See forthcoming reports of the Temporary National Economic Committee on monopoly and restraints of trade.

private regimentation, between two systems of regulation, one in public and the other in private hands. The more rapid the course of change, the greater the likelihood that such controls will be set up in one way or another. The reconstruction of these regulative systems in terms of general welfare rather than the old-time political or the so-called "purely economic" is one of the greatest tasks of the modern planner of social organization. The values and ideologies underlying the old system are not readjusted to emerging values and systems rapidly enough to avoid misunderstanding and friction, and herein lies the largest possibility of unbalance in the social and political order. The maintenance of the moving equilibrium at this point is consequently one of the major tasks of strategic planning in our day.

This, moreover, is not merely a task of democratic statesmanship, but equally of Fascist, Nazi, Communist, Japanese statesmanship, and of any and all other states in which the sweep of technological and other changes is proceeding rapidly and demanding urgently the reorganization of institutions and the reorientation of our ideas and value systems at many important points.[1]

Some basic assumptions underlie modern planning in democracy.

(1) The recognition of the importance and value of an over-all framework of social control of the general type known as the "state."

(2) The reorganization of the regulative system in terms of modern science, technology, education, economics, and politics.

(3) The recognition and protection of value systems other than political within the framework of the political association.

---

[1] On value systems see *Recent Social Trends*, p. lxxv. See analysis of modern planning systems in Bunbury, *op. cit.*

ASSUMPTIONS AND PROGRAM

(4) The relation of various plans and their implications to each other.

This assumption applies to modern industrial states generally, regardless of the differences in organization and ideology and is indeed accepted in part by all of them, but not as a whole.[1] It possesses a special significance for the democratic political association.

(1) That there shall be a general framework of regulation of the general form of the modern state is generally recognized, but with this there goes many times the assumption that there is a "natural" economic order and a "natural" system of "economic" controls which the state must worship. Since the general abandonment of the classical laissez-faire system, this political theology is no longer as clearly stated, but it persists and blocks urgently needed social organization.

The outworn philosophy of Ricardo and Marx, restated by Spencer, is reestablished, and the dogma expressly asserted that there is a well-defined, exclusive, economic domain into which government should not enter. "Less government in business" may become the slogan, or less regulation of industry, or criticism of governmental action as socialistic or communistic, always with the assumption that there is a self-regulating system of economics which *if left alone* will automatically produce the optimum society.

The whole course of Western social legislation for the last one hundred years is against this assumption or conclusion, as we survey the successive waves of governmental regulation of the abuses of private control of mines, factories, housing, investment, insurance, down the long sweep of the modern shore; and the growth of monopoly in industry itself. Industry itself has over and again invoked the aid of government to save itself from unfair competition. In the face of

[1] On the Japanese system see R. P. Reischauer, *Japan, Politics and Government* (1938).

increasing concentration of financial control, in the face of swiftly changing technology with its devastating effects upon economic and political institutions, in the face of the widespread unrest in all classes of society, the persistence of this doctrine must be rated as dubious. But here we observe that the very insecurity of the doctrine has been the incentive to the most frantic efforts to maintain and protect it—even to the breaking of the established molds of order, justice, and liberty in Germany and Italy.

(2) Another basic assumption of planning is that the plans must be organized in terms of modern science, technology, and education. This presupposes a set of general attitudes based upon the acceptance of these elements as essential to the orderly conduct of life in modern societies. It presupposes peoples who are, so to speak, science minded, technology minded, and the education minded, facing the possibilities of modern science and technology and realizing the possibilities of modern educational processes. Many Western peoples are familiar with the trends of science in the broadest sense and with some of the mechanical developments resulting from it, with the manipulation of the new mechanical controls, or chemical and biological controls through agriculture and otherwise. But the relationship of these controls to social processes or to governmental processes is often either incomplete or indeed almost entirely missing. Many accept the results of science, but do not enter into its methods and its spirit—the use of the invention, but not its intellectual origins or social implications.

The machine manipulator looking forward eagerly to every new and latest development in his special field may live in a governmental world of a century ago; and not only this, but he finds a moral purpose and necessity in so doing. He is as proud of tradition in the one case as he is eager to abandon it in the other. He is as ashamed to be old-fashioned in the

ASSUMPTIONS AND PROGRAM

one case as he is anxious to be labeled old-fashioned in the other; and he does not see the incongruity in his attitudes. He may cling to an outworn local government, such as a township, as enthusiastically as he hastens on the other hand to find the latest model of an automobile.

He may be antagonistic to planning in public affairs as much as he favors it in private affairs; and more surprising still, he may oppose planning on the ground that science makes it impossible, that we cannot plan because of the rapidity of change which might outmode the plans in the future. Thus it appears that we must not plan because we cannot change our ancient traditions, and on the other hand because there is too much change.

With even greater folly it may be asserted that the educational system with all of its scientific equipment and its trained personnel must be devoted to the perpetuation of outmoded doctrines, and even that competing doctrines must not be a subject of discussion. Thus creative ability would be employed for the promotion of sterility, and science for training in non-science.

The assumption of the modern state builder, who wishes to advance otherwise than by means of violence and brutal regimentation, must be that the emerging regulative system will recognize the pattern of scientific and technological change in an educational setting as the basis of continuing reorganization. Without this, Western civilization is doomed.

(3) Another fundamental assumption is that of the necessity of recognition and protection of value systems other than political within the political association. The politicians are by temperament, training, experience concerned with political values, and further their prestige is dependent upon the inflation of the political in the social system. The governors are accordingly inclined to look upon government as the most important thing in the community, and to under-

rate the meaning of other associations of social interest and concern, or even to look upon them as competitors to be closely watched and shrewdly checked.

The doctrine of the sovereign state is intoxicating to the lightheaded, who conclude that because they may lawfully do anything, practically they may do all things. The modern totalitarian state is the inebriated state of sovereignty in which unsteady rulers roughly attempt to assimilate every other form of association to that of the state—labor unions, cultural associations, industry, and even the church. If such a result were actually attained, what would happen within the shell of the new totalitarianism would be the rise of old value systems under other names, but performing old functions. Men might salute the state or wear its uniform, but the soul would be another soul and the spirit another spirit. The state itself would find it convenient to encourage independent centers of spontaneity even on its own.[1] The reconciliation of other value systems and their co-ordination in a growing concern may be and usually is one of the most perplexing problems of statesmen, but it may also be said that for this hour came they into the kingdom.

The old tendency was for the state to ride roughshod over other elements, misjudging its own relative significance and the priority of its own projects. For this reason, it is important that it be set up as a basic assumption of the state planners, that they shall constantly bear in mind the importance of recognition and protection of other values than their own, to the end that the constant reminder may serve as a guide in the conduct of state affairs, as a warning against overexaggeration of state claims and failure to face the realities of associated life in a political group.

[1] Local self-government was deliberately stimulated under the old Prussian regime.

ASSUMPTIONS AND PROGRAM

It must be recognized that there are human situations in which the reconciliation of these competing values is impossible on anything but a low level of concurrence in which violence will probably play a large and bloody role. History is unfortunately full of pictures where such methods were employed, whether wisely or unwisely in the special case, as England and Ireland, Germany and the Poles, Austria-Hungary and its dozen nationalities. But history is also full of brilliant illustrations of statesmanship such as that of modern Switzerland which reconciled in incredible fashion diverse and conflicting interests and brought them to a relatively high level of concurrence, partly by arms perhaps but in considerable measure by the arts of persuasion and management. The British Empire and the United States are modern examples of the strategy of interest reconciliation—not to be sure without a darker side in each of these cases, but yet with a conspicuous preponderance of deliberate design to conciliate. These are cases where the negativism of fear was more than offset by the positivism of symbolic attraction to the shelter of a protecting association, hospitable to free development of variety. Pantheons in religion, parliaments in politics, equality before the law, and even-handed justice—these are symbols of conciliation which have played important parts in the cohesion of great states. It is policies of this type that may safely be assumed as basic in a large scheme of national planning.

Value systems it may be said can be crushed out by fire, by sword, by persistent cruelty and unrelenting persecution, as religions and races have been crushed down and out. But the price paid is high, and even then the result may not follow. Was the wrath of Spain against the Jew socially valuable, or of Germany against the non-Aryans of our own time? Or of the French against the Huguenots, or of the

Austrians against the Hussites in Bohemia? A surgical operation with a battle ax may be inferior to medication, diet, relaxation, and the modern series of roads back to normalcy.

In the wider circle of international relations it is likewise essential that plans be considered in relation to each other. This is true even in the absence of an established jural order in which the elements of justice are consistently administered. Indeed the failure of such an order makes it all the more necessary that each member of the family of nations be familiar with the high strategy of the planners of other states, and consider their bearings on their own plans. And again this is equally true whether intentions are friendly or hostile. On a friendly basis there are modifications and interrelations that may be suggested; and on a hostile basis the plans of other states are essential for an understanding of the nature of the enemy power.

Under modern conditions other groups than the state often make their plans across national lines, as science, religion, labor, and high finance, and will unquestionably continue to do so whatever national walls may be built for political purposes. At this point the political association lags behind other important forms of associated life; and the lag if prolonged will precipitate serious consequences for social adjustment—has already done so on a colossal scale. In any case, and whatever the theory or program of international relations, the national planner cannot neglect the affairs and the plans of other states. At every step, as in the use of minerals, water power, food supplies, market security— even on the simplest level—the international aspect of national planning becomes evident. Intercommunication will make this increasingly apparent and isolation correspondingly difficult. The radio and the airplane are products of science with wide-ranging influence on the form and method

ASSUMPTIONS AND PROGRAM

of political association; and they are only the token payments of what technology will bring.

(4) A final assumption of planning is that various types of plans and their implications must be considered in relation to each other. Central and local plans of government, plans of quasi-public agencies, plans of private industry, plans of voluntary associations of a great variety—all of these must be related to each other. Government will not make all of these plans, but it must know what is happening, what the tendencies and implications of various designs may be, in order that the central planners may govern themselves accordingly, in order that plans may not work against each other. It must know the general patterns of plans in order to frame an intelligent plan of its own—to find the basis for an over-all type of planning. Each motorist, in order to steer his own course, must know what the courses of others are likely to be as to speed, direction, modifiability, and so on. So the state must know what it may reckon upon in speed, direction, and concurrence or collision in relation to other associational groupings within its jurisdiction. Thus a public works program, or a public educational program, or a credit program is related to other like programs and must be considered in this light.

Fundamental social and economic policies are more closely than ever interrelated in our times especially, and unless exceptional and unremitting care is taken they will clash and conflict to the detriment of society and the state. Economic stabilization, or social pathology, for illustration, involves the consideration of many factors in a highly complex problem. Fiscal policy, monetary policy, wage and price policy, agricultural policy, foreign policy are all important, but only in the skillful interrelation of these elements can any security be found and maintained. The problems of social pathology run down to the roots of Western civilization in their widespread ramifications through law, medicine, administration, economic and cultural environment.

Montesquieu's admonition to consider carefully the "spirit of the laws" is even more important now than it was two hundred years ago when he made his brilliant observations. We now know more about the many intricate elements in our social organization and process, and the tempo of change is more rapid as the stream of invention and discoveries is translated into the wizard technology of our time.

The planning mechanism provides not merely the clearing house of information, experience, and ideas, but a framework for thought on long-time and fundamental problems of the locality or the nation, whether large or small in its extent and numbers.

If the foregoing propositions are accepted as true, it is of great importance to search diligently for the strategic devices of guidance and direction in any given society in order that the system may operate with the least friction and wastage of effort. The formalism of the law, however, the mechanistic nature of much governmental theory and practice, and the neutral attitude of many classical or neo-classical economists make this by no means an easy task in our time. The will to search, the spirit of imagination, inventiveness, and social insight are essential, to say nothing of the popular attitudes upon which any such program may rest in last analysis.

There have been, however, and still are constructive jurists, inventive statesmen, and contriving economists who are available for this high enterprise—students and practitioners of social technologies whose faculties are equal to the occasion. Some of these workers may be engineers, some may be teachers, research men, and scientists of all types— some may be doctors, some may be psychologists, psychiatrists, psychoanalysts, or whatever color they fly in this division. Others may be statesmen, administrators,

ASSUMPTIONS AND PROGRAM

priests, industrialists, leaders of labor, workers with men. Some will be leaders acclaimed by thousands, others obscure workers. The overwhelming danger is, as few statesmen have recognized, that we will not be able to keep pace with the tempo of modern invention, and the barbarians will take the tools of science for their own purpose. The slow-moving battalions of science will arrive one day, and the reorientation of understandings and value systems based on earlier systems of intelligence now outgrown will also come; but it may be too late.

There are quiet periods in the stream of human history, times of little change, when drifting is the order of the day; but this tumultuous era of change is not one of such times. Our boat, undirected, will not drift idly down a pleasant stream but meet a sterner fate on the rocks.

f. CRITICISMS OF PLANNING

But is not all this equivalent to "economic planning"? No, this term is too broad at one point, and too narrow at another. By this time it is perhaps clear, however, that the "economic" has been much overemphasized in the discussions of human association, and that we shall find it necessary to do our planning in different terms from the transactions of the market place, important as these are.

Planning involves ranges and levels of values that are not within the purview of what is ordinarily regarded as "economic." The modern problem is a social problem rather than an economic one—national in the broadest sense of the term rather than industrial in the narrower. The fluid nature of money as a claim for services, commodities, and recognition often obscures the immense mass of values that lie outside the pecuniary circle, and overlooks even the uncertainty of "money" itself. Money is not the source of science, invention, technology, management, labor; its values

THE NEW DEMOCRACY

depend on them in the modern order of things. Modern wealth and property are the creation of the technology of a machine age, which made and could unmake our civilization.

Our planning may well begin with the sources of our present power, rather than the accidents of its application—with an analysis of the creative forces of modern technical civilization. National "production" is not merely, as many seem to suppose, the building of factories in which goods are made, but the production of a civilization out of which comes the skill to invent the machinery of the factory, and the skills to operate it after it is set up. A planned technology or a planned education might be more important than a planned "economy."[1]

In the largest sense of the term, planners must consider all the resources of the nation, and strive for their highest and best use by the whole community, but not necessarily by the state. All details are subordinate to this major directive. The assumptions of democracy as the framework of association and of science as the genius of production are the guide to planning.

At this point, however, we meet the assertion that "planning" is per se impossible. Occasionally, all "planning" is lumped together as "collectivism," or "creeping collectivism," but usually this is not attempted.[2] Of course, if all kinds of "planning" as such are inherently impossible under the operation of natural laws, then no form of association can enter this forbidden field. All efforts would prove futilitarian in the end. But usually this position is abandoned, in view of the vast amount of modern plan making in cities, counties, industries. Curiously enough, agricultural planning is not reckoned as "economic" in this calculation—or public

---

[1] See National Resources Committee report, *Research a National Resource* (1939).
[2] See Walter Lippman, *The Good Society* (1937).

ASSUMPTIONS AND PROGRAM

works, or highways, and perhaps even railways and airways. Retreat is made to a special definition of "planning" as "economic planning" or "totalitarian planning."

I shall not undertake to follow here the ramifications of the struggle over the question whether there could even be a pricing system under a "planned economy" as urged by von Mises and von Hayek on one hand and denied by Lange and Taylor on the other.[1]

Another position is that the democratic form of political organization is inherently incapable of dealing with planning of any comprehensive character at any rate. Or in milder form that it is relatively ill-adapted to the purposes of planning, in comparison with totalitarian states of modern or ancient type. Still milder would be an assertion that whether or not the democratic society is incapable of comprehensive planning, it has not been able to act effectively in this field because of the internal conflict between the social and economic forces of modern industrial society.

It is easy to observe that the modern world has not achieved a solution of all the problems of industrial stabilization or all the problems of a jural world order. But the conclusion that democratic society is inherently incapable of dealing with either of these puzzles, let us say that of stabilization, does not follow automatically, whether we follow the way of rational analysis or that of observation and experience or both in combination.

If we appeal to observation and experience, where shall we find the proof that democratic societies are incapable of

[1] A. C. Pigou, *Socialism versus Capitalism* (1937); von Hayek, *op. cit.*; Lippincott, *op. cit.*; Gerhard Colm, "Is Economic Planning Compatible with Democracy?" in *Political and Economic Democracy* (edited by Max Ascoli and Fritz Lehmann); Walton Hamilton, editor, *Price and Price Policy* (1938), pp. 549*ff.*; Arthur R. Burns, *The Decline of Competition* (1936), Chaps. XI, XII; Lindsay Rogers, *Crisis Government* (1934), pp. 153*ff.* Eduard Heimann, "Literature on the Theory of a Socialist Economy," in *Social Research*, VI, 88, gives a summary of competing points of view.

programs of social and economic stabilization? Both modern democracy and modern industrial technology are very young, and their interadjustment is by no means a simple problem yielding to a fiat and a sword. It may of course be said that because a solution has not been found, none can be found; but the reasonableness of this contention depends upon the nature of the issue, whether it is a long-time or a short-time problem, and what the probabilities are of ready reconstruction of disordered elements of social, economic, and technological confusion. An immense array of social legislation has been proliferated in recent years, directed toward the amelioration of social maladjustments and deficiencies. Authority in government and authority in the market place have been reconciled at many points, though many problems yet remain.

It is freely asserted that democracies cannot plan, unless they are willing to abandon democratic procedures and adopt the methods of the new despotisms. Only undemocratic states, it is charged, can successfully operate planning on any considerable scale. The situations involved are so complex and the decisions to be made are so urgent and important that no democratic society is able to deal successfully with them. And there could be no adequate continuity in a democratic policy.

This conclusion springs from a failure to analyze carefully the nature of political organization. One who looks at the complications of modern social life and the variety and rapidity of change may of course become bewildered, and gazing in awe at the scene may announce the impossibility of dealing with these situations successfully. He may abdicate in behalf of *laissez faire* or fly to the other extreme of totalitarianism. These are the counsels of impatience and confusion.

ASSUMPTIONS AND PROGRAM

In reality there is nothing in the nature of democratic government to prevent decisions upon broad general policies and the administrative management of these policies in action. There is nothing to prevent such reasonable continuity of broad policy as may be desirable from time to time. Determinations of policies affecting industry, agriculture, labor, welfare, and their application are within the competence of modern governments, and are constantly in operation. Policies as to tariff, banking, land, industrial regulation, foreign affairs are constantly being discussed and determined in democratic communities. To assume that the people are incapable of laying down broad general policies and providing for their management and their supervision by the policy-determining body in turn, is to assume the general incompetence of the community for any democratic action. This is only the old anti-democratic argument based upon the alleged ignorance of the mob and the general incompetence of the many. Experience has amply shown the unreliability of this contention and demonstrated the feasibility of popular control of complicated affairs in a well-built system of democratic organization.

The incapacity of democracies is "a lie that has become a legend," especially with those who half hope it is true, because of specially privileged situations which might be jeopardized by democratic action.

The democratic assumption is that discussion and persuasion instead of violence may be applied to policies as they emerge with more presumption of success than the assumptions of non-consent and force. That the sword, the prison, the terror are the methods of dealing with the problems of the modern technology does not follow from any reasonable analysis of the nature of the complicated problems involved.

We may assert that there is more power—political power—in persuasion than there is in violence—more power in reason than in force which forbids reasoning. Reason too is power. We may assert that morale based upon mutual consent is stronger than the discipline of fear.

If we are to reason about power, we decline *ab initio* to abdicate our reason and bow to force. We may be forced to surrender our weapons, but not our intelligence. The difficulties of our day were brought about by the application of reason to materials, and we look to its further application to relations among men.

It is also charged that democracy is so susceptible to industrial "pressures" as to render planning impossible. The truth is that industrial or other unbalance may happen in any system of government, whether of One, the Few, or the Many. The actual seat of power at a given time may be the religious group, or the military group, or the landowners, or the traders, the producers, or the bankers. From time to time and perhaps for long periods of time, some one of these influences may effectually control the acts of the nominal holders of authority. Indeed a great section of human history is that containing the record of the struggles of the nominal rulers to maintain themselves against the pressure of the unofficial claimants of power.

The dangers arising from unbalance, whether of wealth, military strength, or other social factors, have been discussed by political writers for centuries—by Aristotle, Harrington, Montesquieu, in particular. Unbalance is the perennial problem of politics. Equilibrium is one of the main reasons for the state's existence.

In more recent times Communist and Fascist protagonists have taken up the theme of economic unbalance in democracy. Both Fascists and Communists are united in an "unpopular front" to prove that since modern capitalism and modern democracy developed in modern times concurrently, they must go down together. What they really

ASSUMPTIONS AND PROGRAM

wish to show is that modern democratic society is not strong enough to deal with the abuses of capitalism and to succeed in establishing a solid form of economic stabilization.[1]

There is no ground in general political theory or in experience to conclude that economic unbalance is a special problem of democracies as such, rather than of other forms of political association. The border lines between economics and government are a perennial problem of all governments. The family of power will never be entirely harmonious. "When the waters are too quiet," says Montesquieu, "there is danger of stagnation." Governors who cannot deal with the problem of social balance are incapable of performing their function.

The industrial class was ruled wholly out of the circle of the elect in the classical systems of Plato and Aristotle, but the ban was not obeyed then or now. Large landed proprietors have often lined out the course of government whether the owners were political lords, or landlords, or both. Merchants, moneylenders, shippers, traders have mingled in the affairs of state from time immemorial, sometimes commanding and sometimes being commanded. Usually the commercial class is not willing to assume the responsibility of direct exercise of political authority, leaving this to the governors, the politicos, the brass hats, the clerks, the lawyers, to the priests and the savants, or even the demagogues. Thus the problem of their relation to government has often been one of great difficulty, and still is.

It cannot be said, however, viewing the course of history, that economic authority is more of a menace to democratic association than other forms of extra-legal authority, military, agrarian, or otherwise. If the system of money values with the trail of pecuniary prestige becomes the dominant

---

[1] Harold J. Laski, *Democracy in Crisis* (1933); William E. Rappard, *The Crisis of Democracy* (1938).

THE NEW DEMOCRACY

one in a given society at a given time, it is clear that the influence of financial rating will rise, no matter what the form or type of governance, Many, Few, or One. But the economic-value system is constantly in competition with other values in human life; with military values of glory and fame, with religious values of righteousness, with patriotic values of devotion to the commonweal, with familial values, with scientific, philosophical, and cultural values, with many changing forms of satisfactions which are not classed as economic in nature—at any rate, they have no open market price. These values constantly hold the economic in check, and thrust it back when it presses too far forward, just as others in their turn are held back when they seek to dominate all of their brethren in the family of power.

Strong emphasis on pecuniary values, strong concentration of economic-value holdings, will constitute a challenge to any form of government, not excepting the communistic, where managerial, military, bureaucratic groups may take the place of property groups and press the government hard. But there is no reason to conclude that such interests will prove any more influential with democratic governments than with any other type. When property was land, it influenced all governments; and when property is capital, the same result will follow; or if economic control is technology and management, the same consequences will ensue.

The strong equalitarian tendencies in the democratic type of association, the heavy emphasis on the dignity of man and on the importance of the fullest possible development of his personality, the doctrines of persuasion and peace as normal ways of life: these are factors which place the democracy on guard against the overencroachment of economic values and of economic overconcentration.

Democracy, it may be repeated, is not related to any particular form of production of commodities or services. There

ASSUMPTIONS AND PROGRAM

may be a rural-agrarian democracy or an urban-industrial democracy, or any other variation, depending on the circumstances of the period. What is called "collectivism" might exist under a monarchy, an aristocracy, a democracy, a dictatorship, a theocracy, or other types. In the same way democracy might exist in connection with either so-called "individualism" or so-called "collectivism." Capitalism in modern times has been developed under an ancient autocracy in Japan, under monarchy in Germany, under democracy in England. Socialistic and communistic colonies have existed for a thousand years under many types of political and religious organization.

The battle between collectivism and individualism is in many of its phases a sham battle, since all government is collectivist in one sense, and all governments recognize individualism in another sense.[1] We need not limit ourselves to the possibilities presented by two sets of slippery slogans evolved one hundred years ago and now becoming an obsession so obstinate as to threaten war and revolution and widespread instability.

We need not agree to the "either-or" in regard to so-called "individualism" and so-called "collectivism." I have already indicated elsewhere in the discussion of strategic controls in planning that the community policy utilizes the factors of control most important in the given stage of the state's development, and that this involves alternate advances and retreats, alternate tightening in tension moments and relaxation in periods of less excitement. The index of regulatory activity is not the number of points but their location and trend.

I do not agree with the division of the world into an exclusive domain of pure "economics" and an exclusive domain of pure "politics," and the separation of one from

[1] See my *Role of Politics in Social Change*, Chap. II.

the sovereign domain of the other. Much economics presupposes politics and is an integral part of it; and much politics is economics and an integral part of it. Is public finance economics or politics? Are currency, credit, and banking politics or economics? Are international relations economics or politics? The problems of our times are not primarily "economic" alone, but technical, economic, political, ethical in nature.

It is precisely the preoccupation with these untenable alternatives and the insistence on an "either-or" answer that is upsetting the peace of much of the world. For myself I repudiate these false alternatives, and look for another way through our difficulties.

To those who assert their confident belief in what they choose to call either "economic determinism" or *laissez faire* and its basic influence on all systems of thought and patterns of action, I repeat my previous assertion that this is only a convenient avoidance of what is difficult to explain. Current "economic" interpretation is an explanation that explains too little; for it fails to indicate clearly what is the "economic" or to differentiate it from the generality of social influences and forces. What is it that determines what?

There is a wide field of choice awaiting any open-minded and inventive people who prefer to deal with realities rather than with the phantom interpretations of outworn systems. Between complete "public ownership" and exclusively "private ownership," there is an immense variety of intermediate forms and stages. It is not easy at any time to identify absolute forms of either public or private control in a social organization, and this becomes still more difficult if we include the great tension moments such as war or other emergency in a nation.

ASSUMPTIONS AND PROGRAM

Government-owned corporations on the one side and public utilities on the other approach each other, one reaching toward non-governmental modes of organization and action and the other leaning toward governmental and away from non-governmental. Other forms of organization of a semi-public, semiprivate nature spring up to the bewilderment of the old-timers—combinations of employers, workers, experts, consumers. Trade associations, cooperatives, trade-unions arise and take on many regulative functions much like those commonly attributed to government only.

There is scarcely any limit to the number and variety of such types of "semi-demi-quasi-governmental" associations and processes. That they will continue to spring up and proliferate in the present phase of social development there is little doubt.

At the same time many individuals become both quasi-private and quasi-public in their forms of service, as in banking, and the hard and fast line between the public official and the private citizen tends to break down. In other instances private citizens obtain powers—bottleneck powers —that give to them the ordinary functions of the government, as in the case of dictation by a corporation or a trade-union in critical moments, or price fixing at any time. The citizen may be forced to obtain a permit from the union to obtain milk in a strike, or accept the increased price of bread fixed by a controlling monopoly. It is true that the power to price is the power to tax in many instances.

Millions of persons are unemployed and the government finds it necessary to assist them to find employment or employ them itself, or maintain them without employment, in varying situations. And this problem of the time calls for re-adjustment on the boundary lines of so-called "private" and "public" activities.

THE NEW DEMOCRACY

There is a wide variety of methods by which the system of democracy guides, regulates, and aids the social equilibrium, using the devices of strategic planning to attain its objectives. These are limited only by the insight and inventive ability displayed as time goes on, and by the degree of cooperation it is possible to obtain in a given period of development. And if it is not assumed too confidently that there are two segregated kingdoms of economics and government each with its own divine right to independence, notable advances may readily be made in this way.

If it is held, however, either (1) that there is a divine right to complete immunity on the part of "industry" or (2) that the whole social order must be drawn into the net of the state before any progress can be made—that a totalitarian, omni-competent Leviathan must be set up as the only way out—the outcome is likely to be as troubled as it has been in Russia, Germany, and Italy—disastrous to many of the interests and values in the community.

The planning program of democracy involves then the development of types of strategic organization, processes, and attitudes in which economico-political association and values are newly developed under the new situations of our time. There are other values than are contained in the economic, and the recognition of such values and their identification is an indispensable part of the new order. The richness and variety of human-value systems make possible an indefinitely superior organization of human relations on the associational side, and the encouragement of creative types of life within this ampler framework. This may be a hard saying for the traditionalists, but it is, indeed, the mold in which these very traditions were first cast.

The possibilities of increased production of commodities and services are far greater than have yet been attained

ASSUMPTIONS AND PROGRAM

under any system. In accordance with the preceding outline of the program of democracy, it would be the opportunity of a state to encourage science, technology, and social arrangement to expand production progressively, with the assumption that the gains of production are essentially mass gains. The persistent and skillful utilization of the stream of invention and new techniques would make it possible to establish new minimum standards of life and raise the level of human satisfactions on a wide scale. To those who are devoted to violence in terms of red or black, this is an unwelcome view, and must be brushed aside as unworthy of serious consideration by those who have received the revelation that revolution is necessary as the next step in our development.

But to those disposed to look more calmly and constructively on the evolution of our political and economic social order, there are broad possibilities in the democratic way of discussion and consent.

The social program of democracy will vary with the special circumstances of different peoples, and could conceivably be wide-ranging in its governmental activities or relatively restricted in its functions, depending on the social objectives of the given society at a given time. The control points in a program of democracy are not of necessity confined to what would be called an "economic" program, although by no means neglecting it. They might include a population program, a health and educational program, a scientific development program, a cultural program, a resources program in the field of land, water, minerals, and also in the field of human assets. Much attention may be given to what might be called the "non-economic" factors in social organization.

Finally and perhaps with some repetition of what has gone before, but for purposes of greater certainty restated, the

THE NEW DEMOCRACY

planning program of democracy presumes types of organization and procedure in which new forms of economico-political associations and relations are developed in zones little explored or inhabited. National values need not all be controlled by the government or by private individuals, for there are innumerable alternatives to so wide a contrast. It is, of course, possible to take hard and fast positions, begin to throw up intrenchments and prepare for a long and colorful struggle. But it is also possible to take the other alternative position and proceed to consider the ways and means of strategic planning for a new and better set of relationships.

As a student of government it is not for me to dictate to embattled controversialists who wear the red or the black what they shall do. I can only indicate alternative ways and express my own judgment on the superiority of the methods here suggested. I know that many of the present-day combatants do not want advice; they wish for aid and comfort. They have ceased to think and are impatient to fight. They wish to exercise their combative instincts, not their intelligence. And it must be conceded that if either side insists on fighting, the other will be obliged to defend itself either by prayer and fasting, or more probably by counterorganization for purposes of practicing violence as effectively as possible.

In the end, those who survive will fall back upon their intelligence. But many will be missing.

g. CONCLUSIONS

Summing up the criticisms of democratic planning, it may be pointed out that they rest upon a misunderstanding either of the nature of planning or of the nature of democratic government. Long-range planning of interrelated national policies or community policies means the release of human capacities to accomplish more easily what men wish to do,

ASSUMPTIONS AND PROGRAM

not the restriction or regimentation of their activities on a totalitarian scale. Real planning opens out human opportunities instead of closing them.

Opposition to all planning because of the fear that all may be planned is as blind as opposing all government because everything might be governed. The word itself, "planning," was not originated by the totalitarians, but borrowed from our city planners, and there is no reason why we should surrender the term. It is a useful name for intelligent interrelation of long-time national policies.

Planning is a good American word, which we have used in the home, on the farm, in business and government, and which we do not propose to abandon to anyone who may have borrowed and misused it—a good drink, even if some take too much of it.

Those who charge that a democratic government cannot plan, although other governments may, are in fact re-echoing the age-old snobbery that popular rule is as impossible as undesirable. Democracy, it was said, cannot exist except in a small-sized state. Democracy cannot survive the shock of war. Democracy cannot find competence to govern among its people. Democracy cannot guarantee justice, or order, or liberty even. These have been the stock charges for centuries, one after the other in a grotesque series of what we now know and recognize as hobgoblins. And now democracy cannot plan, it is said, but must leave that task to the new despotisms of the states repudiating the rule of the Many and entrusting their destiny to autocracy and absolutism.

The organization of the democratic state, it cannot be too often or too strongly stated, is preeminently adapted to the

(1) Determination of broad national policies commanding the consent of the governed, and

(2) Administrative management of these policies under

(3) The general supervision of the policy-determining body.

THE NEW DEMOCRACY

Those who are unfamiliar with the organizational principles of the democratic government may be misled or confused at this point by those who see only the complexities and difficulties of social action. But in the new democracies we take counsel not of our fears, but of our hopes.

Some of the defeatist critics are indeed quarreling with modern life rather than with democracy, for their wishful thinking looks back to days of primitive simplicity. Our social life is complicated and it will be more and more complicated as we advance in the next generation. The remedy is not to retreat but to advance, not to suspend liberty and call out the troops but to apply the techniques of modern intelligence in the field of organization and administration to the emerging problems. The difficulties of modern industry and society present no problems that need make us tremble and quiver with fear; they are all capable of solution by the exercise of our intelligence, will, and faith.

5. *Consciously Directed and Peaceful Social Change*

a. CHANGE IN GOVERNMENT

The democratic movement broke through the crust of custom and established the principle that governments are made by men and may be changed by them at their pleasure.

"Government," said Jefferson, "is not like the ark of the covenant, too sacred to be touched." Down to the nineteenth century, however, this doctrine was profoundly distrusted by the defenders of the *status quo*. From their point of view the deliberate making of a government or of a constitution of a government was a fantastic impossibility. Constitutions are not made; they grow. And those who attempt to change them at will are as foolish as if they decreed growth by fiat. The Constitution of the United States was the first great piece of consciously organized political construction, set down in elaborate and written form, in defiance of the

ASSUMPTIONS AND PROGRAM

prevailing opinion that governments could not be made by human decree.

The continuing validation of this principle in democratic societies may be brought about ordinarily by constitutional provisions for orderly change in the institutions of the commonwealth, as in modern states. If, however, these provisions are made too difficult of amendment, they may play into the hands of vested minorities, and defeat the purpose of their establishment. Or if too narrow a principle of interpretation is applied to their operation, the same result may follow, as in the United States from time to time.[1] In general, however, this has not proved to be a serious problem in the bulk of the modern democratic societies, as the experience of Sweden, England, France well illustrates.

The process of change may be more seriously blocked by habits of mind that stand in the way of change by taking the form of overemphasis on tradition or by resistance to special forms of change such as those in the world of industrial enterprise. Clearly, this is not a problem in the structure of formal institutions, but its bearing upon the operation of democratic society is vital. Stability is an important factor in the governance of states, but overemphasis on it may lead to the prevention of sound and desirable change—to fossilization instead of growth.[2]

Sluggishness may obstruct the way to necessary alterations important for the successful workings of democracy in our times. The enemies of democracy like to assert that democracy is incapable of survival because of its inflexibility. When the friends of democracy also act upon this assumption, they make the full development of popular machinery impossible. The principle of democracy is prior in importance to particular mechanisms of government, and

[1] See my *The Written Constitution and the Unwritten Attitude* (1931).
[2] See my *Civic Education in the United States*, Chap. VIII.

THE NEW DEMOCRACY

obsession with the means may be the death of the ends of democratic association. To worship the graven images of government and forget its great spirit is a form of political idolatry—at times a more accurate characterization would be the worship of the golden calf.

b. CHANGE IN INDUSTRY

In the domain of industrial life especially, the democratic principle of the importance of deliberate social change in institutions has not been favorably received in many quarters. Just as the old absolutists maintained that political institutions could not safely be altered by human hand, so the moderns have maintained that economic institutions cannot wisely be altered by human hand. It is held not that these institutions are divine, as were the political, but that they have the approval of the laws of nature, the natural laws of economics. Adam Smith himself would have been startled at some of the ideas accredited to him in the nineteenth century, as Herbert Spencer was shocked when he visited the United States.

In the political field this doctrine has long since been abandoned, but it still survives in the economic domain, although no longer stated in the older terms of *laissez faire*. This political theology stands in the way at various times of the validation of the democratic assumption involved in the idea that commonwealth gains belong to the community, and often impedes forms of social legislation and the realization of ideals of social justice. At times this theory has challenged or checked hasty legislation, but on other occasions it has proved the rallying point of opposition to social advances that posterity has overwhelmingly approved.

c. CIVIC EDUCATION AND CHANGE

One of the modes of validation of the democratic assumption at this point is the development of civic education

ASSUMPTIONS AND PROGRAM

upon a sounder basis, the significance of change in the modern world being recognized. Stability is one side of government, but variation is another; and in the whirling world of modern change, emphasis may well be laid upon the importance of control of the conditions under which present-day progress is made.[1]

In the world of adult education, the organization of controversy may well serve as the medium. The radio, the press, the forum, the movie offer wide and rich possibilities for analysis of the facts and theories upon which conflicting issues are raised, and upon the precise form in which these issues may be joined in public discussion. The elaboration of the ways and means of bringing this about is not within the purview of this volume, but it presents a major problem in the organization of democratic intercommunication—a necessary factor in the functioning of democratic society.

The techniques of dealing with mass psychology are increasingly developed in our day, and new instruments of propaganda and persuasion are rapidly perfected on the mechanical side. Democratic civic education must reckon with the new devices for organization of opinion and the mobilization of morale. When these instruments are in common use, they tend to neutralize each other, but if in the hands of a special few they constitute a dangerous differential advantage, which in some cases may prove to be decisive.

d. FORCE AND CHANGE

It is an assumption of democracy that political changes may normally be made by peaceful methods rather than by violence.[2] The doctrine that change may be brought about by the slow process of custom was an ancient doctrine

---

[1] See my "Some Social Implications of Inventions," *American Institute Monthly*, November, 1937.
[2] See my *Role of Politics in Social Change*, Chap. III.

employed in the defence of the *status quo;* the doctrine that important change comes by the way of violent revolution or by the instrumentality of the club—these are the assertions of communism and fascism.

The democratic assumption does not exclude the use of force, but maintains the priority and normality of peaceful change. One of the thorniest problems of the modern state is the dual organization of persuasion and of violence; and, so to speak, how to keep the peace between them. The rivalry between the brass hats and the frocks is one of long standing. An organization of violence is necessary under modern conditions for the purposes of national defence and the preservation of internal order—an essential condition of survival in our time. Democratic statesmanship can ignore this only at its peril. But military rule and martial law, projected permanently as a dominant institution, are inconsistent with the genius of a government operating on the principle of persuasion and the consent of the governed.

Two obvious ways to the democratic end are

(1) The organization of the jural order of the world.

(2) Minimum emphasis on violence in the administration of internal affairs.

(1) With the organization of a jural order in the world, the chief inducement to the organization of violence would tend to disappear, and the whole character of political relations would undergo a change of profound significance. The development of a body of international law and practice, the growth of arbitration in one form or another, the rise of the idea of international association—these are all evidences of progress in the direction of the outlawry of war as an instrument of national policy. In this movement the democratic states of the world have been in the lead, and will doubtless continue the effort to validate their assumption of peaceful change by construction and trial of one and another

ASSUMPTIONS AND PROGRAM

method of organization and association, directed toward the ending of international anarchy.

Paradoxically, the reign of violence may be ended or aided by the counterorganization of counterforce directed toward another end, namely, the reign of international order. If the jurisdiction of intelligence is challenged, an alternative is the intelligent organization of such force as will ensure the acceptance of the rule of reason. This is not good pacifism, perhaps, but it is good politics. Hermits retreat from reality and find refuge in their reveries perhaps; but the social man may pursue the devils of life in association with others. He may attempt to isolate evil, not himself. War is a weapon with which democracies are not unacquainted, and that they are able and ready to use when necessary. This also might be written in letters of fire, to be read before it is too late by those who mistake reluctance for incapacity. One of the heroes of the late war started as a pacifist.

(2) The rule of force in the administration of internal affairs of states is weakened by the elimination of brutality in punishment and in enforcement of law. The whip has almost disappeared in many places from the school and the prison alike, torture and the duel are on the road out, and the ways of brutality tend to retire as better methods of treatment are developed. Education, medical and psychotherapy tend to replace the older modes of dealing with social deviations, and prevention is more and more emphasized and practiced in lieu of punishment.

In these ways the dignity of man is more highly respected than before, and the process of persuasion emphasized as over against the argument from superior force.[1] There is still a long way to go in this direction before the goal is reached; but looking back a hundred years or so, it is plain that enormous progress has been made in the intelligent applica-

---
[1] See Margaret Wilson, *The Crime of Punishment* (1931).

THE NEW DEMOCRACY

tion of social policy to individual deviation from it. Torture, death, confiscation, mutilation, physical humiliation are no longer the typical ways of procuring compliance with the dominant political, religious, or economic policy.

The relationship between the organization of consent and the organization of violence still remains imperfectly adjusted, and constitutes a problem of all democracies. Civil government and military government are still unreconciled in great measure, although both are arms of the commonwealth. In general it is fair to say that drift and not planning have characterized the policy of political associations upon this point, at almost all times.

In modern military crises, however, it becomes increasingly evident that the tension is not merely military in the narrower sense of the term, but also economic and also one of morale. Thus economic organization on the one hand and propaganda organization on the other become important and perhaps decisive factors in the outcome of war. It was von Ludendorff who said in the World War, "The enemy's pen [propaganda] is mightier than his sword." It was said from another point of view, "Food will win the War." Organizations such as those of a national council of defense draw into their membership not only army, navy, and air services, the technical organization of force, but also civilians who know how to deal with the economic, organizational, political elements involved in the maximum application of national strength.

When the use of gas masks must be taught in the schools, it is plain that we approach a common ground between the civic training of those who are concerned with systematic application of force and those who are concerned with the systematic organization of intelligence. Persuasion and force may be set together in their proper place, alike in the mind of the soldier and of the citizen.

D. CONCLUSIONS

In the preceding paragraphs, methods of validating the assumptions of democracy have been traced in broad outline and in general principle. Evidently particular policies and programs will vary widely with the special situations arising from time to time, but the general direction and trend will be of the broad type indicated.

In sum, the short-time program of democracy, based upon its assumptions, may be summed up with reasonable clearness in general terms. There is involved

(1) A positive social program including the guaranty of full employment, of economic stabilization and security, of increasing productivity with equitable distribution of national gains; and a guaranty of minimum standards of living appropriate to our stage of civilization.

(2) Adequate machinery to make democracy work, including the sharpening of legislative organization and objectives, the further development of public administration, attention to plan making and planning of national resources.

(3) The development of a system of jural order in the world, by force if necessary, through which war may be outlawed as an instrument of national policy by some effective form of understanding or association and, in the interim, more intelligent adjustment of the relations between the organization of violence and the organization of consent in commonwealths.

(4) Faith in democracy's political ideals with (*a*) greater stress upon human values in the larger sense and (*b*) greater emphasis on the broad possibilities in the coming era of abundance.

THE NEW DEMOCRACY

Democracy's program must conform to the newer ideals and possibilities of our new day. It must guaranty a fair share in the vast gains of civilization, material and higher, to members of the democratic society if it is to survive under modern conditions. It must validate the assumptions of democracy in the everyday life of the community.[1]

[1] This study is a discussion of democracy in generalized terms only. Special comment on the trends and program of democracy in the United States is reserved for another occasion.

Part II

THE NEW DESPOTISM

A. BEGINNINGS OF THE ANTI-DEMOCRATIC MOVEMENT

By the middle of the nineteenth century the theoretical attack upon democracy was in full retreat, but a new assault was forming in the background.

The doctrine of the divine right of kings was practically abandoned, and the principle of hereditary transmission of political power was given up, the theories of absolutism were replaced by doctrines and institutions of constitutionalism, the *Machtstaat* gave way to the *Rechtsstaat*, the political and legal equality of men was widely accepted, the consent of the governed expressed through the franchise and through representation was generally adopted in one form or another, the value of peaceful change as the normal method was widely accepted as against the techniques of force, and the network of a jural order of the world was being rapidly developed. Defences of caste and slavery had long since disappeared.

These ideas were not everywhere accepted in principle, or always carried out in practice, but by and large they were the prevailing theories of political action in the Western world, and they were making headway in the Orient, as in China and Japan. In many states of the world, which were called "democratic," there were thinly veiled oligarchies or even military despotisms, giving lip service only to the forms of democratic practice. In some of these cases there was no serious attempt to validate the assumptions of the democratic system. Even in more readily accredited democracies there were wide ranges of undemocratic practice, particularly in the matter of suffrage.

THE NEW DEMOCRACY

Yet on the whole, the earlier anti-democratic theories were in abeyance. No notable defenders arose to proclaim the values of despotism, absolutism, inequality[1] and to deny the basic principles of the democratic form of association.

There were few voices to glorify force and proclaim the desirability of war as the supreme end of life, or to eulogize international anarchy. At best there were defensive compromises which marked the decline of the *ancien régime*—hereditary kings and nobles without large powers, second chambers serving as a brake on popular bodies, checks and devices designed, cleverly or clumsily as the case might be, to halt in some way the rule of the people.

The revival of the anti-democratic theory developed in the first half of the nineteenth century and owed its origin to various converging tendencies.

Increasingly toward the middle of the century it became evident that there was developing a cleavage between the defenders of liberty and the defenders of equality, or from another point of view between political liberty and equality and economic liberty and equality. Thus the low-income groups at the bottom of the heap were inclined to lay less emphasis upon political liberty and more upon a program of economic equality and security. On the other hand the upper-income groups were inclined to lay less emphasis upon equality and more upon liberty—especially economic liberty —upon which they believed their income differentials rested.

The defence of democracy remained with the middle-income groups, who looked with disfavor upon large concentrations of economic power whether in the form of land or capital, and on the other hand with dislike upon a revolu-

[1] The last blast was that of Ludwig von Haller, *Restauration der Staatswissenschaft*, 1816–1834 (six volumes of vituperation). Von Haller denounced in set terms the idea of human equality and proclaimed the doctrine that all authority rests on superiority on the one side and inferiority on the other. See also Nora E. Hudson, *Ultra Royalism and the French Restoration* (1936).

tionary program of collectivism. They held to the values of liberty and equality in a democratic frame of political association. They were weakened however by the defection of elements of the proletarian group willing to sacrifice liberty for equality, and by the defection of a capitalistic group who were willing to exchange equality for liberty in the form of *laissez faire*.

It was this struggle between the competing claims of political and economic liberty and equality that helped to prepare the way for the anti-democratic sentiment, theory, and forms of the twentieth century. The struggle was made all the sharper by the failure of social organization to keep pace with the rapid advance of technology, and to develop appropriate methods of economic and political stabilization. These difficulties were accentuated still more by the growth of intensely nationalistic sentiments on the one hand and on the other the failure to develop a jural order of the world in which local security might be set.

Under these circumstances came the rise of the doctrines and institutions of communism on the left and fascism on the right, both challenging the democratic jural, political, economic order, and substituting an order of their own in which it was asserted that social values might be more readily satisfied than in democratic society.

Some of the elements in the slowly developing anti-democratic theory were philosophical, some were cultural, some were biological-psychological, some were Nietzschean (compounded of Darwinism and Wagner), some were economic.

The massive philosophy of Hegel, court philosopher of Prussia, stated clearly the doctrine of the Few in newer terminology, bridging over the gap between the older times and the emerging era. Elevating the state to a position as the highest possible expression of the moral principle in human association, he sanctified the Leviathan of Hobbes. In this

THE NEW DEMOCRACY

idealized *Staat*, the constitution is essentially undemocratic in nature. The will of the people must be served, but there are leaders who will interpret that will—men who will be able to distinguish the "apparent" will of a majority from the "rational" will of the community, which they are able with their superior insight to discern and express and make effective.

Hegel's definition of the people is "the thing that knows not what it wishes." He who "does not learn to despise public opinion, which is one thing in one place and another in another, will never achieve anything great."[1] Popular representatives cannot understand the advantage or the will of the community, but must be directed and guided by the few who possess true capacity for interpretation. This doctrine reappears in Nazi theory.

Early in the nineteenth century the unique Saint-Simon led the way with a proposal for a new order of aristocracy. In every organized society, said he, there are two powers, one holding its moral and intellectual direction, the other holding the material one. These two functions are performed by two organized minorities which, united, form the ruling class. The basis of Saint-Simon's philosophy of history (which Comte imitated) is the necessary correlation between the moral, intellectual, and material conditions of a society and the few who rule it.[2]

Saint-Simon's proposed society "rests on Industry. Industry is the sole guarantee of its existence, the sole source of all the riches and of prosperity. Therefore the status which is most favourable to Industry is the most favourable to Society."[3]

---

[1] *The Philosophy of Right* (trans. 1896), Sec. 318, p. 325.

[2] For the relationship between Saint-Simonism and aristocracy see G. Mosca, *Elementi di scienza politica* (1923), Part I, Chap. X; Part II, Chap. II; S. Charlety, *Histoire de Saint-Simonisme* (1931), pp. 49–60; G. Weill, *Saint-Simon et son oeuvre* (1894), pp. 121–135.

[3] *Oeuvres de Saint-Simon et d'Enfantin* (1875–1878), Tome XVIII, p. 13.

THE NEW DESPOTISM

The aristoi to whom the rule of society is entrusted are to be grouped in three chambers. The first, the chamber of invention, is composed by 200 civil engineers, 50 poets or writers, 25 painters, 15 sculptors or architects, 10 musicians. Its task is to prepare a yearly plan of public works. Its members were to receive 10,000 francs a year, and to be elected for a five-year term. They were to establish the conditions of the future elections.

The second chamber, the chamber of examination, was to be composed of 300 members: 100 physiologists, 100 physicists, and 100 mathematicians; it would be their task to examine the plans of the first chamber and to direct public education and moral festivities.

The third chamber, the chamber of execution, is a transformation of the Chamber of Commons or of the Deputies. It was to be recruited amongst the leaders of all the branches of industry, who will serve without salary, since they all are rich. It will execute the plans prepared by the other chambers.[1]

The Marxian philosophy developed the doctrine of class conflict as inevitable and revolution as the unavoidable road to social salvation. Force was proclaimed as the method by which capitalism was to be overthrown and the rule of the proletariat to be established.

A part of this body of doctrine was a wholesale attack upon the bourgeois systems of religion, politics, and industry. Democracy, God, the state, and liberty were denounced as tools of the industrial oligarchy about to be destroyed. In general, all forms of "idealism" were assailed in the countername of "materialism," and all "utopian" plans for the future discredited as essentially palliatives when radical cures were

---

[1] To industrialists and scientists who are the rulers-to-be of the industrial society, Saint-Simon adds the artists, because of their "heart-warming" functions. The artists will inspire ideals of glory as well as generosity in the industrialists.

necessary. Democracy was held to be futilitarian in a capitalistic order of things—a screen to cover plutocracy.

Thus at the moment when the democratic ideas were sweeping triumphantly over Western Europe, a broad movement was organized and directed against this entire apparatus of doctrine and institutions. Only in somewhat later stages did socialism become evolutionary instead of revolutionary, and enter into political struggles and responsibilities. One wing accepted the doctrine of the dictatorship of the proletariat as the way out.

Linked with the Caesarism of Spengler and the Nietzschean superman was the later defence of violence by the French engineer Sorel.[1] His notable essay, influenced by syndicalist sympathies, propounded the morality of force and the futility of political and legislative compromise. Elections, parliaments, laws, compromises do not make for progress, but inevitably lead to the betrayal or the destruction of the public interest. The moral values of violence, on the other hand, are very large and their meaning must be given a larger place in the attitudes of our society. Only through struggles that involve disrespect or disregard for the law can substantial progress be achieved. This was the theme of Sorel.

From quite a different point of view came the prophets of the gospel of force as a basic factor in social change. Impulse to this was given by the early builders of military technology such as Clausewitz and later the historian Treitschke.[2]

In this manner the philosophies of socialism, syndicalism, and militarism were united in (1) a defence of violence as a mode of social change, and (2) a criticism of democracy as

---

[1] *Reflections on Violence* (trans. 1914).

[2] Karl von Clausewitz, *On War* (trans. 1911); Heinrich G. von Treitschke, *Treitschke, His Life and Works* (trans. 1914).

incapable of dealing with the problems of social and industrial organization.

In short, just as democratic institutions were coming into general acceptance a great mass movement attacked the bases of democratic ideas and systems, whereas at the same time the organization of force pressed hard upon the organization of popular consent.

It may also be observed that there was a shift in the position of nationalism. Whereas in the early part of the nineteenth century nationalism and democracy were united against localism and monarchism or feudalism, as in Germany, in the later period nationalism tended to become imperialistic and anti-liberal and anti-democratic in nature. Nationalism became a basis for attack upon international socialism or communism or other forms of collectivism whether religious or political. The centralizing forces in nationalism were also developed in some instances into centralized authoritarianism, and this in turn, step by step, was extended to include unfriendliness toward liberalism, radicalism, democracy itself in the course of time.

Thus although the new nationalisms in the early part of the century were liberal and democratic, the nationalisms of a century later tended to be non-liberal, non-democratic. The theory of inequality began its new growth under various circumstances.

Thus it appears that democracy, while engaged in the titanic task of adjusting a social, economic, and political order to the revolutionary developments of modern technology, was at one and the same time assailed

1. From below by a group of workers, fearing the capitalistic tendencies of democracy.

2. From above by a small group of plutocrats, fearing the proletarian trends of democracy.

3. While on the world scale, class, nation, and world order were challenging each other.[1]
This is the background of anti-democratic theory.

1. *The Superman and Caesarism*

Other statements of the anti-democratic theory find their origin in different sources. These doctrines comprise the earlier ideas developed by Nietzsche, Treitschke, Spengler, and the postwar formulations of neo-aristocracy by Spann, Mosca, Pareto, and in more popular form by Mussolini and Hitler, presented now as the philosophies of elitism and *Führerschaft*.

These later ideas are cast in a different mold from the earlier. Heredity and property are in general repudiated as bases of the new Superiors. Likewise the intellectuals, the clergy, the wealthy, and the warriors are removed from any central position in the new picture.

The central elements are now the doctrine of supernationalism, the gospel of force, and the rule of the few, as the solvent of the problems of statesmanship.

The strangest figure in nineteenth-century political theory is Nietzsche, through whose bold, often obscure, and contradictory essays was evolved a form of political attitude and philosophy that fundamentally influenced the Western world. In Nietzsche the doctrine of the survival of the fittest, the pessimism of Schopenhauer, the somber music of Wagner were the overtones in a new doctrine of human relations. Little noticed at first, this doctrine spread slowly through the philosophy of the West.

Its basic features involved

1. The repudiation of Christianity as essentially a slave philosophy of weakness and impotence.

---

[1] Note should also be taken of the Japanese Samurai at this point. *Cf.* William C. MacLeod, *The Origin and History of Politics* (1931), Chaps. XI, XII, XIII, XVI, and XVII.

2. The glorification of a "master" philosophy expressed in war and conquest.

3. The exaltation of the *Übermensch* with his will to power and his superior qualities for leadership and rule.

4. The repudiation of the rule of the Many and of the doctrine of equality and human consent as the basis of authority.

These doctrines must be read along with their analogue, the Marxian doctrines, which likewise repudiated Christianity, expounded the doctrine of materialism, preached class hatred, asserted the inevitability of violent revolution as the basis of reconstruction of civilization, and the futility of "bourgeois" government by the consent of the governed.

These philosophies supply much of the background for the emergence later on of a new form of political theology. With them should be placed Sorel and his hymn of praise to violence.[1]

The "lords of the earth" were proclaimed by the German philosopher Nietzsche. "In this age of universal suffrage," said he, "in which everybody is allowed to sit in judgment upon everything and everybody, I feel compelled to re-establish the order of rank."[2]

A Superior Type may and must emerge

> ... a new vast aristocracy based upon the most severe self discipline, in which the will of the philosophical men of power and artist-tyrants will be stamped upon thousands of years: a higher species of men who, thanks to their preponderance of will, knowledge, riches and influence, will avail themselves of democratic Europe as the most suitable and supple instrument they can have for taking the fate of the earth into their hands and working as artists upon man himself.[3]

Not mankind, proclaims Nietzsche, but the superman is the goal. Power and great deeds are his titles, and his limits are only his own imagination and facility in achievement.

---

[1] Sorel, *op. cit.*
[2] *Works*, Levy ed., *The Will to Power* (trans. 1913), Vol. II, p. 295.
[3] *Ibid.*, p. 365-366.

THE NEW DEMOCRACY

The aristocratic attitude of mind has been most thoroughly undermined by the lie of the equality of souls; and if the belief in the "privilege of the greatest number" creates and will continue to create revolutions, it is Christianity, let there be no doubt about it, and Christian values, which convert every revolution into blood and crime! Christianity is the revolt of all things that crawl on their bellies against everything that is lofty: the gospel of the "lowly" lowers. . . . [1]

Thus he flings a rude challenge to Christianity, to democracy, to romanticism, to Rousseauism, to socialism, to the "predominance of the gregarious instincts in whatever field they may be found, even in music or science."[2]

The order of castes, the highest, dominating law, is only the sanction of a natural order, over which no arbitrary innovation, no "modern idea" has any power. . . . Nature separates from the rest, those individuals preponderating in intellectual power, those individuals excelling in muscular strength and temperament, and the third class which is distinguished neither in one way nor the other, the mediocre. The superior caste—I call them the fewest—has as the perfect caste the privileges of the fewest. It devolves upon them to represent happiness, beauty and goodness on earth. Only the most intellectual men have the right to beauty, to the beautiful; only in them is goodness not weakness.[3]

In the end the Few must assume the supremacy of the group—"these lords of the earth must now take the place of God, and they must create for themselves the profound and absolute confidence of those they rule. Their new holiness, their renunciation of happiness and ease, must be their first principle." The master morality must stand out in sharp contrast to the slave morality.

These supermen, endowed not only with the "will to power," but with the capacity to make their will effective in human relations should be given the right to rule—the responsibility for the ordering of affairs.

[1] *Works*, Vol. XVI, p. 187. *The Anti-Christ*.
[2] See F. W. Coker's excellent Chap. XVI on "Reason of State" in *Recent Political Thought* (1935).
[3] *The Anti-Christ, op. cit.*, pp. 217*ff*.

THE NEW DESPOTISM

Modern political theories, constitutions, modern sociology, socialism, and liberalism[1] are all essentially decadent in that they rest upon the decay of organizing power—"the power which separates, cleaves gulfs, and establishes rank above and below." Until the natural system of ranks and classes is recognized and accepted as the basis of social life, the race will continue to decay and decline. Only in the glad acceptance of the "aristocratic attitude of mind" is it possible to attain the heights.

Nor can it be expected that in the fullness of time the lower groups will approximate the higher. Progress is a delusion, for the process of evolution does not involve "elevation, enhancement, and increasing strength." Here and there higher types will emerge and forms of supermen, but these are "lucky strokes" which in some instances may be shared by races, tribes, and nations. To express one's self in a formula, one might say, "All means which have been used hitherto with the object of making men moral, were through and through immoral."

It is interesting to observe that an indictment of the Jews also appears in Nietzsche—the forerunner of modern anti-democracy. "The Jews," he declares, "are the most *fatal* people in the history of the world. Their ultimate influence has falsified mankind to such an extent, that even to this day the Christian can be anti-Semitic in spirit, without comprehending that he himself is the final consequence of Judaism."[2]

War is eulogized by Nietzsche:

It is nothing but fanaticism and beautiful soulism to expect very much (or even, much only) from humanity when it has forgotten how to wage war. For the present we know of no other means whereby the rough energy of the camp, the deep impersonal hatred, the cold-bloodedness of murder

[1] "Liberalism, or in plain English, the transformation of mankind into cattle." *Works, Twilight of Idols*, Vol. XVI, p. 94.
[2] *Ibid.*, p. 155.

with a good conscience, the general ardour of the system in the destruction of the enemy, the proud indifference to great losses, to one's own existence and that of one's friends, the hollow, earthquake-like convulsion of the soul, can be as forcibly and certainly communicated to enervated nations as is done by every great war.[1]

The doctrines of Nietzsche were further developed in the writings of the German historian Treitschke (lecturer at the University of Berlin, 1874 on), who criticized the workings of democracy, glorified aristocracy, and exalted the meaning of war as a factor in human progress.[2]

In milder Americanized form these ideas were disseminated by the relatively cautious Mencken in numerous writings,[3] tempering Prussian ideas to America.

Oswald Spengler's *Decline of the West* was an elaborate attempt to demonstrate the inevitable decay of all Western civilization—a conclusion somewhat modified in view of the rise of Hitler to power.[4] Our civilization is doomed first of all, he finds, because of its confidence in the value of free human reason as a principle of organization and action. The world suffers from too great reliance upon reason and intellectualism. Furthermore, this faith is misplaced by reposing confidence in the democratic organization of society with general suffrage and parliamentary action. These features of Western organization, unless modified, make the overthrow of our institutions inevitable. In the emerging world, Caesarism, breaking the chains of money and of democracy, will take charge of human affairs, and direct and determine the order of things—Caesarism based on race and blood.

2. *The Noble Few*

From quite a different point of view, the idea of a cultural aristocracy has appeared in various quarters, early in Carlyle

[1] *Human, All Too Human*, Part I, p. 349.
[2] *Politics*, "The multitude must plow and forge and dig in order that a few may write and paint and study." 1: 41, cited by Coker. See Coker, *op. cit.*
[3] H. L. Mencken, *Notes on Democracy*, 1926 and *passim*.
[4] *Decline of the West* (trans. 1926–1929), 2 vols.; *The Hour of Decision* (trans. 1934).

THE NEW DESPOTISM

and Ruskin, later in the writings of Inge, Eliot, Keyserling, Belloc, Ortega, and others of the same general school.[1]

The flaming Carlyle led the way for a number of literary and cultural critics of democracy and friends of the government of the Few, running in our own time to Inge and Ortega. To them, the equality of men and the organization of popular consent are vicious in their effect upon social growth. Democracy runs counter to the laws of the universe. The great achievement of the American democracy is that "They have begotten with a rapidity beyond recorded example eighteen millions of the greatest bores ever seen in the world before."[2] Parliaments, he asserted, are merely "talk shops," incapable of achievement.

The existing English aristocracy was not, however, Carlyle's ideal, for he condemned them bitterly as idle and incompetent. The real hope of leadership he found in the captains of industry. Here he found the new and true aristocracy, and he hoped from them "a noble just industrialism and the government by the Wisest."

Ruskin wished it were possible to keep the common people from thinking about government, and looked forward to the time when the populace would be through with democracy. The ideal government is the rule of the upper classes—the old landowners, the captains of industry, and professional groups.

The later doctrine of the Spanish thinker, Ortega y Gasset,[3] is directed primarily against the general trends and implications of mass rule. The rise of the masses, he indicates, is the striking feature of modern life running through every way of social existence. The masses, however, are essentially vulgar, whereas minorities are essentially noble. The masses will

---

[1] See Francis W. Coker, *Recent Political Thought* (1934), Chaps. XI and XII.
[2] Thomas Carlyle, *Latter Day Pamphlets*, p. 21, cited in Benjamin E. Lippincott, *Victorian Critics of Democracy* (1938), p. 39.
[3] *The Revolt of the Masses* (1930).

emphasize force rather than that reason. He finds, for example, that lynch law is typical of the greatest of the mass-ruled systems.

Ortega refers not merely to political democracy but to the rise and imposition of mass judgments and standards. He dislikes Ford as much as Jefferson, or perhaps more. For that matter, he finds socialism and fascism equally at fault in flattering the masses and exalting their supremacy in national life.

The greatest of all dangers is that of the "politicization of life" through the spread and dominance of this mass movement. Not concerned particularly with mechanical arrangements, the verdict runs against mass rule. In general Ortega raises the standard of the "noble few" whose judgment, taste, quality are in danger of sinking under the surface of mob rule. But the distinguished Spanish thinker is obviously protesting not merely against mass rule in the political world but in the cultural worlds as well, against the tide of mass standardization of culture, as in the cinema, in the press, the radio, the "vulgarization" of art; and he clearly entertains the fear that this trend projected will destroy the best in modern civilization. All of this recalls Nietzsche with his hatred of the herd mind, "the much too many," the mass overriding the distinguished few. He joins here a considerable group of critics of modern democracy who find in mass mediocrity, in vulgarity, in mass incompetence, in mass jealousy, envy, and stupidity the greatest menace to the growth of civilization. Democracy from this point of view is only one aspect of a general phenomenon of mass weight working upon the traits and tendencies of the noble few, and this evokes a broad general condemnation of the inherent tendencies of the mass.

Not closely united in advocacy of any special form of aristocratic association, these thinkers have a bond of union in their common distrust of the masses as governing forces. They deplore the leveling tendencies, which they assume to discover in the crowd, and fear the fate of civilization if entrusted to the rough hands of the generality of mankind. They emphasize the importance of leadership in the hands of the natural aristocrats, who in general are men of superior sensitiveness, highly developed spiritual and mental faculties, keener appreciation than common of the nobler values of life, and ability to direct the course of the commonweal accordingly. A political aristocracy might well be recruited from among such guiding spirits in some manner not clearly described, or at least follow the lines indicated by these natural leaders of men: this is their credo.

3. Economic Inequality

But the whole meaning of the modern anti-mass movements would be lost if we were to omit from it the attitudes of those who resented and resisted the attempts of the mass rulers to deal with the lines of their industrial enterprise, and to set a limit to the activities of the leaders. It is in other words a short way from *laissez faire* in economics to elitism in political and social theory. Democracy may be tolerated or welcomed as long as it leaves the domination of industry to a few, but repudiated when it begins a process of social control.

The full significance of the recent doctrines of the elite cannot be judged except as it is seen in the context of the industrial elites in protest against the regulations of the mass in political form, in the light of mass rule which aims at economic as well as at political content.[1]

Without the support of eminent figures in the field of industry, for example, the present movements in Italy and

[1] See William H. Mallock, *Aristocracy and Evolution* (1898), for plain statement of this doctrine often left to inference.

THE NEW DEMOCRACY

Germany would have been impossible to finance or to press forward effectively. The politically ambitious invoked the aid of the industrial few against the Marxians and the democracy alike. The development of the totalitarian state was from this point of view an unexpected and unwelcome outcome of anti-mass movement. The fate of industrial enterprise under a regime of elitists is a story the last chapter of which is yet to be written.

Since advancement, it is maintained by Mallock and others, depends primarily on the efforts of the industrial aristoi, they should be assigned a preferred position in the general direction and government of industry, and should not be fettered by regulative measures in the area of industrial operation. These leaders cannot make haste if a ball and chain are fastened around their ankles. They should not be bound too closely therefore by the ordinary canons of practice, nor should they be held to a strict responsibility to others either within their field or by the wider processes of social control. In the market place are determined the chief values of life and the true differentials in recognition as between individuals. The process of competition will eliminate the persons and institutions which do not function productively.

It is important to note the changing attitudes, however, toward the rise of leaders in the business world. On the one hand, the older, landed aristocracy was obliged to meet the severe competition of the rising men of money who overshadowed them, in a world where pecuniary values were of increasing significance. Property now tended to become fluid, however, instead of stable as in the landed era, and the new fortunes towered over the older type. The older aristocracy tended to become weaker, and was driven to rely upon alliances with the new men of strength in the financial sense.

THE NEW DESPOTISM

From this point of view the old-time aristocrat looked with disfavor on the rise of the financial oligarchy. But from another point of view the devotees of aristocracy in the theoretical group were often inclined to look upon the captains of industry as the real beau ideal of the aristoi—the true type of social leader, assuming initiative and sweeping all obstacles aside in the general interest of the community.

However, the doctrine of the industrial elite differs from that of other elites, in that this group of leaders is not presented as the actual holder of formal political authority. Governmental control is here a means to an end—the end of industrial advancement. The industrial aristocracy does not assume the direct responsibility for the determination of political policies or for their administration or adjudication. In this sense the captains do not command, but have the right to command or to veto when it is deemed appropriate. They do not constitute the responsible government, but they are its ultimate control.

Whether the industrial elite chooses to cooperate with mass government or with Fascist and Nazi types the events of the next years may disclose; and of course a wide variety of relationships may be developed, including possible rapprochement between government and industry.[1]

---

[1] The development of technocracy as a proposed system of industrio-political government gave an opportunity for the elaboration of a theory of the Superior, but little progress was made in this direction by the proponents of the new system. Chiefly engineers interested in the problem of production of commodities and, in less degree, of services, they did not address themselves primarily or adequately to the governmental implications of the new regime which they advocated. See Harold Loeb, *Life in a Technocracy* (1933), based on the ideas of Howard Scott.

B. POSTWAR DEFENCES OF THE FEW

The anti-democratic doctrine has reappeared in numerous theories of the elite and of leadership, notably in the writings of Mosca, Pareto, Spann.[1] In these new forms, the doctrine of hereditary descent as a basis of superiority has disappeared, and another system is substituted.

These doctrines were earliest stated by Mosca[2] and later by the better known and more voluminous Pareto. In the theory of Mosca, the doctrine of the rule of a minority is presented and the theory of the *classe politica*—the best adapted in a particular moment to exercise the functions of governing—set forth as inevitable and desirable.[3]

Later the term "elite" was popularized by the engineer-sociologist, Pareto: "Let us take a class of those who have the highest indices in the branch in which they are occupied and let us give to this class the name of elite. . . . "

Pareto sets up groups of persons in every activity who would be graded highest in their respective callings or

---

[1] Gaetano Mosca, *Elementi di scienza politica* (1895); Vilfredo Pareto, *Traité de sociologie générale* (1917–1919), 2 vols.; *Les Systèmes socialiste* (1902); Othmar Spann, *Der wahre Staat* (1931).

[2] Controversy on this point is summed up in Renzo Sereno, "The Anti-Aristotelianism of Gaetano Mosca and Its Fate," *International Journal of Ethics*, August, 1938. See also Roberto Michels, *Political Parties* (1915), for a discussion of the rule by minorities in democracies; and Pitirim Sorokin, *Social Mobility* (1927), for a suggestive discussion of social stratification, Chaps. X–XIV. On the relation of Mosca's doctrine to the earlier theory of Saint-Simon, see Mosca, *op. cit.*, Part I, Chap. X; Part II, Chap. II; J. P. Mayer, *Political Thought* (1939).

[3] *The Ruling Class*, Trans. 1939. In somewhat romantic form, Pellizi enthused: "In us aristocrats, there shines the light of a noble myth, the myth of a race of men no longer men, of a liberated race, without good or evil, without need, without desire, without passion; a race of conquerors that no longer believes but is, in a life of sheer cosmic power . . . alone, gazing without fear into the shadows where God no longer exists and where they themselves are the creators of God." Camillo Pellizzi, *Fascismo e aristocrazia*, pp. 101–102.

occupations. Society is thus divided into the elites and the non-elites. The elite again are subdivided into the "governing elite, comprising individuals who directly or indirectly play some considerable part in governing and a non-governing elite comprising the rest." These groups are in constant process of change—characterized by him as the circulation of the elite.[1]

According to Pareto, the Superior do not derive their authority from birth, education, election, appointment, but from the fact of their capacity in the given situation.

The upper stratum again nominally contains certain groups of peoples, not always very sharply defined, who are called aristocracies. The aristocrat may or may not belong to the elite, and vice versa. Many persons nominally enrolled in the aristocracy do not belong there, if classed in accordance with their capacity. The aristocracy, in short, may not be the elite, or vice versa.[2]

Revolutions are caused by the weakening in quality of the nominally dominant group and the rise of elements of superior quality in the non-governing group.[3] History is a graveyard of aristocracies and a continuing circulation of elites—military, religious, commercial, and plutocratic—in a continuous flood. "If human aristocracies were like thoroughbreds among animals, which reproduce themselves over long periods of time with approximately the same traits, the history of the human race would be something altogether different from the history we know."[4]

---

[1] See Marie Kolabinska, *La Circulation des élites en France* (1912). On "vertical" and "horizontal" mobility, see Sorokin, *op. cit.*, Chaps. XIV–XIX.

[2] Pareto accepted the Fascist regime, whereas Mosca viewed it as a resurgence of barbarism.

[3] On this process see Pareto, *Mind and Society* (1934), Secs. 1220 *et seq.*; see also Brooks Adams, *The Theory of Social Revolutions* (1913); Michels, *op. cit.*; Sorokin, *op. cit.*, pp. 310ff.

[4] Curiously enough Pareto names the best government as that of Switzerland, especially the direct democracy of the small cantons, *Mind and Society*, Sec. 2240.

THE NEW DEMOCRACY

It is to Pareto a matter of relative indifference how these especially capable persons are chosen or what their methods and purposes are, or their attitudes toward the mass of the community. They are if they are.

But the wide vogue enjoyed by Pareto among the modern representatives of the Superior does not arise from his discussion of the so-called elite, but from his assaults on the workings of democracy especially in its plutocratic phases, and from his glorification of the use of force in the maintenance of political authority.

Popular representation is a fiction—"poppycock grinds no flour." Universal suffrage is a delusion, since the oligarchy always governs. "Who is this new god called Universal Suffrage? . . . Worshippers of Universal Suffrage are not led by their god. It is they who lead him—and often by the nose, determining the forms in which he must manifest himself."

The maintenance of power depends upon a combination of consent and force. As far as possible consent may be obtained by one device or another—corruption, chicanery, fraud, appeal to interests, or other means; but in the end force is essential. Humanitarians may shrink from utilizing violence, but if so they will be overthrown by those who do not hesitate to destroy. Excessive violence is a danger, but is balanced by the counterliability of unwillingness to exert force in critical moments.[1]

The detail of the indicia of the elite is very slender in Pareto, and scarcely bears close analysis.[2] But the symbolism was effective and was seized upon by the rising group in Italy, who were glad to declare themselves the elite—the natural rulers of Italy, (1) free to use violence, and (2) relieved of popular or formal responsibility.

---

[1] *Ibid.*, Secs. 2477 *et seq.*

[2] Elaborate critique of Pareto is given in *Journal of Social Philosophy*, Vol. I, October, 1935, by McDougall and others.

THE NEW DESPOTISM

Thus Rocco declared that

> The great mass of citizens is not a suitable advocate of social interests for the reason that the capacity to ignore private interests in favor of the higher demands of society and of history is a very rare gift and the privilege of the chosen few. Natural intelligence and cultural preparation are of great service in such tasks. Still more valuable is the intuitiveness of rare great minds, their traditionalism and their inherited qualities.[1]

Mussolini himself vigorously assailed the democratic theory of equality as absurd, untenable, ruinous, and projected the doctrine of unequality in the terminology of "hierarchy."[2]

"Whoever says hierarchies is committed to a scale of human values; whoever says a scale of human values says a scale of human responsibilities; who says hierarchy says discipline."[3]

This principle requires the organization of a superior group who interpret the general interest of the nation, who supply the lines of leadership and direct the process of administration. Whether this ruling group has a legal status or not is relatively unimportant, since they can always seize the government, if they find themselves outside the formal machinery of the law. And it is repeatedly asserted that the uses and necessity of force must not be ignored in the world of practical affairs. As a principle of selection, violence ranks high in the scale of alternatives.[4]

---

[1] Alfredo Rocco, "The Political Doctrine of Fascism," *International Conciliation*, No. 223, October, 1926. "Fascism," said Gentile, "is war on intellectualism. The fascist spirit is will, not intelligence . . . disdaining the culture that is an ornament or adornment of the brain, and longing for a culture by which the spirit is armed and fortified for winning ever new battles. . . . One of the major merits of fascism is this, to have obliged little by little all those who once stood at the window to come down into the streets, to practice fascism even against fascism." *Che cosa é il fascismo* (1925), p. 98.

[2] *Enciclopedia italiana* (1932), Vol. XIV, "La dottrina del fascismo," Part II.

[3] *Gerarchia*, Jan. 25, 1922.

[4] The Italian theory of the elite was undoubtedly influenced by some of the writings of Renan, notably his *La Réforme intellectuelle et morale* (1871), in which, under

THE NEW DEMOCRACY

The doctrine of aristocracy is likewise proclaimed in Germany, both theoretically and practically. The theory and practice of the Nazis involve the recognition of a double racial and class superiority of the Aryan and especially of the pure German type.[1] This is characterized as the *völkisch* principle—the doctrine of the indisputable superiority of a particular cultural-racial group over all others—a proposition rejected by Mussolini and the Fascists until recently.

This system of aristocracy is further developed through the elaboration of the doctrine of leadership (*Führerschaft*).

This doctrine was stated in the early stages of Naziism by Spann[2] in his *True State*. "We should not count the votes," runs his argument, "we should weigh them—not the majority, but the best should rule."

There must be leadership from the top down, in a developed hierarchy of rank and order. The most spiritual, the best will dominate most, the lesser will dominate to a lesser

---

the influence of the crushing defeat of France, he declared in favor of a dynasty and a nobility. "One suppresses humanity," said he, "if he does not admit that some entire classes ought to live for the glory and enjoyment of others." Later he urged the establishment of a socialistic democracy under some form of dictatorship.

[1] For the basic doctrines of National Socialism, see, among others, Ernst Rudolf Huber, *Verfassung* (1937); *Wesen und Inhalt der politischen Verfassung* (1935); Adolf Hitler, *Mein Kampf* (1939, English edition); Alfred Rosenberg, *Der Mythos der 20. Jahrhundert* (1933); Otto Koellreuter, *Grundriss der Allgemeinen Staatslehre* (1933); *Grundfragen des Völkischen und Stattlichen lebens im deutschen Volksstaate* (1935); *Deutsche Verfassungsrecht* (1936); Carl Schmitt, *Staat, Bewegung, Volk* (1935); Ernst Krieck, *Nationalpolitische Erziehung* (1933). For analyses of the National Socialist Weltanschauung by "non-Nazis," see H. Mankiewicz, *Le national-socialism allemand: Ses doctrines et leurs réalizations* (1937); Kurt Wilk, "La Doctrine politique du national-socialism: Carl Schmitt, exposé et critique de ses idées," *Archives de philosophie du droit et de sociologie juridique* (1934), No. 2, pp. 169ff.; Aurel Kolnai, *The War Against the West* (1938); Herbert Marcuse, "Der Kampf gegen den Liberalismus in der totalitären Staatsauffassung," *Zeitschrift für Sozialforschung*, 1934, 3: 159-195; Hans Kelsen, "The Party Dictatorship," *Politica*, 1936, 2: 19-32; Calvin Hoover, *Dictators and Democracies* (1937).

[2] Now fallen from favor with the Nazis. See his *Der wahre Staat*, p. 86.

extent, and a pyramidal hierarchy will eventuate in which the various estates (*Stände*) will be placed in their correct levels.

Democracy, it is asserted, is based upon the assumption that there is a popular will, a general will, whereas actually there is none. What really happens is that the leaders mold the popular will before it expresses itself as the popular will. This must first be created by the leaders, who, according to the false democratic theory, follow it. In truth, there was never a real democracy in the whole course of history. And "from Plato till Hegel, from Euripides to Goethe, all great philosophers and poets have denied democracy, for democracy means the permanent death of culture."[1]

If the masses choose the leaders, proceeds Spann's counter-argument, the leaders play to the instincts of the mobs; radical leaders win over the moderate, and those who appeal to the lower emotions score over those who have insight and ideas. Then what happens is that even if the first leaders of the masses are great, like Pericles among the Greeks, there follows the tanner Cleon, and the masses who demand only circuses and bread. The better leaders lose control of the reins. Thus, in modern times we have seen Austrian socialism make way for the criminal murderous leadership of the communists. A century ago, we saw the same procedure in the French Revolution. The choice of leadership, Spann insisted, is one of democracy's great weaknesses.

In hierarchies, on the contrary, the subordinate leaders are educated and appointed by the superior. These may err in their choice, but certainly they do not choose originally on the basis of mere ability to sway the masses. And those chosen are responsible to their superiors. *There is leadership from the top down, and responsibility from the bottom up,* instead of the reverse as in mass rule.

[1] *Ibid.,* p. 91.

THE NEW DEMOCRACY

As for minorities, even democracy does not tolerate minorities when the issues are really fundamental. Then the issues make the opponents real enemies where struggle determines the contest, as was the case in the Greek democracies, in the Roman Republic, and in the United States Civil War. The atomizing of the state in democracy leads eventually to Caesarism to save it. Philip, Alexander, Caesar, and his successors, Napoleon and many other figures in history prove this. From the condition of division, from the anarchy of democratic regimen, the absolutistic state must of necessity develop.[1]

In order to exist, the state or society must be organized, set up in ranks according to the value of the parts. Here the coercive power of the state may become necessary, especially where there are separate and perhaps inimical systems of value which must be consolidated. But within each sphere, the right of leadership, of domination should belong to the best fitted: "The best form of the state is that which brings the best to dominate. The shoemaker should dominate in the sphere of shoe-making; the teacher, in education; the general, in warfare; the king and his councilors in the sphere of the political whole."[2]

In the new state, which Spann sees as the successor of democracy, there will be group organization, based on the following principles:

1. Organic inequality of the parts.

2. Hierarchization of the parts according to their different values.

3. A recognition that the parts of society consist of people in association, not of autonomous individuals.[3]

---
[1] Spann, *op. cit.*, p. 93.
[2] *Ibid.*, p. 163.
[3] *Ibid.*, pp. 151–152.

THE NEW DESPOTISM

This excursus into the theory of leadership by a professor of political economy and sociology once allied with German Naziism is indicative of the nature of Nazi thought on the subject. It appears *pari passu* in a criticism of liberalism and democracy, as a challenge to the position that democracy finds the best leaders since it has the widest field of choice. Its conclusion is that the qualities that get one chosen by the masses are not necessarily those which make one a good leader after the choice is made.

Democracy, majority rule, and parliamentary government are found to be inadequate to the purposes of a nation—since they emphasize unintelligence and cowardice. The large mass of workers, said Hitler, want nothing but bread and play. They have no understanding of any ideals, and we cannot reckon on winning the workers in any large groups. We choose a selection of the new ruling class which is not driven by any sympathetic motive, but which is clearly possessed of the right to rule because of its better race and which will maintain and secure this leadership over the masses regardless of anything.

In more recent formulations of aristocracy, the doctrine is involved with a general theory of the nature of the state, running back to the older theories of the "organic state."[1] The *völkische Führerstaat*, of Nazi Germany, is based upon the double principle of the *völkisch* state and the leadership principle.[2] The "cultural" or "organic" state has as its head, not as its representative or agent, the leader, through whom the life and being of the state are perfected and expressed. This corresponds closely to the old doctrine of the King as the chief organ of the Organic State—not its agent,

[1] See F. W. Coker, *Organismic Theories of the State* (1910) for full discussion of these ideas; see also his *Recent Political Thought* (1934).

[2] *Völkisch* is an untranslatable word which is not precise in meaning, but has cultural and "racial" connotations.

but its chief organ. The Leader thus escapes responsibility to the state, while being an essential part of it. This is conceived to be a "vital" relationship as distinguished from a purely "formal" relationship of the democratic type, or even a "functional" relationship.[1]

The postwar system of aristocracy has attempted to develop a body of principles and practices differing from the conventional arguments for the domination of the Few over the Many. The historic basis of this is found in dislike of communism and socialism, in the distrust of "democratic capitalism," in the strong desire for wider national self-expression. National socialism utilizes the symbols of national collectivism based upon ethno-territorial grounds (*Blut und Boden*) rather than economic collectivism.

[1] See for example Ernst R. Huber, *Wesen und Inhalt der politischen Verfassung*, pp. 84*ff.*; *Verfassung*, Part III; Hitler, *op. cit.*, pp. 116–117 and *passim;* Mankiewicz, *op. cit.*, pp. 110*ff;* very fully discussed in Aurel Kolnai, *The War Against the West;* important comment in Fulton and Morris, *In Defence of Democracy* (1935), Chap. VII.

C. THE THEORY OF THE NEW DESPOTISM

> I can add colours to the cameleon,
> Change shapes with Proteus for advantages;
> And set the murderous Machiavel to school.
> Can I do this, and cannot get a crown?
> —*Henry VI.*

The new doctrine of the new despotism involves the wholesale repudiation of many of the accepted democratic ideas. The new autocracy disavows the theory of political liberty and its guaranties whether procedural or otherwise, the theory of political equality, the doctrine of government by the consent of the governed, the doctrine of determination of general policy through representative discussion. It proclaims the unrestricted absolutism of the state over all the ways of life and decrees the concentration of all authority in one individual autocrat. It announces the general doctrine of the superiority of force internally and externally, repudiating the rights of individuals and the sanctity of treaties alike—autocracy within and autarchy without. Finally, it emphasizes faith in the ethnic or tribal urge in place of reason and intelligence in social affairs.

These doctrines are to be taken together as a system of ideology and a way of life, which is calculated to enhance the welfare of nations, and incidentally that of their nationals. Hegel, Nietzsche, Sorel, Pareto, Spengler are the historic figures in the field of theory whose doctrines have been woven by Hitler and Mussolini and their courts into this latest web. The proponents of these ideas may perhaps allege that their patterns are those of action rather than of reflection, of will and force rather than of inquiry and deliberation. But there have been men of action before this time who have taken their ideas unconsciously from others; and these are the progenitors of the modern Autocrats and their system of neo-despotism. The background of these doctrines has already been sketched in the foregoing pages.

Political liberty and political equality are rejected, and with them the guaranties in the form of civil liberties historically developed and of voting participation in the process of choice of representatives. The liberty of the individual is swallowed up in the liberty of the nation of which he is a part and through which he must function. His highest and truest liberty is action as an element of the nation. Liberty is a chimera of democracy, never attained in practice and never attainable among men. Men are happiest when they outlaw liberty from their lives and join in the chorus of the state. Nor are exceptions noted in favor of economic liberty, or of religious liberty, or of cultural liberty; for all are subject to the same general principle of sublimation in the state.

Appropriate are the words of Shakespeare who might be nominated as a Jurist of the New Order: "Such joy I never saw before [said the third Gentleman in Henry VIII]. . . .

"No man living could say, 'This is my wife,' there; all were woven so strangely in one piece."

There remains of course the liberty of the nation, of Germany or of Italy, which is absolute and unassailable. All other nations are also free, unless of course they impinge upon the liberties of the aforesaid states.

Political equality is disposed of in an equally summary fashion by the new Autocracy, by lines of reasoning already described in the preceding pages. The equality of men is a myth without reality now or ever—or ever to be. Equalitarianism is a lie of democracy, operated to please the fancy of the many, but designed to thwart their good. The truth is that men are unequal—races also are unequal. Inequality is not the root of injustice but the sound basis of political association and order.

On the rock of inequality, a sound and enduring structure of association may be built. Leadership may be recognized and the worship of leadership established definitely and securely. The few natural leaders will assume their natural authority and firmly administer the affairs of the commonwealth without disturbance from the jostling many. Each master and man will find his appointed place, and with due deference and humility fulfill his appointed functions in the service of the nation. The confusion and loss caused by the struggle for equality will disappear, and the body politic benefit *pro tanto*. The philosophy of superiority will prove the solvent for many of the evils that democracy has found beyond its power to cure.

The selection of these leaders will lead straight up to the highest point in the Fuehrer or Duce himself. And each higher leader will appoint the next lower leader in accordance with the true principles of leadership as interpreted by the leaders themselves.[1]

Representative and responsible government is likewise repudiated. Representative bodies are retained, but for purposes of showmanship rather than statesmanship.

> By its denial of the authority of the individual and its substitution of the mass present at any given time, the parliamentary principle of the consent of the majority sins against the basic aristocratic principle in nature. . . . [2]
>
> That contrivance [parliament] can be desirable and valuable only for the most mendacious sneaking creature who avoids the light of day, while it must be hateful to every honorable straight fellow who is prepared to take personal responsibility. Hence this type of democracy has become the

---

[1] See Adolf Hitler, *Mein Kampf*, on the mass as primarily influenced by will and power. "What it wishes is the conquest of the stronger and the annihilation of the weaker, or its unconditional submission." P. 469, see also p. 669, and *passim*.

[2] *Ibid.*, p. 103.

instrument of that race which in order to forward its own aims has to avoid the sunlight now and in all future time. Only the Jew can praise an institution which is as dirty and false as he is himself.[1]

The "true Germanic democracy" provides for the Leader who assumes entire responsibility for acts of state, in place of the principle of the dignity of the majority.[1]

The military model of this type of association is indicated clearly in referring to "the principle which made the Prussian army the most wonderful instrument of the German people . . . the basic principle of the building of our state constitution—the authority of every leader over those below and the responsibility towards those above."[2]

Further the modern anti-democratic theorists assert a superior insight into the nature of political organization. They profess to have a more efficient organization of centralized authority.[3]

The totalitarian-authoritarian state involves the assumptions of (1) the omnicompetence of the state, and (2) the importance of concentration of power in authoritarian form.

The totalitarian doctrine is built (1) partly upon the older doctrines of the sixteenth-century absolutism and legal irresistibility of the state, and (2) partly upon the doctrine of the German philosopher Hegel who sanctified the state and eulogized it as the highest expression of human idealism.

Not only is it asserted that the king can do no wrong but that he must make everything right. This doctrine is aimed at the democratic state which it is held allowed private

---

[1] *Ibid.*, p. 116.
[2] *Ibid.*, p. 670.
[3] For discussions of the leadership principle and the role of the party, see Ernst R. Huber, *Verfassung* (1937), Chaps. III, IV; *Wesen und Inhalt der politischen Verfassung* (1935), pp. 81–84; Otto Koellreuter, *Deutsches Verfassungsrecht* (1935), Parts VI, VII; Ernst Krieck, *National politische Erziehung* (1933), pp. 81*ff.*; Carl Schmitt, *Staat, Bewegung, Volk* (1935); Grete Stoffel, *La dictature du fascisme allemand* (1936), Chaps. I and III.

organizations to overshadow the state, as parties, churches, labor unions, business associations, cultural groups. These groups have so far weakened the unity of the state that the political association is no longer capable of performing its proper functions.

This is true not merely in crises but in all the ways of life. Thus the theory that might more commonly be invoked as a rationalization of a passing period or process of closer social integration is elevated to the dignity of a universal philosophy.[1]

These wide-sweeping powers of the state are to be concentrated in a single-headed executive in whom the totalitarian powers are vested. The Reichstag remains formally but not for purposes of discussion, but of ratification. Likewise a party and a voting system remain, but under restrictions that deprive them of responsibility. The head of the state is the old-time despot ruling without legal limitations upon his authority, either in civil or in military affairs. This despotism is not founded upon the ownership of land, upon hereditary descent, or divine sanction, but upon the assumed trusteeship of the nation, vested in himself by his own decree.

The theory is not that of dictatorship, since the ruler is in no sense a temporary figure as were the dictators, but permanent head of the state, after the fashion of the historic autocracies, or despotisms. Neither in Germany nor in Italy is the autocrat termed a dictator, but Duce in one case and Fuehrer in the other.

The general theory of "leadership" rests in first instance upon the alleged necessity of unified centralization of author-

[1] Even the Kantian distinction between the realm of politics and the realm of ethics—between the kingdom of internal motives and the kingdom of external conduct is forgotten in this doctrine. See John Dewey's analysis of *German Philosophy and Politics* (1915). Interesting comment is given by Adolf Löwe in his *The Price of Liberty*, Day to Day Pamphlets (1937), No. 36.

THE NEW DEMOCRACY

ity in one point. It relies further, however, upon a theory of political inequality, in many ways like the old system of feudalism.

The consent of the governed is eliminated as an undesirable and unworkable element in political organization, and the irresponsibility of the rulers is substituted as a principle of association.

The essential principle of the new autocracy is then the irresponsibility of the governor to the governed. He is their interpreter but not their representative. He promotes their interests but not in accordance with their mandate or their power of review.

The democratic doctrine of the value of mass judgment is repudiated flatly and the countercontention is made that the mass is incapable of understanding their own interests, of choosing agents to act for them, or of reviewing the acts of their leaders. Further, it is held that the masses are not interested in control over their leaders, but are content to follow. The one-time voters are no longer troubled with the making of decisions regarding personnel or policies but pass over the task of political decision to their superiors, or the One Superior—at once legally omnipotent, morally unassailable, and politically irresponsible. (Paradoxically, however, they still vote.)

Thus liberty, equality, representation, and responsibility are at one stroke wiped out. Justice[1] and order will be interpreted by the leaders as the ultimate molders of the national interest and destiny. But they are in no sense responsible to those in whose interest they act, theoretically. The relation of ruler to ruled is that of freedom from judgment by those of inferior rank. What the nation needs, it is maintained, is Interpretation by the Few and not representation by the

---

[1] Del Vecchio elaborates the new theory of justice in modified Hegelian fashion, *Saggi intorno allo stato* (1935), pp. 149–170.

mass—the leader principle rather than the "consent of the governed."

It may always be asked, How do the leaders come to be leaders? Whatever the answer may be finally, the answer now is, They are.

A formal instrument for the maintenance of continuity of leaders has been developed in the form of the one-party system in Italy, Germany, and Soviet Russia.[1] In Italy, Mussolini declares that the Fascist Party is the Nation, and similar comment has been made by Hitler in Germany. Taking the terminology of the democracy they despise, these groups have set up a so-called "party system," consisting of one party only. In this are presumptively contained the elements of the aristocracy in political control. Once the elite are established in this form, they may continue to add and subtract members, maintain a continuity in eliteship, select or approve the higher command from time to time, and to perform such other duties as may appropriately be discharged by an aristocracy.

Some light might be thrown on the identifying marks of the elite by an examination of the characteristics of those chosen for the Nazi party, the Fascist party, the Communist party in their respective spheres of action.

These parties may determine the qualifications for admission, promote, demote, discipline, and expel their members; may determine the general policies of the party and inferentially of the nation. The Fascist party may even change the line of monarchical succession in Italy and may select the successor of the Duce. Such a party might be broadened out until it reached a point where it included the bulk of all of the adult community, in which case the system would approach democracy again. Or it might be narrowed down until the numbers were closely restricted. The terms and

[1] See Hans Kelsen, "The Party Dictatorship," *Politica*, 1932, 2: 19–32.

conditions of entrance and expulsion are of very great importance at this point, and careful analysis of these criteria might reveal much regarding the significant elements of a particular elite, aside from the requirements of belief and loyalty to the special cause in question.

But on the whole, these tests do not reveal much regarding the qualities of the elite. The requirements seem to be in the main

1. Belief in the doctrines of the group.
2. Loyalty to its leaders.
3. Absence of negative demerits indicating unfitness for any group service, such as excessive dissipation or disorderliness.
4. Positive qualities of a type useful in any group.

But these qualities do not seem to differentiate the elite from any other group of a social nature such as a union, a lodge, a church. They would not separate Nazis from trade-unionists or Fascists from Masons. They point only to capacity for membership in any working organization— except for the element of special belief and particular allegiance.

Of special interest in this connection are the leadership-training schools of Nazi Germany which have been set up in recognition of the problem of the perpetuation of party rule. The function of these *Führerschulen* is to serve as a continuous selective mechanism for those "best fitted" for political and administrative leadership in the party, the state, and the subsidiary organizations. The basis of this system of selection is some thirty projected provincial schools, called *Adolf-Hitler Schulen*. Ten of these have been constructed already, according to German sources. The District Leader (*Gauleiter*) of the party has the responsibility of selecting a determined quota of candidates of the age of twelve years. "The standard of admission is proof of service

THE NEW DESPOTISM

in the 'Jungvolk' of an outstanding, 'leader nature' (Führernatur) character, along with requirements of race and health. . . . "[1] The schools are supported entirely by the party, even to the extent of giving the students pocket money. In these preparatory schools the candidate is given a full-length preparatory education with special emphasis upon sport and Nazi race and political ideology.

Leaving these schools at the age of eighteen, the candidates are free to go out into the world for a period of seven years to join the party as adult members, perform their labor service and military training, learn a trade or profession, or study at a university. At the close of seven years one thousand of a projected total of some four thousand are to be chosen by the party from among those who wish to continue the training, for entrance into the "Castles of the Order" (*Ordensburgen*). There will be four of these castles.

No new principle of leadership education is introduced in this complicated system of recruitment. The inculcation of a body of dogma as a means of perpetuating a loyal leadership was explicitly used by the Jesuits. The great emphasis upon physical strength, endurance, and the type of character referred to by Ley is as old as Sparta. These prospective Nazi leaders are avowedly not trained for thinking, but for action. The assumption of the system is that the truths have all been given. Ley recognizes that this type of training is not schooling.[2]

The molding of popular opinion and the formation of popular consent are possible through the agencies of propa-

---

[1] *National Zeitung* (Essen), Jan. 30, 1938, Special Supplement, p. 3.

[2] "If I use the word school and schooling here, I know that this is the wrong term; for what we want is not schooling in the actual sense. He who is not predestined, he who does not bring with him the inner experience, cannot teach this world, and also can never learn it. Our doctrine is a matter of faith; here the instinct of blood must speak. You must feel and know that our Race doctrine is correct, that our culture in Germany is the product of our blood, and our race." Robert Ley, *Der Weg zur Ordensburg* (1936).

ganda, press, radio, and school, within certain limits. The avoidance of any right of participation or of any formal mode of expression of consent or dissent rests, however, fundamentally upon a fear of failure and the counter use of fear as a means of inducing what cannot voluntarily be obtained. Force steps in at this point to supplement the apparatus of consent without consent, of manipulated allegiance and agreement. Leadership thus becomes "irresponsible responsibility." The top leader is chosen by himself by force or by whatever mode of survival may be indicated in the given situation. This is to be sure a dangerous logic of power. Since only force is valid, it invites the use of force against force. This involves the difficult assumption that although force is legitimate in order to obtain authority, for let us say X, once X is in authority the use of force against him becomes unlawful—by what law, it might of course be asked.

The long-time test of such so-called "leadership" is whether it can survive the absence of the Terror, and the presence of free discussion and free association. Or whether under such circumstances the idol of leadership is seen to have feet of clay.

Various forms of representation are retained, and some types of voting even. Thus the Reichstag is not yet dissolved in Germany, or the Senate and Corporative Council in Italy; while the party councils continue in full activity. Yet the formal legislative bodies are not for the purpose of discussion, but of ratification; and the party councils may discuss but not decide. In any case their recommendations are subject to the supervision and rejection of the Autocrat in authority.

The general theory upon which such organization rests is that of lack of confidence in the competence of the community to choose representatives adequate to express its interests. The alleged proofs are deduced from the acts of contemporary legislative bodies who are found to be ignorant, corrupt, dilatory in their behavior. In Italy argument is made in behalf of the occupational organization of representation through the various corporatives, but it is not conceded that these agencies should possess any genuine legislative power independent of the will of the head of the state.

Voting is also retained, but freedom of discussion is not permitted, or freedom of association. The whole polling process goes on under the shadow of intimidation, direct or indirect, with the Terror not far in the background. Voting is not merely possible at times, but obligatory or at least salutary—a form of insurance which apparently costs nothing. One is reminded of voting under the Second Empire in France, which was termed the "*plébiscite pour le rétablissement de l'opinion.*"

Thus Interpretation and Intimidation take the place of Representation. The consent of the governed is obtained by force if necessary.

The Communist doctrine is also autocratic with variations. In the basic assumptions of its dogma, communism is anti-Christian, anti-capitalistic, and indeed anti-political.

There are really three phases of this doctrine:

1. In Soviet theory the ultimate goal of communism is the complete annihilation of any form of political association. The state is conceived as an instrument of capitalism designed and maintained for the purpose of class exploitation. It is held that when the one-class proletarian society is established, the state will wither away.

2. In the meantime, the Soviet form of political association is dictatorial and aristocratic in organization and action. Ultimate power is centered in the dictator and the working power in the Communist Party with now some two million

members. There are, however, many elective consultative agencies.[1]

3. But there is also another stage between 2 and 1 in which there may be a form of "proletarian democracy" of the type outlined in the new Russian constitution.

In theory the main factor in human life is the "economic," which is regarded as the ultimately determining element in institutions and ideologies (except economic determinism itself, which is a doctrine otherwise derived).

In this economic theory, emphasis is placed upon a type of equalitarianism which is to be achieved through the collective ownership of the instruments of production. This is held to be, however, not a "bourgeois" form of equality, but a "comradeship" based upon social justice and possible and effective through the economic institutions of communism.

The Soviets do not deny individual differences in capacity and differential wage scales and status, but repudiate the differential status acquired by any of the processes of profit making under the capitalistic system.

The more general assumptions of the democratic theory are not denied by the Soviets, who now speak of a proletarian democracy, but it is contended that democratic ends are unattainable in a capitalistic society. Furthermore, the means of arriving at these ends are radically different. Major decisions are not reached by the free consent of the bulk of the community in open elections, but by controlled electoral processes from which freedom of speech and assembly are excluded when signs of effective opposition are evident or suspected.

[1] Sidney Webb and Beatrice Webb, *Soviet Communism* (1936), Vol. I, Chap. II and *passim*; Sir. E. D. Simon, Lady Simon, W. A. Robson, and J. Jewkes, *Moscow in the Making* (1937), Chaps. I, VIII, IX, X; Samuel N. Harper, *The Government of the Soviet Union* (1938), Chaps. V, VI, VII; Albert Rhys Williams, *The Soviets* (1937), Part I; Bertram W. Maxwell, *The Soviet State* (1934), Chaps. III, IV, VI.

THE NEW DESPOTISM

The possibility of conscious control of social processes is accepted and emphasized, but not the assumption that important and fundamental changes are normally made by peaceful methods.

Government by the Few, then, headed by a Dictator is the accepted mode of organization and process of action, with ultimate elimination of government as the final goal and possible widening of the scope of democratic consent as an intermediate stage.

In general the new autocracy places strong emphasis upon the role of force in political affairs. Within the state, force is to take the place of consent as a factor in decision; and externally force is to take the place of the international jural world order advocated by the democratic theorists.

Autocracy and autarchy are made to go arm in arm—despotism within and isolation without. The Terror within and War without. In either case the "softness and persuasiveness" of the democratic process is to be avoided and the sterner rule of violence substituted.

In any event action is better than thought, it is held, and decision is superior to deliberation. Impatience and autocracy are happy companions. They make possible swift, stern, and ruthless decisions which promote the welfare of those whom it may concern, it is said. "We think with our blood," runs one formulation of the new doctrine of activist autocracy.

Obviously this does not mean that there is no room for reflection in the new despotic regimes, but that reflection on the acts of the governors by the governed is unnecessary, and superfluous—and even dangerous. There are many well-trained and competent minds in Germany and Italy, but their thinking must not stray beyond the bounds set for them by those who arrived at the Final Decisions as checked

THE NEW DEMOCRACY

by the Secret Police. If we ask, By what process are these Final Decisions reached by the Few? the answer is vague; even more the question is irreverent and unhygienic perhaps. "Creative Skeptics" are not needed in the moments when the Great Decisions are being made by those who are entitled to make them in their own right as determined by their own personally made Law. The King could do no wrong, and the modern Autocrats can do no wrong—by definition—because they are the Law.

D. ANALYSIS OF THE DOCTRINES OF THE NEW DESPOTISM

We may now examine more closely the political theories indicated above. And first a word as to terminology. "Dictatorship" in its historic sense was merely a temporary device to meet an emergency, and was employed by the Roman democracy for this purpose.[1] The word tyranny, or despotism, or autocracy would commonly be applied to what is termed dictatorship.

A "one-party" system is a twisting of the whole idea of a party system, which requires more than one party (in order to make its operation). One party without another party is no party at all. One party with a "monopoly of legality" and without freedom of counterassociation and discussion is a political institution that deserves another name.

Likewise voting and plebiscites without freedom of discussion are pseudo-votes and pseudo-plebiscites. They are not freedom of consent but the control of consent.

The terms ordinarily employed would not be "dictatorship," "party system," "plebiscites," but despotism, repression of freedom of association, discussion, and expression. This phase of the new doctrine may be regarded as lip service to the theory of democracy, but in fact repudiation of its assumptions and institutions.

National Socialism, breathing fire and slaughter against socialism, is likewise an interesting example of verbal twisting. It might be termed anti-socialistic socialism.

[1] See Carl Schmitt, *Die Diktatur* (1928), pp. 1–6; Ralph H. Lutz, "European Dictatorships," in *Dictatorship in the Modern World* (Guy Stanton Ford, editor, 1935), Chap. II; H. R. Spencer, "Dictatorship," in *Encyclopedia of the Social Sciences*.

THE NEW DEMOCRACY

This twisted use of terms extends even to the use of the word "democracy," which is still retained, surprising as it may seem in view of the bitter denunciation of the ways and works of democratic political association in general.

Thus Hitler defends the "Germanic democracy," as the true democracy, against the impure forms of contemporary states.[1] The autocratic system is the true democracy in this type of reasoning.

In sum, an analysis of the new doctrines shows that though they have eliminated some of the older features of despotism, and have borrowed some of the features of the democratic system, they are essentially the old-time autocracies dressed up in modern garb.

The ancient hereditary factors in government have been abandoned largely in the new despotisms, although the orders of nobility have not been destroyed. In Italy the King remains, and in other states the old aristocracy continues. The supremacy of the military, sometimes but not always seen in the older forms of despotism, has been denied, and an effort is made to utilize military force without submitting to its control.

The development of nationalism, which was in the nineteenth century the task of the liberal democratic movement, has been recognized and accepted as a guiding principle, but has been exaggerated so far as to set up a nation that draws in all human values and makes them its own. This is a throwback to the doctrines of Thomas Hobbes, who supplied all the necessary material for totalitarianism and authoritarianism. From another point of view, the new supernationalism is a type of recurrence to tribalism in its opposition to international order and in its rivalry of the claims of religion.

---

[1] Adolf Hitler, *Mein Kampf*, pp. 116–117.

THE NEW DESPOTISM

The effort to construct a sounder type of national central control is modern in direction, but antiquated in method. It aims at a tighter and more effective ordering of the nation's forces, but is awkward in finding a way. The principle of "authority" invoked—the supremacy of the state—is only the old doctrine of sovereignty which has been the common property of the Western world for three hundred years. English writers since John Austin have described the omnipotence of Parliament with great clearness. But the British never concluded that because Parliament might legally do *anything*, it should actually proceed to do *everything;* or that the citizen should be deprived of the legal and moral right of passing judgment upon the sovereign. An act of Parliament, said Dicey, providing that all blue-eyed babies should be put to death is the law; but this is modified by what Bagehot called the spirit of "illogical moderation." The new autocratic theory takes the doctrine of supremacy, but wipes out the attitude of "moderation." Instead there is *Gleichschaltung*, or the general assimilation or incorporation of social activities in the political.

Democratic elements reappear in different form under the new regime. Thus, the democratic institution of representation and discussion has been ridiculed as a device for mere "talk"—legislative bodies are mere "talking societies." This is not to say, however, that there is now no "talk," in despotisms, but there is no back talk. Shouters take the place of "talkers," and shouting is spread through the air by the use of modern mechanical devices. There are still conferences and statesmen's headaches, but they are private rather than public, and are unreported. The press remains free—only to say what it is told to say.

The device of voting is continued as in democracy, and great pride is taken in favorable votes up to 99 per cent. It would, of course, be easy to make the 99 per cent favorable vote 125 per cent. Indeed, I am uncertain whether this is moderation or due to the poverty of autocratic imagination. Since the voting is controlled by Terror in the background, it can be characterized only as pseudo-voting. In time the control may be relaxed, but thus far this relaxation has not developed. Yet if nothing is ever to be decided, it will be difficult in the long run to get men to vote, except as a part of a parade from which it is important not to be found A.W.O.L. by the secret police.

The party system which was roundly denounced as one of the central asininities of democracy has not been wholly cast out—in form at least. A pseudo-party system has been set up, with a "monopoly of legality." That a group of retainers of the group in power should be called a "party" when all opposition is unlawful and perilous is to be sure an ironical jest. But the explanation is found in the desire to retain some of the features of the democratic system in name at least. Voting and parties are the emblems of the government by consent of the governed and are retained in order that the fact of non-consent may be partly covered over by the gloss of procedural imitations.

The consent of the governed in institutional form is abandoned as unimportant and unnecessary. It is maintained that the "interpretation" of what the community ought to endorse is better seen and stated by those who are irresponsible to the people of the nation. Yet the faithful steward welcomes an accounting, whereas the unfaithful fears and shuns it. The desire for irresponsibility is related to the fear that a review would be not merely troublesome but might be unfavorable. Being weighed in the balance involves the possibility of being found wanting.

Organized propaganda is a substitute for general discussion, and this is supplemented by intimidation and by the Terror.

THE NEW DESPOTISM

A new form of the balance of power appears. The new forces are
1. The Party
2. The Army
3. The Administration
4. The Secret Police

with the Leader as the hierarchical head.

In Italy the Corporatives play a still somewhat undefined role.[1]

Thus far no substantial organizational contribution has been made in the despotic states. Consultation between a Ruler, a General, a Bureaucrat, and a Party Leader offers nothing new to the student of organization. Even the propagandists offer nothing startling to a world of advertising and public relations, except the unusual privilege of bearing the sword in one hand and the microphone in the other—a new means of breaking down sales resistance.

The Reichstag and the voters still remain, curiously enough, but they do not debate or decide questions of national interest. They are told. It is, of course, true that they may one time be restored and revived, and become active factors in the determination of community affairs. The consultative functions and the voting functions are durable factors in the political constitution of modern times and will find their place again. Only in the voters will the *chef d'état* find a counterbalance in the long run against the engrossing tendencies of the military group, or the heads of other groups as they arise.

[1] G. Lowell Field, *The Syndical and Corporative Institutions of Italian Fascism* (1938); William Elwin, *Fascism at Work* (1934); Chap. VI; Gaetano Salvemini, *Under the Axe of Fascism* (1936), Part I; Herbert W. Schneider, *Making the Fascist State* (1928), Chap. IV, Appendix, Part IV. See also Oreste Ranelletti, *Elementi di Diritto pubblico italiano* (1933); Virgilio Feroci, *Elementi di Diritto pubblico italiano* (1935); Sergio Panunzio, *Il sentimento dello stato* (1931); Francesco Carnelutti, *Lezioni di diritto industriale* (1927); H. Arthur Steiner, *Government in Fascist Italy* (1938).

THE NEW DEMOCRACY

The military are still involved in endless struggles with the party and the secret police, and the constant trend toward infiltration and control of the army. The party as a whole must struggle with the party bureaucracy which strives to dominate it, and with incessantly uprising cliques within the inner circles of authority. All this would be immensely complicated by actual warfare from which great generals returned to celebrate their triumphs for endless days.

The modern despots speak the language of force and war, but in reality this may be their undoing. Victory and defeat are equally dangerous to them. In the old phrase, "The evening of victory is more dangerous than its dawn"—for despots who are not soldiers.

The science of management has little to learn thus far from the modern despotic authorities. The main problems of government in the larger sense are typically solved by ignoring them at inconvenient points, as in the improvement of practical methods for dealing with the balance between liberty and authority, between the organization of force and that of consent, of the balance of national and international order.

It is often forgotten that the maximum amount of desirable concentration of power is not determined by the form of organization alone or chiefly, but by the tension of the time, by the severity of the crisis in the life of the particular state. Lincoln and Wilson, Lloyd George and Clemenceau in war, Roosevelt in peace held wide power, returnable to the voters.

Pestilence, war, famine, flood, panic, depression—these are crisis moments when decisionism is concentrated in the hands of one or a few who may act before it is too late. In a democracy this power is returned when the crisis is over; but in a despotism it must go on, even after any immediate occasion has gone by. Dictators return their power when the need for it is over, but Despots must still wave the sword when they should be cultivating with the plow.

The balance between despotism and democracy is wholly in favor of despotism in the new regimes. Democratic institutions are either suspended altogether or are maintained in pseudo form, as in the case of pseudo parties, pseudo voting, and unilateral discussion. In the juristic sense the totalitarian theory is not new, but in its practical application it harks back to the naked despotism of the earlier days, when the king was the state and a divinely ordained creature. But whereas in the days of the Bourbons, politics was said to be second religion, in this system, politics is a first religion perhaps. How far this spree of sovereignty may last beyond the period of national reassertion internationally is, of course, an open question to which no answer can be given.

From one point of view the whole program of assaults upon intelligence and persuasion in common affairs, the glorification of force, the abandonment of human liberty and equality, the slavish worship of the state, the despotic organization of power may be looked upon as an attack upon the whole Greco-Roman Western philosophy of life, not merely anti-Jewish but anti-Christian as well. The Greek regard for intelligence, the Roman regard for law and contract, the Christian respect for human personality, the medieval-feudal regard for the consent of the governed, even the absolutist entente between the altar and the throne —all these seem to be swallowed up in a doctrine of the superman and a gospel of power. Christianity, said Nietzsche, with its gospel of the lowly lowers, its slave morality, its repudiation of the superman is the weak spot in our civilization. All this was made explicit in the savage assaults of Spengler on the whole structure and texture of Western civilization. All this is inextricably interwoven in the present-day theories of autocracy and the national drive for expansion

THE NEW DEMOCRACY

and glory through the organization of violence and conquest.

The new Autocrats promise a sounder system of social and economic order on the one hand and on the other a sounder system of international relations. Thus far this has not appeared. In the task that lies before us of reconstructing sections of the social-economic order that have been outgrown, cooperation and consent are of greater importance than arbitrary decision and violence. Psychiatry will be more effective than surgery. The mass industrial organization of our times will require mass cooperation for its successful operation rather than decisions handed down from above, and if resisted, re-enforced by the Terror. The organization of violence and the chicanery of propaganda will be found inferior at this point to the organization of consent and the processes of discussion and persuasion.

Externally a sounder system of international relations is modern in tendency, but to assume that this reorganization will be brought about by force of individual states places a heavy strain upon the imagination, unless we assume that one nation triumphs over all the others, or that several groups swallow up the others. But unless one alone emerges, there is no peace until some form of jural order is constructed. If any one is strong enough, he may end the anarchy of nations by the stern rule of his law; but otherwise we arrive at nothing but international chaos, with its inevitable effect upon local organization and process. Higher standards of human living will emerge more steadily from peaceful industry than from war.

Will and force are important factors in human organization and association; but they are not the only elements in our composition; nor are they the most significant in the long run. Organized force itself rests not upon a theory of violence as such but upon a form of idealistic devotion and

THE NEW DESPOTISM

indeed of personal abnegation and sacrifice. It is, of course, theoretically possible to substitute nationalism for religion and to set up the tribal worship of the state. But there are values transcending national values in the human scheme of things, and there is no reason to believe that they will melt away. On the contrary as the world shrinks in size through better modes of intercommunication, the prospect for cultural values beyond the autarchy becomes stronger and stronger. The prospects are for larger jural units and for wider ranges of cultural relationships throughout the world.

Likewise, in the reconstruction of the internal life of the nation, force and will are not the only builders of the future, or the most important. The spirit of cooperation, of consent, of persuasion, and guidance are of far profounder meaning in the long run. The economy of abundance was not brought about by the sword, but by science, technology, the machine. The weapons of force are the products of reason. Intelligence as well as will was active in the modern process and consent more than violence.

Indeed an observer familiar with German and Italian backgrounds may well inquire how much of this new doctrine is mere tawdry façade and how much of it is a substantial part of the present reconstruction. A pessimist may say, This is a revolutionary movement the implications of which involve the overthrow of Western political-economic culture and the rise of a new form of political-social structure, profoundly altering our economic, our political, and our religious life.

What will happen then when this tide meets the rushing westward movement of the Orient sweeping forward toward world dominion?

On the other hand, it may be said that when once the immediate urge of the crisis has passed, it is possible to forecast the recurrence of rational discussion and analysis of common affairs, of the role of popular participation in government, of institutions of responsibility in place of personal interpretation of the commonweal.

The present movement is an outcome of an international situation in which there is no authentic jural order, and an internal situation in which technology has not made its peace with the economic and political life of commonwealths. Given a solution of these problems, the pagan protest against Western civilization might recede and disappear, and what remains of our Despotism would be a weary bureaucracy struggling to hold its outworn personal position against the rising demand of the many for a voice in their common affairs. The millions now silent will find their voice again. Their status is not that of abdication, but of frustration for the time. One day they will rise again and resume their throne.

There is always room for retreat from Autocracy through the vitalizing of the ballot by the removal of intimidation; through the recognition of representative bodies, beginning perhaps with the localities; through the expansion of party membership to include a far larger percentage of the population; and by the relaxation of the over-all brooding Terror.

But personal despotisms find it difficult to retreat—more difficult than democracies. The despot's retreat may mean his death; but the people are immortal. All the more difficult is the way of retreat for despots who have repudiated the ways of rational discussion, the forms of conference and compromise, the procedures and participations which are the guaranties of liberty, order, and justice.

Part III

CONCLUSIONS

A. GENERAL CONSIDERATIONS

Whatever the type and form of the state, a great and increasing body of governmental relations is likely to be handled by some highly competent technical administration, dealing with the immensely complicated scientific aspects of social relationships, constantly growing more and more complex with the more intimate understanding of man and nature. Organized social intelligence holds the key to much of the government of the future.[1] Such an intelligence and administration will be at the disposal of any form of rule on the level of the civilized states of the world.

One of the causes of frequent confusion in the consideration of the respective roles of the Few and the Many is the failure to distinguish between the

1. Division of labor in government.
2. Ultimate decision and responsibility in questions of social and political policy.

In the division of social labor it is obvious that the personnel of government is always relatively small except in collectivized states. This may be, however, a matter of social convenience rather than a recognition of special superiority on the part of those governing. The doctor, the lawyer, the engineer in the service of the state may be in no way superior to the doctor, the lawyer, the engineer in private service—may, indeed, be inferior. He may be the convenient instrument of the political authority of the community. He does not really rule, but administers the policies of the commonwealth. Many others might do as well as he or better, and there is constant change in the administrative service.

[1] See my *New Aspects of Politics*, Chaps. VI and VIII.

THE NEW DEMOCRACY

In the field of political leadership, the numbers are relatively few and the rotation is more rapid and pronounced, following the shifts in the attitudes of the nation. Here more fundamental decisions are reached on broad questions of policy, and the extent and mode of responsibility to the community are in question.

Another source of unclear thinking is the assumption that all of the persons of unusual political capacity will be in the governing group at a given time. The distribution of talent does not work out this way. What happens is the presence of special capacity in a number of groups in the community—a distribution of ability. Even under an iron-clad caste system or the oldest and best established aristocracy, the superior arise in every area and on every level—in every group within the wide family of power. There is never an alignment between all of the superior on the one side and all of the inferior on the other. The line is between some superior and some inferior on the one hand and some superior and some inferior on the other hand (on the assumption that political differentials are established). Races, religions, classes, sections, high, low, and middle contain leaders of conspicuous ability—and they help to interpret and organize the minorities against the majority, or one group against many groups, or some groups against some others.[1]

Furthermore, there is an ever-developing supply of leaders, available when occasion offers or demands. In a sense leaders are not leaders because they are widely different from everyone else, but because they are much like many others, and therefore, able to understand them, to hold their confidence, to act in their behalf with assurance that they will be supported by others.

[1] Hans Kelsen, *Der Staat als Integration* (1930); Jacob Wackernagel, *Der Wert des Staates* (1934); Rudolf Smend, *Verfassung und Verfassungsrecht* (1928).

CONCLUSIONS

What is sometimes pictured as the reign of the Superior, as over against the inferior who are governed, is a distorted view of what actually occurs in the development of political power relations.

All government involves forms of consent to common action, even for the preservation of morale, if nothing more.[1] In most modern political types of organization, it is conceded that government is a trustee, and in Western nations this relationship has been institutionalized. Political leaders draw much of their strength from their rapport with the mass of the community. In this sense governance is not a matter of the few but of the mass or the many; it involves a continuing and vital relationship between the few who are technically "governing" and the mass who are the basis of their authority—the condition of the effective exercise of power. In this sense government instead of being always the private affair of the few is the public affair of the many. Instead of being merely a form of specialization, governance is, in a sense, a form of generalization. It is true that there may be specialists in generalization. The issue between the Few and the Many has been the extent to which the Many—the basis of authority—shall participate in the making of ultimate decisions concerning the common welfare.

When it is said that political leaders really induce the mass to accept their own ideas—compel the community to believe or do what the leaders have decided—this may be taken with qualifications. For in many instances just the opposite is occurring, namely, that the leaders are endeavoring to find out what the community wants in order that they may proclaim this as the policy of the state. History is full

---

[1] See my *Political Power* (1934), Chap. VI, on "Poverty of Power"; W. H. R. Rivers, *Psychology and Politics* (1923), on leadership pp. 45, *et. seq.*; T. N. Whitehead, *Leadership in a Free Society* (1936).

THE NEW DEMOCRACY

of the competing claims of statesmen that they are the authentic interpreters—not the inventors—of the popular will. Aside from the role of occasional prophets and teachers or political giants of some other form, great decisions are not reached apart from mass, class, national, social, and economic movements of the special time and place. Hitler did not create German nationalism; nor Mussolini, Italian nationalism. Without undertaking to settle the position of the great man in history, it is clear that in modern times at least, with the rise of democratic, national, and class enthusiasms, political leaders are in large measure followers and interpreters rather than the inventors of the special formulas or forms they express. There is a movement from below up as well as from above down; a creative group movement thrusting upward and in a sense creating and crowning its leaders, as well as a creative inventive movement from the top down.

In the deepest and truest sense no government can ever safely be considered from the top alone, but must also be regarded from the bottom as well. The governing process is not exhausted by the command of a technical superior in a given system of order, but it must be completed by its reception and acceptance by those to whom it is directed. Authoritarians and legalists, in the narrow sense of the term, often consider only a part of the situation which they are interpreting, but students of political power in the more fundamental sense must look to power as a whole in its many-sided incidence and operation, from discussion to declaration, from declaration to administration.[1] Most of

---

[1] In recent times this has been observed by students of industrial management, who point out the significance of consent as well as command in industrial personnel management. See Ordway Tead, *The Art of Leadership* (1933), Chaps. XII and XV; *Human Nature and Management* (1933), Chaps. XII, XIII, XIV, XVII, XVIII; *Creative Management* (1935), pp. 17*ff*., and passim; Ordway Tead and Henry C. Metcalf, *Personnel Administration* (1933), pp. 193*ff*. and *passim*; L. Urwick, *Man-*

CONCLUSIONS

human action is not ordered; the web of behavior is far more complex; command is blended from consent.

When the ruler was believed to be divine, or to own the land and the people on it, or was able to silence opposition with the club, this was not always so clear; but in modern times with the rise of political consciousness throughout the community, the nature of the governmental process becomes clearer. The ruler-ruled relationship stands out more distinctly, and leadership and authority must be interpreted accordingly. Furthermore the political leaders may be the brokers of ideas coming from outside their own ranks—from idea-men of all sorts and types, from all conditions and classes. The initiators of policies may be and often are not in positions of responsibility, political or otherwise.

It is, of course, possible to combine the elements of aristocracy and democracy in a governmental system, and this is what has most commonly happened, even when one or other of these systems was nominally in complete command. "Mixed governments" have been advocated and established since the days of Aristotle, and probably before that. The books are full of hybrid systems occurring in many widely scattered times and places—of the compromises reached between Patricians and Plebeians, Roman and otherwise.[1]

The possibilities of compromise in organization are indefinite, and not yet exhausted. At the moment the widest range of possibility is in the area of responsibility of governor to governed and the ways and means of bringing this about under modern conditions. Italy, Germany, Russia offer interesting illustrations of the effort to set up the rule of the few as the interpreter of the many but without effective responsibility to the mass. This might be called the substitution of

---

agement of Tomorrow (1933), Part IV; Sam A. Lewisohn, *The New Leadership in Industry* (1926); Mary Parker Follet, "The Process of Control," in Gulick and Urwick, *Papers on the Science of Administration* (1937), pp. 164, 168.

[1] See S. de Madariaga, *Anarchie ou hiérarchie* (1936) for a recent proposal.

interpretation for representation. In the case of the Soviets, it is maintained that the dictatorship is temporarily bridging over a transitional era until a different form of economic order is established. But in Italy and Germany, the rule of the few is held forth as a permanent type of political organization, although not without some hesitation about abolishing voting and representation. Italy, Germany, and Russia alike retain the plausible name of "party" after removing everything but the bones of the party system as it has been historically developed.

An expert in government could devise innumerable forms of mixed governments in which aristocratic and democratic elements were brought together; and there is no reason to suppose that experiments of this general type may not continue almost indefinitely. The characteristics of the culture complex with which the expert may deal, the intensity of the community crisis, the state of education and science, the dominant value systems—these will furnish the material out of which varying forms of political association and understanding will continue to be woven.

The truth is that most of the present-day confusion is caused by the failure to distinguish between (1) general principles of association and (2) special situations arising from particular kinds of tension or crises in affairs. The disturbing problems of our day are

1. The relation of aggressive supernationalism to a jural order of the whole world.

2. The relation of early patterns and attitudes both of government and industry to the revolutionary changes brought about by modern science and technology.

Intellectual confusion, institutional distortion, and desolation of precious human values—all these are due in largest measure to the revolution wrought by intelligence in our time. Intelligence will find the way out also.

CONCLUSIONS

This set of problems has perplexed the minds of many, and the hesitation and floundering that follows is not caused by any particular form of government. Nor will it automatically be cured by any type of political association upon which we may confidently call.

These crises are a challenge to human intelligence in the social field, to the willingness of mankind ot act intelligently and wisely, using due political prudence where exactitude is impossible.

B. THE NEW DESPOTISM

The problem of autocracy is to provide for the selection of its rulers in an unending line and to define acceptably the nature of their trusteeship for the commonwealth. Instability of equilibrium is a constant peril besetting the way of the Few. On the one hand there are dictators who may decide to become kings; and there are masses on the other hand pressing for admission into the sacred circle of the Few. Intelligence and religion are repudiated as means of continuity in the present elites, whereas birth, wealth, and military force are likewise looked upon with disfavor as dominating influences in the aristocracy.

The present groups of autocratic rulers cannot rely accordingly upon the military, or upon the traders and bankers, or upon the church, or upon the intellectuals, or upon labor. They must worry along with the army, with the functionaries, with the politicos as best they may. If military victory comes, it will inevitably enhance the prestige of some generals and emerging heroes receiving wide popular acclaim. The victor, if any, may find himself a national figure with political possibilities. Or in time the party is likely to develop, if the present system continues, a little government in itself, taking on the elements of conference and consent from which it boasted emancipation.

The rule of the Few, if it is to be set up, would rest more firmly upon religion, upon the inflexible devotion aroused by the flame of religious zeal, or upon the constancy to social welfare built into some such civil service group of guardians as that outlined in the *Republic* of Plato. The hope of a continuing rule of intelligence and devotion would

CONCLUSIONS

be found in the leadership of the intellectuals or of the clergy. But this is cold comfort to robber barons who hope for a freer hand than mass rule will offer them.

To them Plato's *Republic* reads like a professoriat par excellence, while the clerical group will take views of the commonweal in which predatory interests occupy a secondary place. And neither the clergy nor the intellectuals desire irresponsible political power.

The modern elites are undemocratic in their professions and institutions, but they are not true aristocracies in the sense in which the term is commonly employed—that of the rule of the most gifted in the art of government.

The organization of the human differentials is a continuing problem of government and society that will never be definitely solved, except as adequate allowance is made for variations in human capacity in a broad framework of opportunity allowing for stability and mutation alike. We may learn far more about the precise nature of psychological and biological differences, and about the techniques and possibilities of their effective management and control, but in the end and in any event there must be left room for the valuation and recognition of these numerous and varying types, and for broad social judgment regarding the wisest institutional framework in which they may be set.

C. THE NEW DEMOCRACY

The modern long-time trend is in the direction of democracy. Pointing this way are the advance of science and education, the growth of respect for human personality, the decline of brute force, the growth of the world's jural order, the nature of massed industrial life, the reorientation of our modern value systems.

Once the principle of democracy is firmly established in institutions and understandings, it is possible to achieve the recognition of the genuine elements of social and political intelligence found in a given community at a given time. It is not necessary to set up a detailed comparison between the systems of autocracy and democracy at all the various points where contrast might be sharpest.[1] I choose for the moment the category of the maintenance of the balance between justice and order. Order makes possible an integration of external behavior in patterns that may be counted upon by the citizenry. Justice makes possible or facilitates

---

[1] In my *Political Power*, Chap. VIII, I have analyzed the elements of the survival of the fittest as follows:

Insight into social composition—social intelligence.

Adequate distribution of rewards and preferments—social values as far as politically determined.

Moderation.

Adequate zoning or diffusion of power.

Capacity for planning and leadership.

Maintenance of the balance between order and justice.

Compare the "tests" set down by Bryce in *Modern Democracies* (Part III); also the Aristotelian discussion of the causes of revolution, *Politics*, Book V; Pareto on the balance between force and cunning, *Mind and Society*, Secs. 2202, 2213, 2227–2236, 2244–2278, and *passim*; J. S. Mill, *Representative Government*, Chaps. IV, conditions favorable to representative government; Eduard Heimann, *Communism, Fascism, or Democracy?* (1938).

CONCLUSIONS

an inner integration of the personality and the development of community morale.

In any case the balance between order and justice is one of the basic elements in stability and progress. Authoritarians are likely to place order first, and it is, indeed, of urgent importance in any scheme of affairs. Autocracy is also likely to place order first and allow justice to come along afterward—but perhaps forgotten in the meantime. The Few are likely to fear the Many and to interpret causes in their own interest. The mass is confident in its own strength and not likely to precipitate action from nervous fear that they may be too late.

Another great object of government is the organization of stability and the organization of change. It is plain that the mass may promote stability while recognizing genuine variations. The fatal weakness of the autocracy is the prolonging of power after its justification has gone—of preserving the authority that once rested upon superior capacity long after the element of superiority has faded out. The brain that won the battle or the war, the hand that waved the wand of economic production, the intelligence that understood the secrets of statesmanship and its practice—these pass away and their successors cannot carry on, except as they cover their inner weakness with the glitter of decorations. Weakness contrives the appearance of strength, encouraging belief in skill that is actually gone. The continuing mass, however, has no reason to deceive itself as to outworn capacities, but may recognize the flux of the difference in human capacity, political or otherwise, and adjust its affairs accordingly.

Those who assert that democracy cannot organize effective management forget that scientific management is the very child of modern democratic societies; and that executive leadership is the great contribution of modern democracy to statesmanship, notably in the United States.

THE NEW DEMOCRACY

Those who assert that democracy cannot organize and utilize force are unmindful either of ancient predictions of democratic incapacity to survive or of recent military events demonstrating democratic strength. The gravest danger threatening the peace of the world today is the illusion that democracies will not and cannot fight because they do not like to fight. This is the philosophy leading to the cemetery—the rendezvous with death—in Belgium or elsewhere.

Those who assert that force is the only solvent of industrial and social ills ignore the history of social legislation and its wide achievements and possibilities. Morale is a basis of group life, and common counsel the mode of its achievement and expression. Constitutions, congresses, courts, civil liberties are ways of reaching the goal of common consent—the soundest foundation for the superstructure of the modern state.

Those who assert that democracy cannot organize to meet the insistent demands for social change, for the recognition and adaptation of the new, and who therefore rely upon the sword within and without ignore the essential nature of our modern difficulties. Our social, economic, technological, philosophical problems are not capable of solution by brute force, but require the exercise of the highest intelligence, the highest wisdom, the greatest patience and skill. Autocracy in regard to economic and social affairs is not an open road to a secure retreat from trouble.

The conclusion is that, under modern conditions in civilized states, it is easier for the Many to maintain efficient administration with responsibility to the community than for the Few to develop an autocracy that is at once socially efficient and a wise judge in its own cause.

Either might maintain an effective administration, although autocracy has usually developed class administration, but in the field of political leadership the responsible choice

CONCLUSIONS

of the mass is likely to be superior to the irresponsible choice of a Few.

If great political Messiahs emerge from time to time out of troubled periods, they may, perhaps, choose themselves and function in some crisis in the national life. But the followers of the Great are seldom equally great, and their successors are better selected by the people they serve through some line of established responsibility. America has shown in Washington, Jefferson, Lincoln, Wilson, Roosevelt the vast possibilities in the field of democratic leadership, ready for the darkest hours of national difficulty, and for periods of peace and prosperity. The history of democracies is full of great men who rose and retired in the framework of popular organization and approval.

In the near future several factors, among them the following, will make the task of democracy easier than before.

1. *The Emergence of Superior Forms of Public Administration.* In earlier times administration was the creature and the servant of the autocrats—the Hohenzollerns, the Bourbons, the Stuarts—and was recruited from the few. But in our day it comes from the mass, is the tool of the mass, and stands at their service. Administration is not only the channel of continuing efficiency but also the open way for the influx of new scientific intelligence in the domain of social affairs.[1] The bulk of government is administration. The new kind of administration will command not only the services of the old-time jurists, but also of the new-time scientists, educators, engineers, doctors, technical workers, managers springing up on every side in modern communities and constantly recruited from the ranks of the people through a system of general education for all. Those who assert that democracy cannot utilize intelligence in its service are un-

[1] See my *New Aspects of Politics*, Chap. VIII.

mindful of the possibilities and actualities of modern civil service, as seen in England, Sweden, France, and elsewhere.

This is not to say that lawmaking agencies will not function. On the contrary, they will work more effectively than ever before. Lawmakers are greatest when they deal with general principles and policies, weakest when they enter into minor details and management.

Furthermore, the development of executive leadership—one of the great contributions of modern democracy to government—will make the task of mass politics easier than before. This form of organization has been most fully developed in the United States, but closely related systems are seen in the prime ministry of England and other countries. Through this type of organization it is possible to blend the elements of effective popular responsibility with those of unification of action, both in peace and in war. An executive of this type, resting on a genuine system of institutionalized responsibility, is a factor of vast strength in the future development of government. In wartimes such an executive is able to deal effectively with the aggressiveness of military authorities on the one hand and the sensitivity of representative agencies on the other, while maintaining the general framework of understandings and agencies in which mass rule is embodied. In peacetime he may provide the energetic leadership and power of coordination required for the development of constructive policies, for dealing effectively with vested interests resisting change for the common good, for application of policies determined by commonwealths. President Wilson is an example of war leadership, and President Roosevelt of social leadership in an industrial emergency.

2. *The Growth of Education*. Another factor of far-reaching significance in mass rule is the spread of universal education. Most of the time in the history of the world, most men

CONCLUSIONS

have lived and died in ignorance, excluded by class or caste barriers from the circle of trained intelligence of their time. Reading, writing, "schooling" were the marks of the gentleman and the ruling class. As late as 1807 it was said on the floor of the House of Commons in England that

> However specious in theory the project might be of giving education to the labouring classes and the poor, it would, in effect, be prejudicial to their morals and happiness; it would teach them to despise their lot in life instead of making them good servants in agriculture, and other laborious employments to which their rank in society had destined them; instead of teaching them subordination, it would render them fractious and refractory . . . it would enable them to read seditious pamphlets, vicious books, and publications against Christianity; it would render them insolent to their superiors; and in a few years, the result would be that the legislature would find it necessary to direct the strong arm of power toward them. . . . [1]

Education will provide outlets for the discovery, expression, and realization of human capacities in a manner hitherto unknown, and it will equip the generality of the community with standards of and equipment for critical judgment on the basic policies and key personalities of the community. In the first stages of growth it is not unlikely that shallow and superficial education may serve as a basis for corresponding types of judgment, but in the long run the general spread of intelligence through both formal and adult education will result in higher levels of appreciation, criticism, judgment. The quality of education itself shifts from the traditional to the transitional and prospective point of view, and to new forms of insight, appreciation, and capacity for adjustment.

3. *The Emergence of the Era of Abundance.* The vastly increased productivity of mankind fundamentally changes many aspects of human behavior. It particularly diminishes the role of fear and force in human relations, and narrows

---

[1] *Hansard's Parliamentary Debates*, First Series, Vol. 9 (1807)—Debate on Parochial Schools Bill, July 13, 1807—remarks of Mr. Giddy.

the field of human domination through exclusive possession of some very limited commodity or utility. Land hunger, poverty, unemployment, and insecurity were easy roads to slavery and submission for centuries of human existence; the differentials in capacity were under these conditions readily magnified into wide disparities of political position and translated into terms of brutality and neglect. The philosophy of submission, instead of consent; the justification of brutality as a necessary mode of social discipline and integration; the rationalization of poverty and destitution as the inevitable burden of existence—all these come out of the period of scarcity and uncertainty. But the entrance into a new domain where land and commodities are more abundant and where insecurity in the older sense lacks a reason for existence, profoundly modifies the whole basis of human life, and makes the way far easier for the development and application of the doctrines of democracy. It is easier to be good neighbors when there is enough to go around.

4. *The Reconciliation of Liberty and Equality*. One of the most perplexing and troublesome problems in the whole field of political association in all times is the reconciliation of liberty and equality. In our day this is a special problem of democratic states, and one which has proved to be most disruptive in its effects. The double interplay between political and economic ideas of liberty and political and economic ideas of equality has produced conditions especially difficult of reconciliation and stabilization.

It is possible, however, to reconcile these diverging elements, and this task is particularly appropriate for a democratic society. It may be said very broadly that the Soviets attempt a form of equality but destroy liberty; that Fascism and Naziism destroy both liberty and equality; but that the democratic state may protect and develop both equality and liberty.

CONCLUSIONS

Where the commonweal is determined by the community, using the consent of the governed as a basis of political theory and action, it is entirely feasible to maintain liberty as against the arbitrary and unappealable decision of autocrats, and it is entirely feasible to maintain equality against the inroads of the Few.

Liberty and equality are not exclusive but complementary. The recognition of the equality of human personalities involves their freedom to develop; freedom of choice is indeed the very condition for the unfolding of the human personality and its progressive development.

The abandonment of political liberty to obtain economic liberty or the reverse; the abandonment of political equality to obtain economic equality or the reverse—these are the counsels of impatience, despair, and defeatism. They rest upon easygoing and indefensible assumptions which by their sheer repetition sometimes obtain acceptance and cause flight into systems that only multiply the difficulties.

5. *The Emergence of Industrialized Democracy.* The burdens of the democratic state will be easier to bear when the commonwealth performs avowedly and actively the function of validating the assumptions of democracy—particularly the assumption that the gains of nations are essentially mass gains and should be distributed through the mass of the community as rapidly as possible. Modern democracy escaped from absolutism, which was established on the ruins of feudalism, only to fall foul of the snares of plutocracy from which it is difficult but not impossible to escape. The transition of modern democracy from a landed base to an industrial base has been a long and severe one; but as this crisis passes and industrialized democracy emerges, the strength of the mass position becomes clearer and stronger.

That a transformation is on its way is clear to anyone who observes the signs of the times—the increasing tempo of scientific invention and technology; the displacement of personnel and capital resulting therefrom; the disunity in social, economic, and political life, and the ensuing trend toward mass integration and unity; the disjointed experiments in social legislation; and finally the emergence of central planning.

The type or types of association emerging cannot be predicted confidently by any responsible person; but the indications are that the units will be the nations, set in some jural order, and that the basic type of organization will be the rule of the Many in one form or another. The precise form of this reorganization is far less important than the general principle, the common understanding regarding the goal.

The exchange of the values of liberty, equality, consent of the governed, rational discussion and persuasion for despotism, inequality, irresponsibility, the terror within and war without, anti-intellectualism and shrill emotionalism is not a bargain in our time. The price is high and there is no guaranty that the goods will be delivered.

The task of the modern state in readjusting its ways and means to the urgent demands of the new technology, to the new inventions in natural and social science is a vast one, but there is every reason to believe that the problem may be solved within a reasonable period of time, and within the general framework of free institutions. The shift from an economy largely agricultural to one largely industrial is fraught with many difficulties, but in no sense impossible to accomplish within the limits of order, justice, liberty, equality, and consent.

The Jeremiahs are in general those who undervalue the capacity of the state for promoting the common weal by the balance and integration of social forces within its area and people. Or on the other hand there are those who think

CONCLUSIONS

of the state in terms of its primitive tools of force and violence. Thus the communists reject the state altogether, and the new autocrats deify the state. There is a zone of moderation between them in which the destiny of mankind will be worked out. Both rational analysis and broad long-run historical trends show that this zone is not that of absolutism and irresponsibility, of force and terror, but one of consent, discussion, persuasion, of expert knowledge under the general guidance of the common judgment.

6. *The Growth of the More Abundant Life.* Finally the dawn of the creative role of mankind is just beginning to be dimly seen. Not only do we observe that the bonds of tradition are being broken in many places, and that the role of change in human affairs is being recognized in modern times. The opportunity before us is not merely that of adapting ourselves to necessary change, but a prospect of constructively shaping the course of affairs and events. The new knowledge of the modern world not only enables us to avoid ancient dangers, but may also make it possible to take a part in the reorganization of the conditions out of which dangers emerge and reshape them for our uses. It is not enough to learn how to step aside from an automobile. We may control the conditions under which traffic risks arise. The avoidance of death is the negative side, the positive is the growth of the more abundant life.

The new world into which youth now comes is not merely an "economy of abundance," but a period of creative evolution—of a destiny not imposed from without, but springing from the creative, constructive forces of man. "Each individual," says Whitehead, "embodies an adventure of existence. The art of life is the guidance of this adventure."[1] There is reason to believe that the future holds for every person some small but precious part in the progressive recon-

[1] T. N. Whitehead, *Aims of Education* (1929), p. 58.

struction of the society within which he dwells—some contribution not only to the preservation of our race and its culture, but also to its further advancement toward higher levels of attainment. In this joint enterprise, power and authority become creative instead of repressive—the leaders are not those who crush and bruise but those who heal and help—and the greatest service to mankind becomes the highest value.

In the day when this new situation is generally understood, not only the concepts of power, property, and prestige, but also the concept of human differences in capacity enter an altogether different phase. Just as government ceases to be chiefly repression, and as leadership ceases to be crass domination and exploitation, and as property ceases to be largely an economic symbol of exclusive possession, and as activity ceases to be chiefly long and grinding toil, the whole nature of power is being transformed from the negative to the positive, and is unfolding in its creative aspects. In these oncoming days men may achieve not merely that personal security and community stability which alone might mean monotony and boredom. Men may look forward to adventurous participation in the process of creative evolution—in the constructive transformation and betterment of life conditions.

The greatest of all revolutions in the whole history of mankind is the acceptance of creative evolution as the proper role of man; for this will eventually transform the spirit and the institutions of education, of industry, and of government, opening a broad way to the realization of the highest and finest values of human life, in a form of association where leaders no longer scream and curse and threaten, and where men no longer shuffle, cringe, and fear, but stand erect in dignity and liberty and speak with calm voices of what clear eyes may see.

INDEX

A

Abundance, an aid to democracy, 257
  possibility of increased production, 176
Acton, J. E., 76n.
Adams, Brooks, 209n.
Administration (*see* Public Administration)
Administrative law, 131
Administrative management, President's committee on, 126
Adolf-Hitler Schulen, 224
Adult education, 96
  prerequisite of rational democratic change, 183
Anarchism, 43
Anti-democratic movement, background of, 191
  (*See also* New despotism)
Anti-democratic theory, elements of, 193
  revival of, 192
  (*See also* Autocracy; New despotism)
Aristocracy, and biology, 26
  failings of, 91
  industrial, 205
  isolation of governing class under, 41n., 42
  new principles of, 215
  premises of, 23ff.
  and race doctrines, 24
  true forms of, 90
  (*See also* Autocracy; New despotism)

Aristocratic spirit, attitude toward human differentials, 74
Aristotle, 47, 170, 252n.
  on defense of mass judgments, 41
  on the Few and the Many, 4
  rediscovery of *Politics*, 51
  on slave nature, 24
  on types of democracy, 66
Artz, F. B., 14n.
Aryan race, alleged superiority of, 24
Ascoli, Max, 167n.
Austin, John, 54, 233
Authority, centralization of, in new despotism, 221
Autocracy, characterized by indecision, 118
  collapse of, in war, 63
  democratic elements in, 246
  diplomacy of, 142
  emphasis upon order at expense of justice, 253
  failings of, 91
  governmental intervention under, 40
  as personal adventurism, 90
  policy of, in new despotisms, 229
  problems confronting, 89, 250
  and public administration, 128
  resort to parliamentary process, 117
  use of force and ballyhoo in, 90
  (*See also* Anti-democratic theory; Aristocracy; New despotism)

B

Balance of power, in new despotism, 235
Barnes, H. E., 61n.
Belloc, Hilaire, 114n., 203

Benes, Eduard, 12n.
Bentham, Jeremy, 44
Beyle, H., 14
Biology, and forms of political order, 26
  (*See also* Aryan race; Heredity; Race)
Birth, as mark of political capacity, 23
  (*See* Aristocracy)
Bismarck, 134
Blum, Leon, 126n., 138n.
Blut und Boden, 216
Bouglé, Celestin C. A., 12n., 17n., 20n., 54n., 58n.
  on democracy, 3
Bright, 14n.
Bryce, James, 12n., 17, 61n., 63n., 65n., 252n.
  on democracy, 4, 47n.
Bunbury, Henry, 145n., 156n.
Bureaucracy, avoidance of inflexibilities of, 124
Burgess, J. W., 76n.
Burns, Arthur R., 167n.

C

Caesarism, 198
  Spengler on, 202
Capitalism, relation to politics, 206
Capitalist class, role of, in government, 171
Capitalists, as menace to democracy, 67
  resistance to change, 182
Carlyle, Thomas, criticism of democracy, 203
Carnelutti, Francesco, 235n.
Caste system, 12
Centralization of authority, in New despotism, 222
Chamberlain, H. S., 24n.
Charlety, S., 194n.
Christianity, attacked by new despotisms, 237

Christianity, influence upon democracy, 51
  other-worldly character of, 92
Church government, influence upon civil government, 52
  recruitment of leadership in, 52
Citoyen, 14
Civic education, and conscious social change, 182
Civil liberties, essential to democracy, 107
Civil War, 137
Civilization, gains of, distribution of, 37
  equitable distribution of, 11, 100
  and democracy, 259
  extravagant claims upon, 37
  necessity for continual survey of, 98
  (*See also* Mass gains)
Classe politica of Mosca, 208
Clausewitz, von, 142, 196
Clemenceau, 134, 137
Coker, Francis W., 28n., 54n., 61n., 200n., 203n., 215n.
Collectivism, in background of democracy, 54
  and individualism, 173
  planning in, 148
Colm, Gerhard, 167n.
Communism, attitude toward democracy, 228
  criticism of economic inequality in democracy, 171
  doctrines of, 227
  origins of, 193
  recognition of differences in capacity, 228
Communist party, 227
  recruitment in, 223
Comte, Auguste, 194
Compton, K. T., 93n.
Concentration of power, in crises, 236

INDEX

Conciliar function, 114
 (*See also* Parliamentarism; Representation)
Condorcet, 34
Conklin, Edwin Grant, 20*n*.
Conscious control, contrasted with brute struggle for survival, 6
Conscious social change, 42*ff.*
 approaches to problem of, 46
 assumption of democracy, 12
Consent, basic understandings, a condition of, 104
 and dignity of mankind, 87
 of governed, early origin of theory of, 51
 organization of, 186
 (*See also* Democracy; Electoral process)
Constitution, amendment of, 181
 as expression of conscious control, 6
 interpretation of, as political function, 131
 theory of customary growth of, 180
Consumption, continual surveys of, 98
 (*See also* Standard of living)
Counts, George S., 12*n*.
Corporatives, role of, in Italy, 235
Courts, political function of, in United States, 131
Cram, Ralph Adams, 75*n*., 114*n*.
Creative evolution, 261
Crisis, and concentration of power, 236
 and democracy, 45
Custine, marquis de, 15*n*.
Custom, as restricting influence upon liberty, 80

D

Darwinism, 193
Decentralization, in administration, 131
Decisionism, in democracy and autocracy, 132
Decisionism, in military affairs, 135
 (*See also* Diplomacy; Military affairs)
Declaration of Independence, Lincoln on, 16
Defeatism, reaction against complexity of modern problems, 180
Del Vecchio, 222*n*.
Democracy, and adult education, 183
 advance of, in nineteenth century, 191
 not perceived in some fields, 14
 allegedly incapable of planning, 168
 aristocratic elements in, 247
 assumptions of, 11, 45
 attack on, by mass movements, 197
 by new despotisms, 218
 balance between justice and order in, 252
 and biology, 26
 capacity for action in diplomacy, 144
 causes of spread of, 50
 and change in industry, 182
 and civic education, 182
 and civil liberties, 107
 and Communism, 228
 Communist criticism of, 170
 and conscious social change, 42
 corruption and incompetence in, 50
 and crisis, 45
 criticism of, by Carlyle and Ruskin, 203
  by Hitler, 215
  by Spann, 213
 and decisionism, 132
 defenses of, against economic concentration, 171
  by middle income groups, 192
 definitions of, 47
 development of ideology of, 50
 and dignity of mankind, 87
 diplomacy of, 142
 and distribution of gains of civilization, 100, 187

Democracy, early restricted franchise in, 59
and economy of abundance, 257
efficiency of, in domestic policy, 145
and emergence of improved administration, 255
examples of successes, 63
Fascist criticism of, 170, 222
and feudalism, 51
form of, varies with historical situations, 64
function of the courts in, 130
function of party system in, 122
future of, 262
general conditions making it possible, 5–6
government as trustee in, 245
and governmental competence, 63
governmental intervention under, 39
groups attacking, 197
and heredity, 19
Hitler on Germanic, 220
and improved executive leadership, 256
and improvement in education, 256
increasing participation in, 65
influence of Christianity upon, 51
influence of Stoicism upon, 51
intelligent participation in, 34
and laissez faire, 67, 205
and liberalism, 36
and liberty, 75, 84
limited role of force in, 85
menaced by concentration of wealth, 67
Mencken on, 202
military efficiency of, 63
modern long-time trend toward, 252
modern problems of, 65
nature of mechanisms of, 86
necessity for flexibility in, 181
need to overhaul machinery of, 187

Democracy, new indictment of, 64
nominal adherence to, 47
not a blueprint, 44
not identical with special governmental forms, 64
not identical with special mechanisms, 71
not identifiable with economic system, 64
older criticism of, 60
refuted, 62
organization of, adapted to planning, 179
and peaceful change, 183
philosophical background of, 54
and planning, 145, 187
policy of, with respect to equality, 18
and political mechanisms, 101
possibility of planning in, 179
pressure groups in, 122
problems of, in industrial society, 69
program of planning in, 176
and prosperity, 36
as protector of plutocracy, 81
and public administration, 126
tool of, 124
range of liberty in, 75
and recognition of talent, 18, 84
relation of, to economic order, 66, 172
to Industrial Revolution, 56
responsibility of, for social justice, 103
role of consent in, 87
role of democratic experience in the development of, 60
role of education in development of, 57
role of the Few and the Many in, 243
role of political techniques in background of, 59
role of printing in background of, 57
role of science in background of, 54

INDEX

Democracy, role of social sciences in development of, 58
  role of social techniques in development of, 57
  role of technology in background of, 55
  and science, 93
  short-time program of, 187
  and social contract theories, 52
  and social equilibrium, 176
  spirit of, in public administration, 125
  struggle of, against divine right theory, 53
  subordination of force in, 183
  summary of program of, 72
  survival of, 4
  in World War, 63
  tasks of, in nineteenth and twentieth centuries, 61
  and technological advance, 34
  tradition and symbolism in, 102
  and types of economic order, 101
  underlying principle of, 65
  variations in program of, 177
  war potentials of, 139
  as way of life, 48
  weakness and strength of, 49
  and world jural order, 60, 184
    (*See also* Electoral process; Military efficiency; Parliamentarism; Popular will; Representation; Voting)
Democratic Assumptions, methods of validating, 4
Democratic liberalism, tools of, 45
Democratic planning, basic assumptions of, 156
Democratic techniques, retention of, in new despotism, 222
Despotism, new theory of, 217
  (*See also* Autocracy; New despotism; Non-democratic order)
Deviational behavior, changing policy toward, 186

Dewey, John, 12*n*., 17*n*., 40*n*., 42*n*., 221*n*.
  on democracy, 4
Dicey, A. V., 14*n*., 233
Dickinson, H. D., 149*n*.
Dictatorship, misuse of term in new despotisms, 221
  really despotism, 7
  (*See also* Autocracy; New despotism)
Differentials, recognition of, in democracy, 21
Dignity of mankind, 73
  approach to problem of, 46
  assumption of, in democracy, 11
  contributing influences to, 74
  and democracy, 87
  fraternal principle, 12
  and the fraternal ideal, 16
  and religion, 52
  (*See also* Democracy; Equality; Liberty)
Diplomacy, criticism of democratic capacity for, 144
  democratic and autocratic, compared, 142
  problems of, 143
  (*See also* Decisionism)
Discoveries, role of, in the development of democracy, 55
Disraeli, 143
Divine right, struggle of democracy against, 53
Duce (*see* Mussolini)
Duguit, Leon, 76*n*.
Dunning, William A., 53*n*., 54*n*.
Dupuy, R. Ernest, 140*n*.
Durkheim, Emile, 12*n*.

E

Economic council, failure of, 148
Economic inequality, 205

Economic order, and democracy, 66
  subordinate to democratic principle, 100
Economics, overemphasis upon, 7
  and politics, 173
Education, for adults, 96
  development of, an aid to democracy, 256
  role of, in background of democracy, 57
  and importance of, 96
Elections, pseudo, 108
Electoral process, alternatives to, 106, 110
  corruption in, 109
  criticisms of, 105
  device for holding governors responsible, 105
  educational value of, 108
  and fear of popular verdict, 111
  and free channels of communication, 107
  as morale mechanism, 114
  presuppositions of, 107
  retained in new despotism, 113
  sphere of operation, 110
  (*See also* Consent; Democracy; Parliamentarism; Representation; Voting)
Eliot, George Fielding, 132*n*., 140*n*., 203
Elite, circulation of, 111
  industrial, 205
  Pareto, on characteristics of, 29
  theory of, 208
Elwin, William, 235*n*.
Encyclopaedia of the Social Sciences, 115*n*., 122*n*.
Environment, role of, in producing differentials, 25
Equalitarians, objective of, 17
Equality, before the law, 59
  definition and discussion of, 18
  degree necessary to democracy, 18

Equality, and liberty, 79, 82
  conflict between, 192
  possibility of reconciling, 7, 258
  of opportunity, 74
  rejection of, in Fascist dictatorship, 218
  and standardization, 81
Executive, modern role of, 125
  reorganization of, 126
Executive leadership, development of, aid to democracy, 256

F

Faguet, Emile, 34*n*., 50*n*., 114*n*.
Fascism, criticism of democracy, 47, 171
  origins of, 193
  (*See also* Autocracy; Dictatorship; New despotism)
Fascist party, recruitment to, 223
Feroci, Virgilio, 235*n*.
Feudalism, political relationship in, 51
Few, repudiation of rule of, 6
  (*See also* Autocracy; Dictatorship; New despotism)
Few and the Many, confusion as to roles in democracy, 243
Field, G. Lowell, 235*n*.
Finer, Herman, 30*n*.
Follet, Mary Parker, 247*n*.
Force, overemphasis upon, 254
  role of, in democracy, 85, 185
Ford, Guy Stanton, 231*n*.
Fosdick, Dorothy, 77*n*.
France, Anatole, 77
Fraternal ideal, attacks upon, 16
Freedom, of assembly (*see* Civil liberties)
  of the press (*see* Civil liberties)
  of speech (*see* Civil liberties)
French Revolution, 16
Friedrich, Carl J., 126*n*.
Führer Prinzip, 29, 212
  (*See also* Leadership)

INDEX

Führerschulen, 224
Future, unfolding prospects of, 262

G

Gentile, 211n.
Gentz, M., 15
George, Lloyd, 134, 137, 139, 143
Germanic democracy, Hitler on, 220
Germany, purge of 1934, 111
    treatment of capitalism in, 88
    (*See also* Hitler; National Socialism; Nazi)
Gobineau, A. J. de, 24n.
Godkin, Edwin L., 61n.
Gosnell, Harold F., 123n.
Government, conscious and peaceful change in, 180
    influence of crisis situations upon form of, 248
    influence of social conditions upon, 5–6
    modern problems of, 248
    organization of change in, 253
    tasks of modern, 260
    trusteeship of, in democracy, 245
    (*See also* Crisis; Planning)
Government-owned Corporations, 175
Governmental intervention, in absolutistic state, 40
    in democracy, 39*ff*.
Governmental mechanisms, overemphasis upon, 104
Grant, Madison, 24n.
Green, T. H., 76n.
Gregory, T. E., 149n.
Gulick, Luther, 126, 247n.
Gunther, H. F. K., 24n.

H

Hague Tribunal, 60
Haldane, J. B. S., 28n.
Hall, N. F., 99n.

Haller, Ludwig von, 192n.
Hamilton, Walton, 167n.
Hammond, B., 10n.
Hammond, J. L., 10n.
Harper, Samuel, 228n.
Harrington, 170
Hart, Basil Henry Liddell, 132n.–134n., 139, 140
Hasbach, Wilhelm, 63n., 114n.
Hayek, F. A. von, 149n., 167
Hegel, Georg W. F., 54n.
    place of, in theoretical background of democracy, 54
    theory of state, 193
Helms, E. Allen, 123n.
Heredity, basis of selection for political leadership, 23
    and democracy, 19
    role of, in producing differentials, 25*ff*.
    (*See also* Biology)
Heimann, Eduard, 167n., 252n.
Hitler, Adolf, 24n., 114n., 116n., 143, 212n., 216n., 219, 232n.
    and Aryan doctrine, 29
    on democracy, 215
    on Germanic democracy, 220
    military service of, 33
    personal fortune of, 31
    problem of succession to, 33
    purge of 1934, 111
    on representation and parliamentarism, 219
Hobbes, Thomas, 232
Hogben, Lancelot, 28
Höhn, Reinhard, 132n., 134
Huber, Ernst Rudolf, 42, 132n., 134, 212n., 216n., 220n.
Hudson, Nora E., 192n.
Human differentials, distorted into inherited status, 73
    state of knowledge as to, 91
Huxley, Aldous, 29n., 40n., 87n., 90n.

[269]

I

Ideology, democratic, development of, 50
Income, principle of distribution of, 180
 (*See also* Civilization, gains of; Mass gains; Standard of living)
Individualism, and collectivism, 173
 economic connotation of, 77
 (*See also* Liberty)
Industrial elite, relation to politics, 207
 supporters of fascism, 205
Industrial revolution, role in background of democracy, 55
Industrialists, resistance to change, 182
Industry, claimed immunity of, to regulation, 176
Inequality, economic, 205
 Nazi theory of, 219
 (*See also* Equality)
Inge, 203
Inheritance, laws of, 74
Intelligence, necessity of, 253
 rejection of, in modern social struggle, 178
Intelligence testing, failure to isolate hereditary factors, 26
Internal affairs, diminution of violence in, 184
International Labour Office, 60
International order, maintenance of, 184
International organization, and democracy, 187
Interpretation of popular will, in dictatorships, 248
Irresponsibility (*see* Responsibility)
Israel, Kingdom of, popular establishment of, 51
Italy, treatment of capitalism in, 88

J

Jefferson, Thomas, 255
 on survival of democracy, 66
Jennings, H. S., 25, 26n., 28n., 31n., 58n., 84n.
Jesuit elements in national socialism, 225
Jewkes, J., 228n.
Jews, persecutions of, 22
Journal of Psychiatry, 28
Judd, Charles H., 57n., 97n.
Justice, administrative, 131
 balance of, with liberty and order, 79
 in democracy and autocracy, 252
 democratic responsibility for, 102
 nominal and substantial, 72

K

Kallen, H. M., 76n.
Kant, Immanuel, 221n.
Kelsen, Hans, 12n., 212, 223n., 244n.
 on democracy, 4, 47
Keyserling, 203
Knight, Frank H., 67n.
Koellreuter, Otto, 212n., 220n.
Kokovtsov, V. N., 118n.
Kolabinska, Marie, 209n.
Kolnai, Aurel, 212n., 216n.
Krieck, Ernst, 212n., 220n.
Kropotkin, P., 15n., 78
Kruif, Paul de, 21n.

L

Laissez faire, and abdication of responsibilities of democracy, 104
 and development of democracy, 67
 and elitism, 205
 immunity of industry to regulation, 176
 modern rejection of, 157
 rallying point of opposition to social advance, 182
Lange, Oskar, 167
Laski, Harold J., 12n., 76n., 147n.
 definition of democracy, 47

INDEX

Lasswell, Harold D., 31*n*.
Law, administrative, 131
Leadership, distribution of talent for, 244
  emergence of executive, in democracy, 256
  Führer Prinzip, 29
  influence of community on, 245
  modern role of, 125
  in non-democratic order, 21
  political, bases of, 23
  distribution of talent for, 244
  purge of, in Soviet, 111
  succession of, in New despotisms, 223
Leadership principle, 212, 219, 223
Leadership training schools, in Germany, 224
League of Nations, 60
Lecky, William E. H., 50*n*., 76*n*., 83, 115*n*.
Legislative bodies, functions of, 120
  necessary modifications in, 119
Lehmann, Fritz, 167*n*.
Lerner, Max, 12*n*.
Leroy-Beaulieu, A., 15*n*.
Lewisohn, Sam A., 247*n*.
Ley, Robert, 225
Liberalism, in background of democratic theory, 54
  and democracy, 36
Liberty, balance of, with other values, 78
  creative or positive theory of, 77
  custom as restricting influence, 80
  definition of, 17
  economic connotation, 77
  economic interpretation of, 81
  and equality, 79
    conflict between, 192
    possibility of reconciling, 7, 258
  as freedom from economic regulation, 67

Liberty, forms of, twisted to tyrannic purposes, 17
  legal and substantial, 72
  priorities in, 78
  range of, in democracy, 75
  reconciliation of competing forms of, 85
  redefinition of, in Fascist dictatorships, 218
  restrictions upon in interest of equality, 82
  as slogan for defense of rich, 17
  types of, 78
Lilly, William S., 115*n*.
Lincoln, Abraham, 16, 41, 74, 118, 137, 225
Lindsay, A. D., 12*n*., 51*n*.
  on democracy, 4
Lippincott, Benjamin E., 149*n*., 167*n*.
Lippmann, Walter, 110*n*., 166*n*.
Locke, John, 39
Loeb, Harold, 207*n*.
Logan, G. B., 76*n*.
Löwe, Adolph, 80*n*., 221*n*.
Lower classes, attitudes of upper classes toward, 13
Ludovici, A. M., 114*n*.
Lumpen proletariat, anomaly of, under modern conditions, 20
Lutz, Ralph, 231*n*.

M

Macaulay, Thomas B., 75*n*.
McClellan, General, 118
McDougall, 210*n*.
Machiavelli, 112
McKenzie, Charles W., 123*n*.
MacKenzie, Findlay, 149*n*.
McKinley, Silas Bent, 132*n*.
MacLeod, William C., 115*n*., 198*n*.
Madariaga, S. de, 247*n*.
Magyary, Zoltan von, 126*n*.

[271]

Maine, Henry J. S., 34*n.*, 115*n.*
Maistre, Count de, 42
Majority rule, validity of, 107
Mallock, William H., 205*n.*
Mankiewicz, H., 212*n.*, 216*n.*
Mann, Thomas, 12*n.*
Marcuse, Herbert, 212*n.*
Maritain, Jacques, 77*n.*
Markham, Edwin, 19-20
Marx, Karl, 157
    emphasis upon role of violence, 6
    overemphasis upon economic factors, 7
Marxism, attitude toward democratic state, 68
    doctrines of, 195
    (*See also* Communism)
Mass decision, approaches to problem of, 47
    assumption of democracy, 11
    conditions necessary to obtain, 44
    forms of expression vary, 38
    instrumentation of, 104
Mass gains, approaches to problem of, 46
    should be diffused to masses, 37
    (*See also* Civilization, gains of)
Mass production, as discouraging variety and spontaneity, 81
Masses, and recognition of talent, 84
Maurice, Frederick, 132*n.*, 137*n.*
Maxwell, Bertram W., 228*n.*
Mayo, Elton, 35, 46
Means, Gardiner, 99*n.*
Meinecke, Friedrich, 53*n.*
Mencken, Henry L., 115, 202
Merriam, Charles E., 3*n.*, 8*n.*, 25*n.*, 28*n.*, 40*n.*, 42*n.*, 51*n.*, 59*n.*, 61*n.*, 62*n.*, 67*n.*, 68*n.*, 97*n.*, 101*n.*, 122*n.*, 146*n.*, 173*n.*, 181*n.*-183*n.*, 243*n.*, 245*n.*, 252*n.*, 255*n.*
Merriam, John C., 80*n.*, 93*n.*
Metcalf, Henry C., 246*n.*

Meyer, S. P., 208*n.*
Michels, Roberto, 208*n.*, 209*n.*
Mikhael, Grand Duke, 15
Militarism, 196
Military affairs, attitude toward, in early democracy, 133
    British experience with, 133
    decisiveness in, 135
    German experience with, 134, 138
    French World War experience, 134
    neglect of, in democracy, 138
    sheltered character of military career, 139
Military organization, civil life in fascisms modeled on, 220
    general problems of, 137
    place of, in democracy, 134
    rigidity of, 137
    subordination to civil organization in United States, 136, 137
Military profession, role in politics, 32
Mill, John Stuart, 76*n.*, 80*n.*, 252*n.*
    overemphasis upon economics, 7
Minimum standards of living (*see* Standards of living)
Mises, Ludwig von, 149*n.*, 167
Mixed government, 247
Montague, F. C., 76*n.*
Montesquieu, 77, 170
Mosca, Gaetano, 194*n.*
    attitude toward Italian fascism, 29
    theory of political class, 208
Mussolini, Benito, 143, 211, 223
    emphasis upon role of violence, 6
    military service of, 32
    on race, 30
    selection of successor to, 33
    on voting, 114

N

National Governmental Organizations, 130*n.*

INDEX

National Planning Board, 149n.
   report quoted, 150
National Resources Committee, 34n., 95n., 100n., 131n., 166n.
   as planning agency, 148
   report on technological trends, 55
National Socialism, militarization of civil life in, 220
National Zeitung, 225
Nationalism, and anti-democratic movement, 197
   in background of democratic theory, 54
   in new despotism, 232
   popular character of, 91
Nazi, theory of inequality, 219
   (*See also* Germany; Hitler)
Nazi party, recruitment in, 223
Nazi theory, 212
Nespa (National Economic and Social Planning Association), 148n.
New despotism, attack upon Western tradition, 237
   attitude toward criticism, 230
   attitude toward equality, 218
   attitude toward liberty, 218
   and autarchy, 229
   balance of power in, 235
   civil life of, patterned after military model, 220
   democratic elements in, 231
   destruction of mass movements by, 88
   emphasis upon force, 229
   failure to fulfill promises, 238
   impermanence of, 239
   internal struggles in, 236
   nationalism in, 232
   party system in, 231
   and religion, 89
   responsibility in, 222
   retention of electoral mechanism in, 114
   role of propaganda in, 234
New despotism, theory of, 217
   voting in, 226, 231
   (*See also* Autocracy; Non-democratic order)
Nietzsche, 237
   attitude toward common man, 75
   basic features of philosophy, 198
   on Christianity, 199
   criticism of democracy, 199
   superman of, 196
   on universal suffrage, 199
   on war, 201
Nietzschean doctrines, 193
Nobility, no agreement as to marks of, 112
Noble few, common ideas of proponents of, 203
Non-democratic order, and dignity of mankind, 86
   popular responsibility under, 113
   problem of morale under, 112
   program of, 86
   qualifications of few for ruling, 112
   rule of Few unstable, 111
   selection of leadership in, 23*ff.*
   treatment of masses under, 87
   (*See also* Autocracy; New despotism)

O

Occupation, as basis of leadership selection, 32
Odegard, Peter H., 123n.
Omond, J. S., 132n., 133n.
Opportunity, equality of, 74
Order, in democracy and autocracy, 252
   in internal affairs, 184
   in international affairs, 184
Ordensburgen, 225
Organic state, modern version of, 215
Ortega y Gasset, José, 34n., 75n.
   on the masses, 203
Owen, Robert, 15

P

Paleologue, Maurice, 118*n*.
Panunzio, Sergio, 235*n*.
Pao Chao Hsieh, 51*n*.
Pareto, Vilfredo, 50*n*., 114*n*., 252*n*.
    attitude toward Italian fascism, 29
    characteristics of the elite, 29
    criticism of democracy, 209
    theory of the elite, 208
Parliament, supremacy of, in England, 233
Parliamentarism, analogues of, in autocracies, 116
    criticism of, 114
    by Hitler, 220
    in new despotism, 226
    preconditions of, 115
    relative recency of, 119
Parliamentary debates, 257
Parties, political, 59, 223
    functions of, in democracy, 122
    in new despotism, 231
    recruitment in, in new despotisms, 223
Paternalism, realization of democratic values in, 47
Pellizi, Camillo, 208*n*.
Personality, influences of environment upon, 27
PEP, English planning agency, 81*n*., 99*n*., 148
Perfectibility of mankind, 34*ff*., 92
    approaches to problem of, 46
    assumption of, in democracy, 11
Personality, relation to liberty and equality, 18
Pigou, A. C., 167*n*.
Pintschovius, Karl, 141*n*.
Planning, allegedly impossible in democracy, 166, 168, 179
    availability of personnel for, 164

Planning, in collectivist states, 148
    coordination of public and private, 162
    criticized as regimentation, 152
    decentralization of, 151
    in democracy, 145, 187
    democratic program of, 156, 176
    and education, 159
    flexibility of, 152
    functions of, 146
    inconsistencies in criticism of, 158
    by individual business enterprises, 149
    and international relations, 162
    intricacy and urgency of, in modern society, 163
    limitations of, 159
    and public administration, 146
    range of, 165
    role of science, technology, and education in, 158
    strategy of, 153
    test of, 154
    types of agencies, 146
    should not be limited to economics, 149
    value of, 7
Planning, 99*n*.
Plato, on aristocracy, 90
    on the Few and the Many, 4
    guardians in republic, 32
    Republic of, 250
    on superiority, 24
Plebiscites, pseudo, 44
Plutocracy, attack upon militant democracy, 197
    elements of, in democracy, 68
Political aptitudes, isolation of, 29
    (*See also* Leadership)
Political capacity, differentials in, 23
    (*See also* Biology; Heredity)
Political messiahs, rise of, in troubled periods, 254
    (*See also* Leadership)

INDEX

Political parties (*see* Parties, Political)
Political techniques, role of, in background of democracy, 59
Politics, and economics, 173
Popular control, 38
  (*See also* Mass decision)
Popular decision (*see* Mass decision)
Popular government, creative role of, 43
Popular will, modes of organizing, 116
Poverty, elimination of, goal of democracy, 35
Power, balance of, in new despotism, 235
  concentration of, in crisis, 236
  as repression and as creation, 83
  zoning of, 153
President, role of, in American government, 125
Pressure groups, functions of, in democracy, 122
Printing, invention of, in relation to democracy, 55
Privilege, special, repudiation of, 7
Production, possibility of gains in, 5, 176
Productivity, necessity for continual surveys of, 98
Proletariat, dictatorship of, 54
  (*See also* Lower classes)
Propaganda, and civic education, 183
  and electoral process, 107
  role of, in dictatorships, 234
Property, ownership of, and political power, 31*ff*.
Prosperity and democracy, 36
Proudhon, 43
Psychiatry, and personality development, 27
Psychoanalysis, 31
Public administration, in autocracy, 128
  corruption and incompetence in, 125
  decentralization of, 131
  and defense of liberty, 129
  developing role of, 123

Public administration, development of, in democracy, 187
  emergence of profession of, 128
  important changes impending in, 129
  improvements in, aid to democracy, 255
  inevitable growth of, 243
  and planning, 146
  potentialities of, in democracy, 128
  quiet revolution in, 124
  reorganization of, 126
  role of executive in, 125
  role of non-governmental agencies in, 130
  tool of democracy, 124
Public Administration Clearing House, 130*n*.
Public law, development of, in relation to democracy, 53
Public ownership, 174
  (*See also* Collectivism)

R

Race, as basis of leadership selection, 30
Racial doctrines, attack fraternal basis of life, 16
  (*See also* Aryan race)
Randall, Henry S., 75*n*.
Ranelletti, Oreste, 235*n*.
Rappard, William E., 75*n*.
  definition of democracy, 47
Rational discussion, advantages of, 6
Recent Social Trends, 95*n*., 156*n*.
  President's Committee on, 35*n*.
Regulation, emerging nature of, 159
Reischauer, R. P., 157*n*.
Regimentation, governmental and private, 154
Religion, in background of democracy, 52
  evaluation of individual in occidental, 52

Religion, and new despotism, 89
   and toleration of oppressive authority, 52
Renan, 211n.
Representation, basis of, 116
   as basis of responsible government, 59
   intimidation substituted for, in dictatorships, 227
   no best form of, 118
   (*See also* Electoral process; Legislative bodies; Parliamentarism)
Republic, of Plato, 250
Responsibility, development of, in government, 53
   lack of, in dictatorships, 7
   lines of, in autocracy, 117
   in new despotism, 222
   organization of consent, 186
   rejected by autocratic theorists, 39
Ricardo, David, 157
Rivers, W. H. R., 245n.
Robson, W. A., 228n.
Rocco, Alfredo, 211n.
Rogers, Lindsay, 126n., 138, 167n.
Roman law, doctrine of popular basis of rule, 51
Roosevelt, Franklin D., 143, 255
   committee on administrative management, 126
Rosenberg, Alfred, 24n., 212n.
Rousseau, 19, 23, 41n., 92
Ruskin, criticism of democracy, 203
Russia, recent espionage trials in, 111
Russian mujik, attitude of aristocracy toward, 15

S

St. Simon, 195n.
   aristocratic theory of, 194
Salvemini, Gaetano, 114n., 235n.
Savoy, king of, 14
Scarcity, political effects of, 258

Schmitt, Carl, 115n., 212n., 220n., 231n.
Schmitthenner, P., 132n.
Schneider, Herbert W., 235n.
Schwesinger, Gertrude C., 27n., 28n.
Science, in background of democracy, 54
   basis of progress, 93
   a national resource, 93
   problems confronting and promise of, 95
   spirit of, in public administration, 124
Scott, Howard, 207n.
Sereno, Renzo, 208n.
Shaftesbury, Lord, 13
Shakespeare, 217, 218
Simon, Lady, 228n.
Simon, Sir E. D., 228n.
Slave nature, marks of, according to Aristotle, 24
Smend, Rudolf, 244n.
Smith, Reginald H., 77n.
Smith, T. V., 74n., 77n.
Social contract, place of, in background of democracy, 52
Social invention, possibilities of, 96
Social Science Research Council, 59n.
Social sciences, in background of democracy, 58
   as educative force for orderly progress, 94
   and planning for better future, 94
Social techniques, in background of democracy, 57
Socialism, 196
Societarian political theories, 54
Sorel, Georges, 196
   and Nietzsche, 199
Sorokin, Pitirim, 208n., 209n.
Sovereignty, exaggerations of, 160
Soviet, purge of leaders in, 111
Spann, Othmar, 208n.
   criticism of democracy, 212
Spartan elements in national socialism, 225

INDEX

Spencer, Herbert, 83*n*., 157, 231*n*.
Spengler, Oswald, 114*n*., 196, 237
    general theory of, 202
Standard of living, achievement of democratic minimum, 187
    the American minimum, 100
    differentials in, 100
        (*See also* Civilization, gains of; Mass gains)
State, functions of, 3
    as private law entity, 53
    as public law entity, 53
        (*See also* Government)
Steiner, H. Arthur, 235*n*.
Stephen, J. F., 76*n*.
Stoffel, Grete, 220*n*.
Stoicism, influence of, upon democracy, 51
    passive attitude of, 92
Studd lectures, 126*n*.
Suffrage (*see* Electoral process)
Superman, 198
    in Nietzsche's theory, 196
Syndicalism, 196

T

Tawney, Richard H., 12*n*., 17*n*., 74*n*.
    on inequality, 73
Taylor, Fred, 167
Tead, Ordway, 246*n*.
Technocracy, 33, 207*n*.
Technology, in background of democracy, 54
    and democracy, 34
Temporary National Economic Committee, 155*n*.
Terror, role of, in new despotism, 234
Thomas, E. D., 51*n*.
Tocqueville, Alexis de, 76*n*.
Tolstoi, 43
Totalitarian doctrine, overemphasis of, political, 7
Totalitarian state, excessive regulation in, 160
Totalitarianism, theoretical origins of, 220
Townsend, Rev. Joseph, 13
Tradition, as resistant to social change, 181
Treitschke, Heinrich von, 196
    political theory of, 202

U

Unemployment, solution of problem of, in democracy, 187
Uniformity, impossibility of achievement of, 161
United States, educational policy of, 97
Universal suffrage, 59
    (*See also* Electoral process; Voting)
Upper classes, fear of democracy, 15
    (*See also* Aristocracy; Industrialists; Plutocracy)
Urwick, L., 46, 126*n*., 246*n*.

V

Vagts, Alfred, 132*n*., 139
Violence, compared with rational discussion, 6
    diminution of, in internal affairs, 184
    emphasis upon, in anti-democratic theory, 196
    in international affairs, 183
    as means to political power, 23
    organization of, 186
    (*See also* Force; Military affairs; Military organization)
Voegelin, Erich, 61*n*.
Völkisch principle, 212
Völkische Führerstaat, 215
Voting, Mussolini on, 114
    in new despotism, 226, 231
    (*See also* Electoral process)

W

Wackernagel, Jacob, 244*n.*
Wagner, Richard, 193
War, potentialities of democracy for, 139
   role of non-military factors in, 186
   (*See also* Military affairs; Violence)
Washington, George, 255
Wealth, as mark of political capacity, 23
   (*See also* Civilization, gains of)
Webb, Beatrice, 10*n.*, 228*n.*
Webb, Sidney, 10*n.*, 228*n.*
Weill, G., 194*n.*
Wells, H. G., 87*n.*, 90*n.*
Western tradition, attack upon, in dictatorships, 237
White, L. D., 126*n.*
Whitehead, T. N., 245*n.*, 261
Wilhelm II, Kaiser, 134
Wilk, Kurt, 212*n.*
Williams, Albert Rhys, 228*n.*
Wilson, Margaret, 185*n.*
Wilson, Woodrow, 137, 255
Wolff, Theodor, 118*n.*
Wootton, Barbara, 150*n.*
World jural order, and democracy, 187
World War, fate of democracy and autocracy in, 63